W9-BZA-475

RAISING CHILDREN TOXIC FREE

RAISING CHILDREN TOXIC FREE

How to Keep Your Child Safe from Lead, Asbestos, Pesticides, and Other Environmental Hazards

HERBERT L. NEEDLEMAN, M.D., AND
PHILIP J. LANDRIGAN, M.D.

WITH A FOREWORD BY T. BERRY BRAZELTON, M.D.

FARRAR, STRAUS AND GIROUX
NEW YORK

Designed by Debbie Glasserman
Printed in the United States of America
Published simultaneously in Canada by HarperCollins*PublishersLtd*
First edition, 1994

Library of Congress Cataloging-in-Publication Data
Needleman, Herbert L.
Raising Children Toxic Free:
How to keep your child safe from lead, asbestos,
pesticides, and other environmental hazards / Herbert L. Needleman and
Philip J. Landrigan.
p. cm.
Includes bibliographical references and index.
1. Pediatric toxicology. I. Landrigan, Philip J. II. Title.
RA1225.N44 1994 618.92'98—dc20 93-38108 CIP

To our wives, Roberta and Mary
To our children: Sam, Josh, and Sara; Mary, Chris, and Lizzie
To their children
And to their children's children . . .

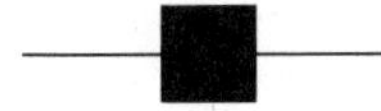

ACKNOWLEDGMENTS

We want to acknowledge with gratitude the help of many friends and colleagues whose advice was essential to the creation of this book. The seeds were planted in the Committee of Environmental Health of the American Academy of Pediatrics in the mid-1980s. We both served on this committee, and profited greatly from many intense and fruitful discussions with our fellow pediatricians from across the country on topics that now appear here as chapters. Dr. Sophie Balk had constructed a household inventory just as we came upon the idea. She freely allowed us to use hers as the foundation for ours. Similarly, Inform, Inc., permitted us to use their list of environmental organizations and resources. We thank them both for their generosity. We are indebted to Bernie Weiss, Ellen Silbergeld, Henry Falk, Ruth Etzel, Richard Jackson, Bill Nicholson, Mary Wolff, Barbara Barish, and Ed Baker, who carefully read and criticized manuscript chapters and gave us the benefit of their long experience. Any errors in the text are ours. Elisabeth Dyssegaard, our editor, helped put our thoughts into accessible prose and provided the perspective of a mother-to-be, and Beth Vesel, our agent, shepherded us from the start, encouraged us, and kept us at the job.

CONTENTS

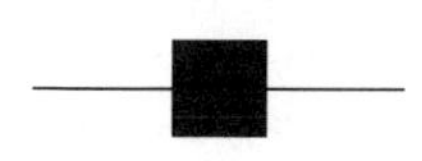

FOREWORD

In my practice, I see loving and caring parents who are increasingly worried about the environmental hazards that seem so prevalent in our lives. They are concerned about eletromagnetic radiation, asbestos, and pesticides. They worry that environmental toxins may be causing cancer in their neighborhood, that lead poisoning and air pollution and other ill-understood toxins could threaten their children.

Maintaining the right degree of concern and caution about environmental hazards is critical to the well-being of the family. Loving parents must guard against excessive and needless worry about unknown hazards. At the same time it is essential to the child's development that parents learn everything they can about environmental health risks and then take reasonable precautions to protect their growing children against them.

This book is about maintaining, in the middle of the tumult, a balance between the all-important needs of children to play and grow without fear and the parents' need to protect the child from environmental toxins. This book gives parents the tools and the information they need to evaluate environmental threats, so that they can make informed decisions about how to deal with them in a rational manner.

The authors of this book are eminent experts in child health and environmental medicine. They have spent years investigating the impact of pollutants on child health, and they recognize the need for trustworthy, plainspoken advice. Both have trained at world-renowned children's hospitals, and their work has had a sweeping influence on regulations and public health practices. Both have spent an important part of their careers at my institution, the Children's Hospital Medical Center in Boston—Phil Landrigan as one of my students and as a resident; Herb Needleman as an attending physician and colleague. They know the world of the child and are sensitive to the aspirations and concerns of parents.

This book fulfills an important need. It gives parents essential information on environmental health, an area that until now has been largely neglected. The book will be widely read and it should be.

T. Berry Brazelton

RAISING CHILDREN TOXIC FREE

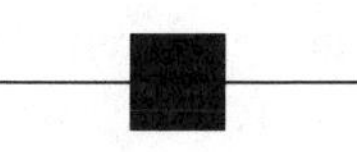

PREFACE

Our children inhabit a fundamentally different world than the one in which we were raised. In many ways their world is a better one. Most children in developed societies today are better fed and better educated than children a generation ago; many once lethal childhood diseases have been virtually eradicated; and the life span of an infant born today is likely to be longer. At the same time, the children of today face hazards that were neither known nor imagined just two decades ago. The amount of available lead in our world is hundreds of times greater than that present in the 1950s. Since 1950, at least 70,000 new chemical compounds have been invented and dispersed into our environment through new consumer commodities, industrial products, and food. Only a fraction of these have been tested for human toxicity. We are by default conducting a massive clinical toxicological trial. And our children and their children are the experimental animals.

Each day carries new hints of the earth's vulnerability and signals that time may be running out. We read of events started by man but slipping past human control. It has become easy to believe that we are swimming in a toxic soup and that every food, paint, pesticide, or appliance carries a singular risk. The forces that produce pollution seem remote and mysterious, and many people are pessimistic about controlling environmental spoilage and disease. Parents, facing this torrent of poorly understood threats, are frequently tempted to turn their attention away to matters they feel they can control. This is one way to reduce anxiety, but it carries its own costs.

This book is an effort to counter that tendency. It works to bring environmental threats into perspective, to inform parents in a realistic and supportive manner, and, in doing so, to contain this source of disabling dread and passivity. Our goal is to help parents understand and deal constructively with environmental hazards. You have the ability to limit the exposure of your children to many toxicants such as lead or asbestos without panic or unnecessary constrictions in living. To take effective action requires sound information about what and where these substances are, how they work, and what remedies are available.

Fear of pollutants can make people easy targets. Frequently, when considering the purchase of an older home, parents may worry about radon, fragmented asbestos, or dangerous lead paint. Many contractors exploit these fears to sell expensive and often unnecessary renovation projects. In this book, we provide information about evaluating your home for these hazards, choosing a reliable testing service, and, if necessary, selecting a contractor.

Informed parents and environmental scientists can be effective partners. By collaborating, they succeeded in the late 1980s in taking Alar, a carcinogenic pesticide used by apple growers, off the market. When parents learned from environmental scientists about the risks to children from Alar, they acted to influence regulation. Alar was withdrawn in months. This important victory occurred after years of governmental delay. It would have taken many more years had the consuming public not taken part in this campaign. This partnership between scientists, environmentalists, and parents has unlimited possibilities for shaping our laws and customs to make the world healthier for growing children.

Sound information on environmental hazards should not be hard to come by, but it is. Pediatricians, who should be the first source of reliable instruction, receive little training in environmental health or toxicology. Because they are expected to be expert, some pediatricians rely on blanket reassurance that the dangers from environmental hazards are overstated. But placebos have no protective value, and do little to reduce anxiety.

We are pediatricians who came to our understanding of this new field of environmental health from our interests in child development and epidemiology. Our points of view, while developed through different pathways, were shaped in the public health tradition. Dr. Landrigan, after training in clinical pediatrics, joined the U.S. Public Health Service and the Centers for Disease Control as an officer in the global effort to wipe out smallpox. He went on to study the impact of lead smelters on surrounding communities. He found that children in these communities had absorbed excessive amounts of lead from the smelters and that their intelligence scores were lower as a consequence. Dr. Needleman trained in pediatrics, and after entering private practice, trained in psychiatry. His work in a community mental health center in the inner city of Philadelphia brought him into contact with teachers and principals whose resources were strained by children with learning disorders or behavioral problems. His interest in the factors influencing developing children's brains drew him to the study of lead. Our interest in the controversy-filled field of childhood lead poisoning brought us together and convinced us that the most significant gains in human health and welfare spring from broad public preventive actions. These require public participation.

There is also need, and room, for you as parents to take preventive actions in your home and school. This is the major terrain of this book. We know that parents, given good data, generally make good decisions. We also know that it is the clear obligation of scientists and physicians to present what they know about environmental risks in coherent and understandable form to parents. Armed with that information, parents can be trusted to act discerningly on their children's behalf.

THE VULNERABILITY OF CHILDREN

■ ■ ■

Many toxicants are greater threats to children than to adults. There are numerous reasons for this:

- Children absorb a greater proportion of many substances from the intestinal tract or lung. For example, children take up approximately half of the lead that they swallow while adults absorb only about one-tenth.
- Children indulge in more hand-to-mouth activity than adults and transfer more foreign substances into their bodies through this route. Because of their smaller size, and the fact that they often play in the dirt, they are closer to the source of many pollutants.

- Children take in more air, food, and water per pound of body weight than adults.
- Children's biology is different. Their immune system is less developed, and may be less protective. For some toxicants, the body has developed biochemical detoxifying mechanisms; in some instances, these are less developed in children.
- Cells that are developing are generally more vulnerable than cells that have completed development. This is particularly true for the central nervous system. The brain increases in complexity at an extraordinary rate during fetal life, and this continues after birth until at least the third year. During brain development, cells move from their initial position in the embryo to their final position in the brain. As they travel, these cells trail branches and send out a complex web of connecting fibers to meet and connect with other preselected fibers from other nerves. The specificity of these connections is highly important in determining the precision and quality of brain function. Small doses of neurotoxins can alter the process of migration and laying down connections. As a result, deficits occur at doses that would be harmless or transient in the adult.

THE NEW PATTERN OF CHILDHOOD ILLNESS

■ ■ ■

The practice of pediatric medicine has changed steadily over the past two decades. Its focus is now what is referred to as "the new morbidity," meaning that the predominant diseases of children have shifted from brief and simple infections to complex, chronic handicapping conditions of multiple origins. Among these are asthma, cystic fibrosis, learning disabilities, attention deficit, the behavior disorders, the rheumatoid diseases of childhood, and other problems of coping with growing up. Some of these conditions have at least part of their origins in environmental factors. Air pollutants clearly worsen and may initiate asthma and other respiratory disturbances. Metals, solvents, pesticides, and other neurotoxins, by affecting the central nervous system, can contribute to the pool of learning disabilities, as well as attention deficit disorder and behavioral disturbances.

Early detection and removal of children from toxic exposure are necessary to successful prevention. Pediatric medicine has a great deal to learn about environmental health. When pondering a diagnosis or setting up a treatment plan, pediatricians need to think of environmental factors. This is particularly the case when the patient is middle-class. Indoor air pollution, lead exposure, radon, and other hazards are democratic; they respect neither race nor station.

The focus of this book is the intimate environment of children, and its primary audience is you, their parents. We will concentrate mainly on toxicants and other threats that can be identified and responded to in the home or the school. We leave for other writers the examination of drugs of abuse and alcohol. Because tobacco inflicts important damage to nonsmokers, whether children or adults, through sidestream smoke, it is clearly an environmental pollutant. We discuss it here. We give an overview of important global issues such as the ozone layer, the energy cycle, and global warming. These are obviously critical questions that will influence the kinds of lives we will be living in the near future, but extended discussions are outside the scope of this book. We hope that this book will stimulate you to read more about these issues and become active in their resolution.

Awareness of environmental health issues is spreading, but there continues to be an excess of skepticism about the reality of these hazards. Parents who take steps to protect their children from unnecessary exposures to pesticides, metals, asbestos, or radiation may meet with disdain and occasional disbelief from officials, some physicians, and even some of their fellow parents. We hope *Raising Children Toxic Free* can give these parents confidence and assistance in dealing with these old but generally uninformed doubts.

The plan of *Raising Children Toxic Free* is simple. The important environmental threats to children are classified according to their physical or chemical characteristics. We then examine the history, properties, distribution, and toxicology of each substance. We provide, for each agent, advice about how you can evaluate individual risk in your home, your neighborhood, and your school, and then we discuss the steps toward prevention. Where more than individual action is needed, we provide the names of agencies or groups to which you can turn for information about what further collective or political steps can be taken to eliminate the threat. A household inventory provides a checklist of items to be evaluated in and around the home. We encourage you to use it. It will assist in determining where, if any, risky circumstances exist.

We aimed this book at parents, but we hope that it will also find a receptive audience among family physicians and pediatricians. They may have received relatively little instruction in these areas in medical school or in their graduate training, but increasingly are the first to be asked by patients for advice. It is clear that many diseases (for example, asthma) that are seen by these physicians are caused to some extent by environmental factors, or are at least modified by them. Comprehensive medicine demands that environmental factors be examined and controlled for the health of our children.

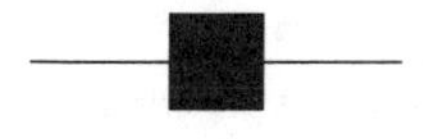

INTRODUCTION

Some diseases are determined at the moment of conception, when our parents' genes are combined and shuffled. The origins of these diseases are largely beyond our control. A much larger number of diseases spring directly from human choices. In this class are the greatest causes of illness and premature death: tobacco, alcohol, drugs, automobiles, handguns, and violence. Environmental diseases are in part the result of personal and collective choices in the way we live, in the way we consume our resources and dispose of our waste products. There is cause for optimism in this observation. If a disease is made by human beings, we should be able to prevent it.

THE GROWTH OF ENVIRONMENTAL AWARENESS

■ ■ ■

For centuries mankind has seen itself as separate from nature. The world's resources appeared limitless and put here only for our benefit. This is a product of the Western vision of the world as our dominion. Given this dominion, we set out not to live in nature, but to conquer it and to use its minerals, vegetation, and animals as raw materials for our own enrichment. When the world's population was sparse, and when the available technology neither consumed much energy nor created much waste, this was a safe, if transient creed. It is now a dangerous misperception.

In the early twentieth century, the major concern of the conservationists was to create conditions that optimized the use of natural resources, the nation's water, minerals, and forests. They saw these resources as fuel for the national economy and joined the effort to speed the flow of industrial production.

Our vision of our place in the natural environment began to change rapidly at the end of World War II. The idea of the environment as an end rather than a means slowly emerged. Samuel Hays, in his important book *Beauty, Health and Permanence*, describes the shift in thinking from the conservation movement to environmental awareness, and describes the numerous forces that accelerated it:

> The early conservation movement had generated the first stages in shaping a "commons," a public domain of public ownership for public use and the public ownership of fish and wildlife as resources not subject to private appropriation. This sense of jointly held resources became extended in the later years to the concept of air, land and water as an environment. Their significance as common resources shifted from a primary focus on commodities to become also meaningful as amenities that could enhance the quality of life.

As incomes grew and life spans lengthened, people in Western societies began to look past questions of immediate survival to questions of life quality for themselves and for their children. They began to spend more time engaged in outdoor activities and grew to value natural beauty and its preservation. Many of the early environmentalists were people of means who wanted to preserve the beauty of the natural surroundings that their wealth had permitted them to live in. This fact has been used by many critics to damage the environmental movement. They have frequently painted environmentalists as moneyed elitists who valued the charm of their sunset views more than the proposed power plant or the jobs needed by working people who would build it. This false tension between jobs and beauty is exploited and stimulated by industrial interests and continues to pervade some of today's environmental debates.

The relationship between human health and the environment is not a new discovery; one finds references in antiquity to bad vapors and disease. The word "malaria" itself means "bad air." The observation that certain occupations produced certain illnesses is centuries old. Appreciation of the significance of this relationship between occupation and disease deepened in the mid-twentieth century. Growing concern over the causes of cancer forced attention to the role of the environment in disease.

With the development of antibiotics, the threat of infectious diseases shrank. Cancer, once seen as a shameful, frightening rarity, became one of the more common causes of death, and could now be discussed in public. Synthetic chemicals as a cause of cancer came under examination. The role of tobacco in causing lung cancer was clearly presented by Surgeon General Luther Terry in the 1960s. The cancer-causing properties of asbestos had long been suspected, but were established in the late 1960s by Dr. Irving Selikoff of New York's Mount Sinai Medical Center. When he traced large numbers of World War II shipyard workers who were exposed to asbestos in their jobs, he found that they suffered an extraordinary rate of lung disease and cancer. Other occupations were determined to be associated with cancer. Benzene workers were found to develop leukemia, and plastic production workers were found at risk for a rare form of liver cancer. If some occupational chemicals were carcinogens (i.e., caused cancer), how many other chemicals were unrecognized hazards?

If workers who were exposed to high doses were affected by these chemicals, were these risks shared by those who lived near the plant? A dramatic and frightening case in point was the Minamata Bay disaster in Japan. In the 1950s, in Minamata Bay, a chemical plant was found to be discharging large quantities of mercury into the bay. The citizens of Minamata who fished the bay developed severe neurological diseases. Infants whose mothers had eaten fish while pregnant showed severe congenital brain damage and cerebral palsy. Poignant photographs by the late Eugene Smith provided unequivocal testimony that residents in nearby communities shared the risk of occupational intoxications.

The effects of methyl mercury were dramatic and relatively easy to identify. Lead's effects were less obvious. In the early 1970s, a new threat inflicted by factories on their neighbors was recognized. A Centers for Disease Control study of children living near a lead smelter in El Paso, Texas, showed that these children had higher blood lead levels and lower IQ scores than children at a distance. An industry-sponsored study of the same neighborhood failed to find this relationship, and this resulted in a controversy that has continued until recently. It is now acknowledged by almost all but the lead industry and its public relations apparatus that lead is a hazard whose safe level has yet to be found.

The widely accepted picture of synthetic chemicals as offering unqualified benefits slowly began to change. DDT was widely publicized at the end of World War II as an unconditional blessing. Few people thought that pesticides had any attached risks. In 1962 Rachel Carson published *Silent Spring* and called eloquent attention to the risks that attended the uncontrolled use of insecticides on wildlife and the biosphere in general. A world that had been dazzled by the future presented by man-made chemicals began to rethink the benefits of their wholesale dispersion.

Doubts about chemicals even intruded into the doctor's office and the hospital. Even the "miracle drugs" sulfanilamide and penicillin were found to have unpleasant and sometimes lethal side effects. This, the decreasing populations of rare and common birds, and the increasing awareness of chemical carcinogens further challenged the absolute acceptance of synthetic chemicals as offering unqualified benefits.

At the same time, the young science of toxicology was undergoing rapid and jarring changes in perspective. The most common tool of toxicologists was once the "LD_{50}" (lethal dose/50). This simply means the dose of a given poison that kills half of the animals in an experiment. For years, toxicologists gave groups of animals a toxic agent at increasing doses ranging from the very small to the universally lethal. The dose that killed 50 percent of the animals was defined as the LD_{50} and this dose was used to characterize the toxicity of the agent. This clumsy and cruel stratagem returned little information and severely limited the vision of the field.

In the study of human toxic exposures, understanding was not much more refined. Toxic effects were recognized only in extremis, when the victim fell into coma or convulsions. For fifty years after childhood lead poisoning was described, eminent pediatricians continued to maintain that there were only two possible outcomes from lead exposure: death or complete recovery. The idea that lasting toxicity could occur in the absence of severe symptoms did not exist until the 1940s, even though lead had been recognized as a brain poison for two thousand years.

THE STUDY OF BEHAVIOR AND POLLUTANTS

■ ■ ■

This blind spot regarding silent toxicity started to shrink when toxicologists began to talk with psychologists. They took this unusual step because the pharmaceutical industry, in the 1960s, was developing a host of new drugs to treat schizophrenia, depression, and anxiety, and new methods to discover drugs and evaluate their safety and efficacy were badly needed. Toxicologists, once they learned to use the tools and language of experimental psychologists, stopped using death as the outcome of interest, and replaced it in some experiments with measures of behavioral change. Quickly they noticed that experimental animals began to behave weirdly at lesser doses of poisons than those that killed them. The field of behavioral toxicology was born; its credo was that changes in behavior were often the earliest signs of poisoning. This was a revolutionary idea; the first meeting of behavioral toxicologists took place in 1972. A pair of psychologists, Bernard Weiss and Victor Laties at the University of Rochester, published the first textbook on behavioral toxicology in 1975.

The field of behavioral toxicology grew rapidly and produced a new offspring: behavioral teratology. "Teratology" means the study of birth defects. In the 1960s it was recognized that some chemicals (designated as "teratogens") could cause physical defects in newborns. Quickly scientists realized that just as chemicals could produce birth defects, some agents, when given during pregnancy, could produce a different type of birth defect: a lasting change in offspring behavior and intellect.

Joann Spyker Cranmer was among the first to show this effect. She gave methyl mercury to pregnant mice and found that at higher doses mercury produced visible birth defects in the central nervous system. At lower doses offspring appeared normal at birth, but when tested at thirty days of life, the mercury-exposed mice showed abnormal exploratory and swimming behavior. Mice also had alterations in their immune systems, and some died prematurely of unexplained causes. This study became a model for other investigations of potentially toxic substances.

Behavioral teratology is a field of extraordinary importance, because many pregnant women take medicines or other agents that affect the brain. Many drugs, including tranquilizers, can produce behavioral disturbances in offspring if given to the mother while she is pregnant. There is also a growing body of evidence that paternal exposure can have consequences for the offspring.

The question of maternal exposure to pollutants became a central issue in what many consider the most significant civil rights case since 1964. In this case, Johnson Controls, a major lead battery manufacturer, recognizing that exposure to lead affected the fetus, banned women from work in lead-exposed sectors of its plants unless they could prove that they could not become pregnant. Although there was evidence that fathers' exposure to lead could affect the baby as well, the body of information was not as great as that for maternal exposure. The industry chose to interpret this as evidence that maternal exposure was more dangerous, not that more male data were needed. In ruling on this case, the Supreme Court unanimously held that women could not be banned from a job because it contained fetal risks. This amounted to saying that the workplace had to be made safe for all workers, without regard to gender.

Recognition of the role of the environment in shaping human health has been a slow process. Science does not take a steady uphill stroll toward objective truth. There are times when scientific behavior more closely resembles a tag-team match. Each manmade chemical has an industry behind it and bears a price and a profit. Reducing a chemical hazard will inevitably cost someone money, and regulation inescapably becomes a contentious process. Industrial representatives often work hard at blurring the relationship between their product and poor health. The tobacco industry is the clearest example; it still argues that there is no proof that smoking causes cancer or lung disease, and at this time is suing the Environmental Protection Agency to remove the statement on cigarette packaging that passive smoking can cause cancer.

Industrial representatives often demand standards of proof of harm that are not possible to deliver in the real world. The task of showing that there is a relationship falls upon epidemiologists. Epidemiologists cannot administer poisons to humans and observe the outcome; instead they must measure the observed variation in exposure to disease-causing agents and then compute the rate of illness after it has occurred. It is their exacting task to measure and separate out associated factors that could influence the rate of an illness and then estimate the role of each factor individually and in concert with other risks. Real-world epidemiology, like the life it attempts to measure and model, is not a perfect enterprise.

Nor is it necessary to know all of the causal links in a disease to control it. John Snow, one of the first epidemiologists, studied the pattern of distribution of cholera cases in London during the epidemic of 1854 and noticed that it was associated with one water company, while a neighboring source was safe. He removed the handle from the Broad Street water pump in Soho, and the disease was virtually controlled. Snow knew nothing about the cholera bacteria; it was first isolated almost thirty years later in 1883.

New tools permit us to see things in a different light. What is true depends on our viewpoint. When we stand at the shoreline and look at the horizon, the world seems obviously a plane that stretches without limit. From a satellite, we see that the world is round and finite. The tools of modern toxicology, psychology, and epidemiology have reshaped our understanding of the physical and chemical world that we live in. These tools have shown us that chemical agents can produce harm that is not dramatic, that may be invisible to the unaided senses, and that may be delayed in onset, but is of great significance to the individual.

We know that children, because they are developing, may be more vulnerable to toxins, and that for some agents the most vulnerable target may be the child's nervous system. We know that prevention of exposure is much more effective than treatment after exposure has occurred and that prevention of illness can in most cases be accomplished.

1

REPRODUCTION

Parents frequently ask us whether their exposure to some environmental hazard will interfere with their ability to have normal, healthy children. This concern is becoming more commonplace as people's awareness of environmental hazards grows. A particular source of anxiety is reproductive effects: birth defects, delayed development, prematurity, and infertility.

These are appropriate concerns; we take them most seriously. Reproductive problems are widespread in modern society and some appear to be growing in their frequency. In the past two decades medical science has identified strong associations between reproductive problems and exposure to certain drugs, environmental chemicals, and radiation.

Here are some basic statistics on reproduction in the United States:

- Each year 3 million babies are born.
- 500,000 of these babies are lost each year through early miscarriages—in the first 20 weeks of pregnancy.
- 24,000 babies are lost in late miscarriages and stillbirths.
- 250,000 babies are born prematurely.
- 250,000 babies have birth defects.
- Infertility is widespread and appears to be increasing in frequency. More than 2 million American couples who want to have children are unable to do so.

What Are the Causes of These Problems?

- Some are due to maternal infection during pregnancy. Rubella (German measles), toxoplasmosis (a parasitic infection), and cytomegalovirus account for about 15 percent of congenital malformations.
- Mumps is responsible for a number of cases of male infertility, and pelvic infections account for some cases of infertility in women.
- Trauma, radiation, and other physical factors account for about 20 percent of birth defects.
- Genetic factors and inherited mutations are responsible for about 5 percent of birth defects.
- Poverty, malnutrition, and inadequate access to medical care are clearly associated with increases in the frequency of low-birthweight babies, premature births, and stillbirths.

For the great majority of birth defects, as many as 60 percent, the cause is not known. Nor are the causes of the recent apparent increase in the infertility rate known.

What is the Possible Role of Toxic Environmental Exposure?

In the early 1960s, awareness began to grow about the role of environmental exposure in the causation of congenital malformations, miscarriages, and infertility. The shock of the thalidomide tragedy alerted the world to this possibility. No other episode in recent medical history so clearly illustrates the connection between environmental hazards and human reproduction.*

> After it was licensed in the mid-1950s, thalidomide was widely marketed as an over-the-counter sedative and tranquilizer. Virtually no animal tests for harmful side effects were performed, but the manufacturer declared that the drug was safe. An aggressive marketing and advertising campaign was aimed particularly at pregnant women with morning sickness. It was a success, and tens of thousands of pregnant women took the drug. Total sales in West Germany exceeded 30,000 kilograms. Over the next several years, thalidomide swept across Europe and deeply penetrated the market in Latin America, Australia, Japan, and England. Because of a com-

* This historical description is adapted from W. Lenz, "A Short History of the Thalidomide Embryopathy," *Teratology*, 1988, 38:203–215.

bination of shrewdness, stubbornness, and good luck, the United States government did not license it for use.

On December 25, 1956, in Stolberg, Germany, a baby girl was born with no ears. Her father worked at Grünenthal Chemie, the manufacturers of thalidomide, and had been given samples of the drug for his pregnant wife. Over the next several months more cases were reported. These mothers had also been given premarket samples. The most common malformations were defects in the limbs, termed phocomelia. Frequently the arms of affected children were only a few inches long and resembled flippers.

At first the relationship between the malformations and thalidomide was unclear, and other causes were considered. The number of cases continued to grow steadily. In 1957, the year the drug was licensed, there were two cases of babies with limb defects. In 1958, there were 24. In 1959, 97 cases were reported; in 1960, 450, and in 1961, over 1,500. Altogether 3,049 babies were born in Germany with limb malformations.

Many parents of afflicted children readily recognized the connection between the drug and the disease. Often thalidomide was the only medication taken during pregnancy. The time trend in malformations lagged seven to eight months after the sales of the drug, precisely what would be expected for a toxin that acts in early pregnancy.

As the number of cases mounted, the link between thalidomide and phocomelia became inescapable, and European governments finally issued warnings. Sales of the drug were halted. Seven months later the epidemic ended. A few late cases were scattered over the next decade in families that had inadvertently kept samples of the drug.

Because of one steadfast woman, the United States was spared the epidemic. Dr. Frances Kelsey, the official responsible for issuing drug licenses at the U.S. Food and Drug Administration, was opposed to licensing any drug for use during pregnancy. From the beginning Kelsey had been unwilling to release thalidomide to the American market. Then, in 1958, Dr. Kelsey received a telephone call from Dr. Helen Taussig, a world-renowned pediatric cardiologist at Johns Hopkins Medical School. Dr. Taussig had just returned from Europe, where she had learned of the epidemic of phocomelia sweeping across Germany and of the possible link to thalidomide. For Dr. Kelsey, that was enough. She immediately halted the proceedings to grant a U.S. license. Only a few cases of phocomelia occurred in American babies. These were in families of servicemen stationed overseas or in families in which the mother had lived or visited in Europe.

Thalidomide awakened the medical profession to the dangers posed by medications and environmental chemicals during pregnancy. Physicians were forced to abandon the long-held myth that the placenta was a complete barrier between mother and child or between the baby and the environment. Doctors realized that toxic chemicals cross the placenta and can damage the developing infant. Thalidomide also convincingly demonstrated that an embryo or fetus can sustain severe damage from chemical agents that cause little or no toxicity to adults.

Another critical event that showed physicians and public health officials that chemicals could interfere with reproduction was the dibromochloropropane (DBCP) epidemic in the 1970s. It affected male fertility.

DBCP, a pesticide used to control insects on fruit crops, was produced at a manufacturing plant in California beginning in 1962. During the 1970s a group of young men working in this plant realized that none of them had been able to father children, although in the past some had been fertile. Others had never conceived a child despite several years of trying.

In 1976, a group of these men underwent voluntary examinations. Neither their libido nor their sexual functioning was impaired, but all of the men had severely decreased sperm counts. In several, the count was zero. When scientists from the University of California compared sperm counts in pesticide production workers with counts in workers from other areas of the plant, they found that pesticide workers had strikingly depressed sperm counts; the rest of the workers were normal. The longer a man had been employed as a pesticide production worker, the lower his sperm count. It was clear that DBCP had caused the reduction of sperm counts. The Environmental Protection Agency was notified; production of DBCP was stopped. The pesticide is no longer used in this country, but continues to be used overseas. Some of the men's sperm counts returned toward normal; others were permanently sterilized.

Chemicals encountered in the environment can damage the male reproductive system. Damage to either the father or the mother may result in serious genetic or developmental injury. The tendency by scientists to focus entirely on the mother's contribution and to ignore the father's role is slowly beginning to change.

HOW DOES HUMAN REPRODUCTION WORK?

■ ■ ■

To understand the various ways in which environmental toxins can interfere with reproduction, we briefly sketch some of the important steps in the complex process.

Each stage of reproduction must be executed correctly to pave the way for the many steps that follow. Any of these steps can be blocked or interfered with by the reproductive toxins that we list in the next several pages. The principal steps are:

- Production of eggs and sperm
- Conception
- Implantation of the fertilized egg in the lining of the uterus
- Development of the embryo and formation of the major organ systems (first 20 weeks of pregnancy)
- Growth of the fetus with further development of the body's organs (latter 20 weeks of pregnancy)

Reproduction requires that the genetic material, deoxyribonucleic acid (DNA), from a father's sperm join with maternal DNA to form the first cell of the new baby. All of the cells that comprise a child's body are derived from this first cell.

Successful maternal reproduction requires that the woman have an adequate store of eggs, that the eggs are fertile, that her fallopian tubes are open, and that her uterus is functioning properly. This requires that all of the necessary hormones are in proper balance.

Successful paternal reproduction requires that there are sperm in adequate numbers and that they are able to swim across the mother's uterus and up the fallopian tubes and are capable of fertilizing the descending egg.

PRODUCTION OF EGGS

All of the egg cells in a woman's body were formed when she herself was a fetus. By the fifth month of fetal life, those cells have localized in the developing ovaries. At birth a healthy female child has about three to four million oocytes (egg cells) in her ovaries. These oocytes remain dormant during childhood. A woman is not able to make any more egg cells to replace those that are damaged or destroyed. Early exposures that damage oocytes may not be recognized until years later when the oocyte supply is exhausted.

With the onset of puberty, under the direction of centers in the brain, fundamental changes in the secretion of hormones occur. Cyclic secretion of estrogen and progesterone begin, preparing the lining of the uterus for implantation of a fertilized egg. In each reproductive cycle, an egg matures, and after release from one of the ovaries, migrates down the fallopian tube to the uterus. If during this journey it encounters a sperm and is fertilized, conception results. If fertilization does not happen, the woman enters her menstrual period, passes the unfertilized egg from her body, and the cycle resumes.

Production of Sperm

Human sperm cells are produced in the testicles by the division of precursor cells called spermatogonia. These precursor cells are formed in males during embryonic life. Formation of sperm cells does not begin until puberty. Unlike women, who have all of their egg cells in place at birth, men continue to form new sperm continuously throughout adult life. This is essential because each sperm lives only a few days. If male spermatogonia are damaged, and production of new sperm is blocked, sterility may result.

Conception and Pregnancy

At the moment of conception, a single sperm penetrates the fertile egg and fusion of maternal and paternal DNA occurs. After fertilization and conception, the egg begins to divide. Within hours, there are 2, then 4, then 8, and then 16 cells. As these divisions proceed, the fertilized egg, now called an embryo, descends slowly through the mother's fallopian tube to reach the uterus. There, in the normal course of events, it will successfully implant in the thickened uterine lining about seven to eight days after conception.

During the first 20 weeks of pregnancy, a human embryo grows from microscopic size to a recognizable human form. During this period all of the major organ systems are formed. The fundamental structures of the brain and the heart and cardiovascular system are initiated and organized. The gastrointestinal tract and its major attachments, the liver and the pancreas, the kidneys, the bladder, and the other components of the baby's excretory system, as well as the immune and endocrine systems, are established.

Any environmental insult to the embryo during the early weeks of pregnancy can result in gross disruption of organ formation.

For example, rubella virus infections in these early weeks can result in terrible congenital malformations in the heart, the eyes, and the brain.

The latter 20 weeks of pregnancy are known as the fetal period. During this time, development and maturation of the baby's organ systems continues. The baby gains most of its weight during this period, and by the time of birth the average baby weighs 7½ pounds. The development of the central nervous system continues during the fetal period. (See Chapter 2.)

ENVIRONMENTAL CHEMICALS THAT ARE TOXIC TO REPRODUCTION

■ ■ ■

As a reference guide, we present an abridged list of common environmental chemicals that have been shown to adversely influence reproduction.

Lead is toxic to reproduction in both men and women. In men, it can reduce the sperm count and produce abnormal sperm. Men employed in the lead trades, such as battery manufacturing and construction, have reduced sperm counts. It is possible that young boys who are heavily exposed to lead during childhood will have impaired production of sperm when they reach puberty.

Lead is also a reproductive hazard for women. Young girls who absorb excessive amounts of lead during childhood will store much of this lead in their bones; bone is the depot tissue for lead in the human body. When these women reach adult life and become pregnant, lead and calcium can be mobilized from their bones. Since lead crosses the placenta, this may expose the unborn child to excessive levels of lead. Lead decreases fertility, increases the rate of prematurity and congenital malformations, and interferes with brain development in the fetus.

Polychlorinated biphenyls (PCBs) are a group of synthetic chemicals that until a few years ago were widely used as electrical insulation fluid. (See Chapter 10.) Intrauterine exposure to high concentrations of PCBs, reported in Japan and Taiwan, has caused congenital deformities and learning defects. Lower-level exposure of infants to PCBs is known to have occurred in the United States, particularly among the children of women who consumed large quantities of PCB-contaminated fish from the Great Lakes. These children have been found to have behavioral difficulties and problems with learning.

Diphenylhydantoin (**Dilantin**) is a prescription drug that is widely used to control seizures associated with epilepsy. Dilantin has been implicated as a cause of congenital malformations of the nervous system. All neuroactive drugs should be avoided during pregnancy if possible. This includes sedatives, major and minor tranquilizers, stimulants, and antidepressants. Where their use is critical, you should consult your doctor and carefully discuss the risks and benefits.

Ethanol (**alcohol**) is a known cause of congenital malformations. It produces an array of birth defects that are referred to by pediatricians as the "fetal alcohol syndrome." This syndrome includes mental retardation, small head size, abnormalities in the face, and behavioral effects. In recent years we have learned that even relatively small exposures of the fetus to alcohol can cause milder degrees of this syndrome. We strongly advise women to abstain from all alcoholic beverages during pregnancy.

Heroin and other opiates can cause neurological problems in newborn children. Babies exposed to these chemicals in their mothers' wombs have extreme irritability that lasts for several days after birth. In fact, the symptoms seen in the baby of a heroin-addicted mother are precisely the symptoms of withdrawal that are seen in an adult who abruptly stops taking the drug. Although these symptoms can be life-threatening when severe, they disappear within several weeks or months. Whether they produce later deficits is under study.

Cocaine has also been shown to damage the nervous system of newborn children. The children of cocaine-addicted mothers manifest profound twitching and irritability at birth—apparently a form of withdrawal. Although these symptoms eventually disappear, recent data indicate that the babies of cocaine-addicted mothers may be left with residual learning deficits and behavioral problems. Clearly, the use of all illicit drugs during pregnancy must be completely avoided.

Diethylstilbestrol (**DES**), a synthetic hormone, was used in the 1950s, 1960s, and 1970s to prevent premature delivery. It has been shown to produce vaginal cancers in young women who were exposed to the chemical when they were fetuses within their mothers' wombs. Young women who were exposed in utero to DES should have frequent gynecologic examinations.

Boys exposed prenatally to DES also have a higher rate of congenital malformations of the reproductive organs and may have decreased fertility. Adolescent boys and young men who were exposed to DES in utero should undergo a thorough medical evaluation of their reproductive tracts by a urologist when they reach puberty.

Estrogenic substances. Pesticides and a number of other environmental chemicals are toxic to reproduction because they have properties that resemble estrogenic compounds. These include certain chlorinated organic pesticides like Kepone and DDT. Kepone, a pesticide manufactured in the United States for export to Central America, reduces sperm counts and causes male sterility. DDT can mimic some of the properties of the female reproduction hormone, estrogen. It can interfere with reproduction in eagles and ospreys and may cause reproductive dysfunction in humans by interfering with endocrine balance. Many pesticides can cross the placenta and may interfere with the organization and functioning of the developing nervous system.

WHAT CAN PARENTS DO TO REDUCE REPRODUCTIVE TOXICITY?

■ ■ ■

Damage to the reproductive organs caused by environmental chemicals frequently cannot be repaired or corrected once the injury has occurred. Prevention of exposure is therefore essential. To be effective, prevention must involve fathers as well as mothers.

Here are some specific steps that you can take.

Reduction of all unnecessary uses of chemicals in your home is the first step in prevention. Review your uses of chemical cleaners, solvents, and pesticides (see Chapter 7 and Appendix 1).

Learn what chemicals you and your partner are exposed to in your work. Under state and federal right-to-know laws, you have a legal right to be provided with the name and the available data on the toxicity of any chemical that you may encounter at your workplace. If you learn that you are being exposed to reproductive toxins, you can discuss the problem with fellow workers, your union, and management to determine if safer substitutes can be utilized or the ventilation and other engineering controls improved.

If those approaches are not successful, you have a legal right to contact the National Institute for Occupational Safety and Health (NIOSH) or the Occupational Safety and Health Administration (OSHA) for assistance.

Avoid all use of tobacco, alcohol, and illicit drugs during pregnancy and in the months preceding pregnancy. Take only medications that are absolutely necessary during pregnancy, and only under strict medical supervision.

Consult the EPA's Toxic Release Inventory to learn what chemicals are being discharged into the environment in your community by local industry. Details on how to obtain this information and how to use it are provided in Chapter 11.

Join with others. As you seek to reduce your exposure to toxic chemicals in your environment you will soon come to realize that your ability as an individual to control major polluters is limited. However, by joining with other parents, friends, neighbors, and concerned citizens, you can greatly magnify the effectiveness of your efforts (see Appendix 2).

Two-thirds of the synthetic chemicals to which we are all regularly exposed in modern society have never been properly tested for their toxicity to human reproduction either by government agencies or by the chemical industry. It is distinctly possible that we and our children are being exposed without our knowledge to unidentified reproductive toxins. This represents another example of the regulatory laxity that we criticize elsewhere in this book. As a parent, you need to understand that in the past government has put very little pressure on the chemical industry to properly test chemicals for reproductive toxicity. There are substantial disincentives to proper testing, most of them economic. Effective resolution of this problem will require the combined action of large groups of concerned parents, pediatricians, and citizens. State and federal officials will need to be persuaded to fulfill their responsibility to protect the health of the public.

2

BEHAVIOR, DEVELOPMENT, AND ENVIRONMENTAL NEUROTOXINS

THE ROLE OF CHEMICALS IN CHILDREN'S ADJUSTMENT TO LIFE

Long before there were psychiatrists there was strange and unpredictable behavior, and people who tried to make sense out of it. From antiquity, all societies, frightened and fascinated by erratic and inexplicable conduct, have looked to religious, supernatural, moral, medical, and psychological sources for explanations. Relatively little consideration was given to physical factors as causes.

Insanity was once accepted as a sign of being touched or inhabited by gods or demons or as punishment for moral failings. In a few instances, the ancients blamed physical and chemical aberrations. What we call hysteria was once thought to be the product of a displaced and wandering uterus (indeed, the Greek word for uterus is *hystera*). Mood disorders were thought to be due to imbalances in body fluids—the humors. The brain was largely overlooked. More recently, in the early twentieth century the dominant view was that bad parenting or early childhood trauma was responsible for most psychological problems.

Science has only relatively recently made great strides in understanding some of the mechanics of the central nervous system, by applying a rigorous approach to examining the relationship between the brain and human behavior. Brain scientists and behavioral scientists, who worked in widely separated tracks, began, over the last thirty years, to notice intriguing connections between their fields. And as we learned more about how the brain worked, the mystery attached to some psychiatric symptoms began to be solved.

This application of brain science to behavioral disorders has, by explaining the origin of some diseases, removed unnecessary guilt from some mentally ill patients and their families. For many years the disease called infantile autism was attributed to bad mothering. This myth had its beginnings with Leo Kanner, a child psychiatrist at Johns Hopkins. Noting, about fifty years ago, that autistic children who were referred to him often had educated and hard-working professional mothers, Kanner leaped to the conclusion that these mothers lacked affection. These "icebox mothers" deprived their children of needed warmth, he pronounced, and that was the cause of this devastating syndrome. Deprivation, Kanner declared, was responsible for the language disturbances, inability to relate to people, and strange stereotyped movements.

This assumption, unsupported by any evidence, was swallowed whole by child psychiatrists and specialists in child development. Many families, severely weighted with autistic children, had guilt inflicted upon them by doctrinaire therapists who insisted that they, the parents, must have done something wrong. Many became depressed, and some marriages ended because the blame was too much to bear. Now, although we do not know specific causal factors producing autism, we are certain that it is not a disease of early rearing or bad parenting. It is a product of disordered brain function—a form of brain injury. The old punishing message of parental guilt is no longer being delivered at modern child development centers and burdened parents are spared unnecessary grief.

This history offers hope. Although we do not believe that all behavioral problems or mental disorders will ever be reduced to chemical disturbances, it is clear that there are chemicals that exert important influences on brain function, thinking, and feeling. A better understanding of these influences has opened the door to appropriate and effective therapies for many conditions. True prevention of some psychiatric and neurologic illnesses in both children and adults is now a possibility.

Along with those chemicals that function in the normal brain there is a growing list of compounds that have harmful effects. These chemicals are known as neurotoxins. In this chapter, we look at some brain mechanisms and then examine some ways in which neurotoxins can cause behavioral problems by interfering with the working of the nervous system. We mean neither to raise new alarms for parents nor to say that every problem has a chemical cause. But these studies point to emerging areas where preventive actions could be important and beneficial.

THE NERVOUS SYSTEM

■ ■ ■

Some Obsolete Models of the Brain and Mental Life

The human brain is possibly the most complex apparatus in the universe. To cope with this extraordinary complexity, scientists construct simplified models that draw on more familiar systems. Sigmund Freud, trying to fathom the role of inhibition and sexual frustration in neurosis, saw the mind as a kind of hydraulic pumping system. If raw instincts were dammed up by civilized conventions or guilt, their energy overflowed into otherwise baffling behaviors—the neuroses. This scheme had some utility, but like all models or metaphors, it clouded a clearer comprehension of human behavior and blocked new approaches. It led to a primitive but still potent belief that simply expressing and relieving blocked feelings was the road to mental health.

Another simplification was that patients with psychological disturbances suffered from a deficiency of good early emotional sustenance: love and affection. Some explanations of autism relied on this untested premise. "Icebox mothers," by depriving their children of needed emotional nutrients, were said to block their child's full development. Therapies were based on this assumption that aimed to satisfy the patient's longing for affection. But clearly this is an oversimplified approach. Certainly children deserve and do better with affection, consistency, and the firm knowledge that they are valued and loved. We all do. But life is more complex than any scheme that assigns the cause of nonadaptive behavior to this alone. Disturbed behavior is rarely a simple deficiency disease.

With the development of communications and electronics, the brain was visualized as a complex switchboard, and then as a computer. The reflex psychology of Pavlov and the learning theories of B. F. Skinner and others tempted many students of psychopathology to explain behavior as chains of reflexes and neuroses as pathological learning sets. While some patients derive therapeutic benefit from therapies modeled on stimulus-response phenomena, and some insight from computer models, these are also diminished visions of the human condition and its disturbances.

NEUROTOXICOLOGY: CHEMICALS AND MENTAL FUNCTIONING

The science of toxicology has also been undergoing a revolution in thinking. In the 1950s and 1960s some toxicologists began to realize that poisons not only damage the liver and the heart and cause cancer but also can disrupt the tightly orchestrated behavior of animals and humans. They began to measure behavior as an effect of giving a toxin. They found that chemicals frequently affect brain function at doses that had once been thought harmless. Clinicians noticed that some neurotoxins clearly affected intelligence, language ability, and attention, and some affected mood and social adjustment. Investigators saw that these effects occurred in apparently normal individuals at levels of exposure that were well below the levels that previously had been set as safe.

To understand how neurotoxins work, we must examine some of the structures of the nervous system.

THE NEURON: THE BASIC UNIT OF THE NERVOUS SYSTEM

Neurons are cells in the nervous system that are specialized to accept and transmit information. This information is taken in by the neuron's input branches, the dendrites, and encoded as electrical impulses. They then transfer the information through the cell body and down its output branch, the axon. The axon, in turn, connects to dendrites on the next neuron in the chain, and the information is thus passed along.

Dendrites vary in length and complexity. They have characteristic swellings at the end of their branches called spines. These spines are specialized to form connections, called synapses, with other neurons. It is at the synapse that nerve cells communicate with each other. The nerve impulse is conveyed down the axon by an electrical current, and when the impulse reaches the terminal of the axon, the signal is sent across the gap between nerve cells

DIAGRAM OF A TYPICAL NEURON

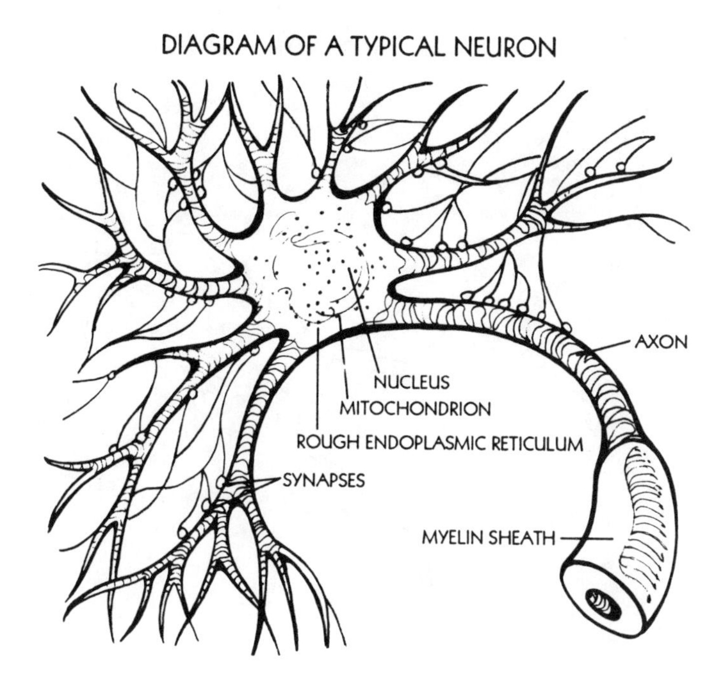

by small packets of chemicals called neurotransmitters. These neurotransmitters cross the synapse and bind to receptors on the dendritic spines.

Many axons are surrounded by a cellular sheath called myelin that folds itself in layers around the axonal shaft. This sheath behaves as a type of insulation, and also is the area along the nerve in which the propagation of the electrical impulse is boosted.

At the synapse, each neurotransmitter is picked up by a specific molecule on the receiving cell called a receptor. Receptors are highly specialized chemicals whose three-dimensional shape fits them specifically to one type of transmitter. Each of these receptors can be a target for brain poisons. After sending their signals, neurotransmitters are taken back up by the sending cell or broken down by enzymes into other molecules. Toxins can alter the synthesis of neurotransmitters or their receptors or can inhibit the breakdown and disposal of neurotransmitters after they have served their function.

Acetylcholine, one of the most important transmitters, is broken down by an essential enzyme, acetylcholinesterase. Many insecticides work by poisoning this enzyme. As a result, the transmitter

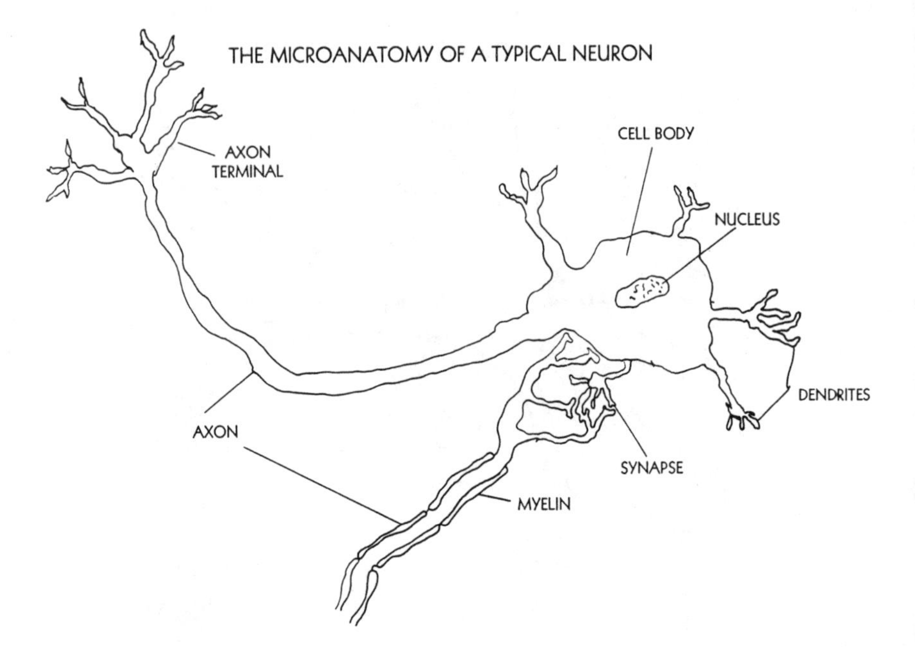

The human nervous system is made up of billions of separate cells, called neurons. Each neuron contains internal elements, the organelles, and each is in constant communication with neighboring neurons by way of synapses, the points of intercellular connection.

is not broken down. Instead it persists in the synapse and continues to stimulate the downstream cell. This will overstimulate the animal and eventually kill it. Humans also use acetylcholine in neurotransmission. Many of the nerve gases stored for use in chemical warfare work exactly like pesticides, by poisoning acetylcholinesterase.

Some neurotoxins, such as the fungicide triethyl tin, are active against the fatty myelin sheaths that surround and insulate nerves. This destruction of the myelin can interfere with nerve conduction.

Development of the Fetal Nervous System

At critical periods in the brain's development it is especially sensitive to toxins. During early embryonic life, a baby's nervous system develops from the same primitive cells as the skin. These

DIAGRAM OF A TYPICAL SYNAPSE

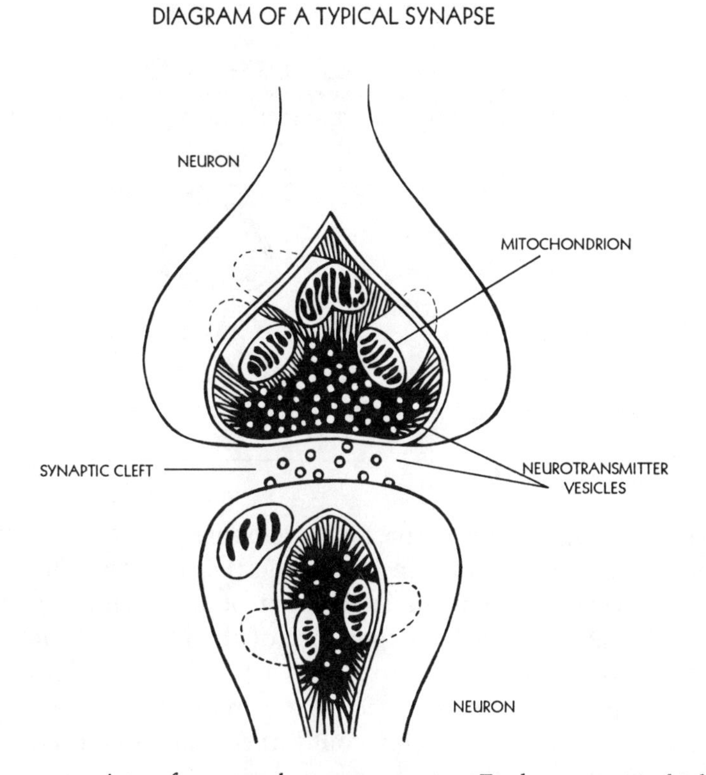

Synapses are points of contact between neurons. Each synapse is highly structured to permit the transmission of chemical messages from cell to cell across the gaps.

cells line up as a strand along the back of the embryo. It then folds into a tube. The tube thickens and folds at the head end as the specialized areas destined to form the brain begin to develop. Nerve cells begin to move along specific paths to their final resting place. This precisely orchestrated sequence of events is critical in the development of the brain, and in the healthy organism is a highly determined and predictable event. Any influence that interferes with the specific hooking up of nerve cells with each other, or with migration of neurons to their final site, can be expected to have serious effects on the child's neurological and behavioral abilities.

Surprisingly, there are more branches and connections in the brain cells of the infant than in the mature adult. After the nerve cells migrate to their final site, they send out thick clouds of branches to connect with their partners. Then a curious thing happens. In many areas, the branches and the connections begin

THE DEVELOPMENT OF THE BRAIN:
THE DEVELOPING HUMAN BRAIN VIEWED FROM THE SIDE IN A SUCCESSION OF EMBRYONIC AND FETAL STAGES

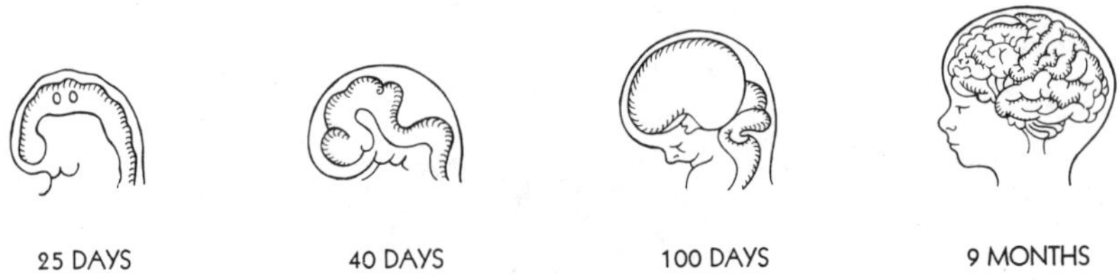

25 DAYS 40 DAYS 100 DAYS 9 MONTHS

to thin out. An important part of development consists of trimming back excess connections in highly specific patterns. This pruning back of cells is in part under the control of the child's genes, but it is also affected by the experience of the nervous system. If the nervous system is exposed to agents that interfere with the specific migration of cells, or the response to stimuli, it will alter the pruning back of dendrites. This could affect the later precision and responsiveness of the child.

The blood-brain barrier, the protective boundary between the general circulation and the brain, is an important defense mechanism for the central nervous system. It isolates the brain from variations in the blood chemistry and, in some cases, shields the brain from exposure to bacteria and poisons. Heavy metals and other brain toxins can interfere with this barrier and make it porous. This can increase vulnerability to other agents. Lead can cause leakage in brain capillaries, and this can lead to brain swelling and eventually hemorrhage.

NEUROTOXINS

■ ■ ■

AN UNDERACKNOWLEDGED PROBLEM

In the paragraphs above, we provided some examples of neurotoxic targets. Neurotoxins can interfere with the migration of embryonal neurons, diminish the number of branches of dendrites, produce immature synapses, inhibit or overstimulate the release of neurotransmitters, slow the degradation of transmitters, disrupt the formation of myelin, and weaken the blood brain barrier. There is clear evidence that agents that have a temporary effect on the adult brain can produce permanent changes if they come in contact with a brain while it is involved in the delicate and incredibly complex process of development. Neurotoxins can have long-delayed effects, and they are receiving careful scrutiny as causes of Parkinson's disease and some dementias.

Many types of chemicals have neurotoxic properties. These include metals, solvents, pesticides, and other organic molecules, including alcohols. There is convincing evidence that some natural products, including foodstuffs, may contain chemicals that under certain circumstances are brain-damaging.

ARE THERE UNRECOGNIZED NEUROTOXINS?

At high doses, neurotoxic attacks on the targets listed above can produce striking symptoms, illness, and disability, including coma, convulsions, respiratory paralysis, and death. At lower doses, some neurotoxic agents can be difficult to detect, but their actions can show up as disturbed mood, altered behavior, impaired thinking and attention. The effects of most of these substances at low doses can only be demonstrated in large-scale epidemiological studies. Clinical observation alone misses them completely. It is likely that we will be finding other agents that affect brain function and behavior. Among the candidates are pesticides, solvents, other metals such as cadmium, and a host of organic molecules that can be found under the sink, in the basement, or in the garage.

Undoubtedly there are many substances that affect the brain and therefore could have an impact on thinking or feeling. We first recognize a toxic disease when a cluster of dramatic cases occurs. Frequently, the people with the highest exposures to toxins, who provide the first cases of disease, are those who work with the toxins and are occupationally exposed. Later, the definition of the disease is broadened to include people who have had lesser exposures and show less dramatic symptoms. This has happened with lead, pesticides, and solvents.

THE DOSE-RESPONSE CURVE: MORE IS WORSE

A critical relationship in understanding the effects of toxins is the "dose-response curve." This simply means that as the amount of drug or toxin experienced increases, the severity of the resulting disturbance increases. The shape of the curve may vary, and for some chemicals which have essential functions, there may be a change in the slope, but this is a universal biological phenomenon of great importance.

In regulating toxins, an important area of debate has been whether there is a threshold for the toxic effect. That is, is there a dose of the agent that is too low to produce an effect? For many substances, there appear to be thresholds, below which no toxicity can be measured. For others, the thresholds are so low that to have any margin of safety, exposure would have to be reduced close to zero. Where thresholds are placed depends on the quality of the science. As scientists use better, more sensitive methods, the effect level for a toxin will often drop, because effects are found that were previously missed.

THE MANY EXPRESSIONS OF NEUROTOXICITY

Toxins can cause psychosis. The Mad Hatter is a fictionalized example of a well-known occupational disease in nineteenth-century England. Hatters used mercury to prepare felt and often took in toxic amounts. Some solvents and organic molecules, as well as lead, have produced psychotic states. When tetraethyl lead was being produced as a gasoline additive in the 1920s, an outbreak of psychotic symptoms occurred in workers in two Du Pont plants in New Jersey. About 300 workers had a psychotic episode; a few died. Because affected workers hallucinated insects crawling on them, and could be seen brushing them off their bodies, the building where tetraethyl lead was synthesized became known as the "House of Butterflies." Any sudden onset of psychotic symptoms should have neurotoxins included in the list of possible causes.

Toxins can cause dementia. Dementia means the loss of thinking ability. Among the symptoms are memory loss, distractibility, disorientation (not knowing where one is, who one is, or a loss of a sense of time). There is growing interest in the role of neurotoxins in Alzheimer-like conditions. One theory holds that aluminum has a role in Alzheimer's disease, but this cannot be considered established.

Neurotoxins can affect sexual development. The resemblance of some environmental chemicals to estrogens raises the question of whether these can affect the gender development of the brain. The brain is sexually dimorphic. This means that after development has occurred the brains of males are anatomically different from those of females. During early fetal life, however, all brains are alike, basically female in organization. The brain of male fetuses, under the influence of testosterone from the developing testes, begins to undergo reorganization. There is considerable evidence that certain hormonal drugs, either masculinizing or feminizing, can alter this process. Also, some synthetic chemicals, particularly pesticides, resemble estrogens and may affect the development of the brain by linking to estrogen receptors. Serious attention is being given to the effects of prenatal exposure to neurochemicals that have estrogenic properties and to their impact on brain development and behavior.

Neurotoxins can affect mood. Workers who use solvents in their jobs, who are in lead fabricating, have a higher incidence of depression, anger, and anxiety than other people. Toxins can interfere with judgment. Neurotoxicity can result in impulsivity and impaired decision making.

The most frequent problem seen in child development clinics is attention deficit disorder and hyperactivity. While it has been recognized as a problem for at least fifty years, it has come under intense examination quite recently. Whether its prevalence is increasing in recent times is not certain. The rate of this disease is between 3 and 10 percent.

Neurotoxins have a particular ability to impede the resistance to distraction, the ability to make discriminations between events, the ability to stick to one task and shift to another when appropriate. There is some evidence that altered neurotransmitter balance constitutes one of the changes in attentional disorders. Studies have indicated that children with hyperactivity and attention deficit disorder have altered patterns of neurotransmitter activity, and this may be the reason for inappropriate responsiveness.

There is persuasive evidence that some hyperactive behavior is an expression of disordered brain function. Whether this qualifies as "brain damage" is difficult to establish and probably not worth arguing about. In the 1940s child specialists reported that retarded children with brain damage differed from those without brain damage by displaying hyperactivity, distractibility, and little ability to inhibit behavior. Others have shown that people with closed head injury (internal head injury without skull fracture) often had problems in social control, and that children with minor signs of neurologic dysfunction had more frequent problems in learning and psychiatric difficulties.

A number of studies suggest that neurotoxins do play a role in attention and behavioral regulation. Lead provides a good example. In one study some hyperactive children excreted more lead in their urine after being given a drug that enhances excretion. In another study American children with higher lead in their teeth had poorer attention and more impulsivity than other children. British investigators found the same relationship. Lead affects many of the sensitive areas that regulate behavior. It alters the output of neurotransmitters, affects myelination, and decreases the branching of the dendrites. Some of these exposures may occur before birth. Because lead crosses the placenta, infants in utero are exposed if their parents' levels are increased.

Because lead's properties are shared to a greater or lesser extent by mercury, solvents, alcohol, carbon monoxide, and probably other agents yet to be identified, we need to determine how much of this attention-hyperactivity disorder is due to brain toxins and can therefore be prevented.

What is obviously needed is a rigorous premarket testing program that would submit any new chemical to a battery of tests for neurotoxicity before it is put on the shelves. Yet the testing protocols of the EPA frequently do not include tests for neurotoxicity.

Types of Neurotoxins

- Metals
  - Lead
  - Mercury
  - Cadmium
  - Tin (organic forms: triethyl tin and trimethyl tin)
  - Manganese
  - Aluminum
- Solvents
  - Alcohol
  - Styrenes
  - Trichloroethylene
  - Vinyl chloride
  - Gasoline (including benzene additives)
  - Toluene
  - Methylethylketone
  - Carbon tetrachloride
- Pesticides
  - Carbamates
  - Organophosphates

WHAT CAN PARENTS DO TO REDUCE NEUROTOXIC EXPOSURE?

■ ■ ■

Making the home safe from neurotoxins is relatively simple. The use of organic solvents should be minimized. If they are used for cleaning or other purposes, they should not be stored in your house or in any other area accessible to children. Inventory your home; decide what solvents are absolutely essential, and store them in your garage or shed. Get rid of the others on a special toxic waste disposal day or through a toxic waste disposal site. When solvents are used, it is important to make sure that the home is adequately ventilated. Pesticide use should also be minimized. Fruits and vegetables should be washed carefully before eating. Do not eat fruits out of season. These are imported from southern countries where the use of pesticides is widespread. More and more, markets are stocking certified organic fruits and vegetables. See Chapters 4 and 5 for advice on protecting the home from leaded paint and mercury.

WHAT CAN BE DONE TO REDUCE THE LOAD OF NEUROTOXINS?

■ ■ ■

We need to encourage new approaches to pest control, to reduce the environmental load of these agents. There are two approaches to accomplishing this: through the market and through regulation. If consumers make their choices known, there will be more pesticide-free products available. This is exactly what happened with Alar and apples. When educated mothers told their suppliers that they would not buy apples treated with this chemical, apple growers quickly responded, and you can now readily obtain safe apples in the market.

There are strong signs that our unhealthy approach to growing vegetables and fruits through the wholesale use of pesticides is changing. The recently issued report on pesticides by the National Academy of Sciences indicates that children need special protection from neurotoxins and that the governmental standards do not accommodate this need. Farming practices that use little or no pesticides can be practical and profitable, and more farmers are turning to these practices.

The federal government, particularly the EPA, needs to test all chemicals for neurotoxicity before clearing them for production. Clear labeling of potentially toxic products is needed. At the present time, far too many compounds are released to the market without being exposed to rigorous testing for neurotoxicity.

We need extensive epidemiologic studies of nervous system function in relation to the toxins described. We believe that in the next decade a large number of heretofore unknown interactions between chemicals and brain function will be demonstrated, and that some of the disorders now being treated by psychiatrists will be shown to be due in part to low-dose neurotoxic exposure. When that happens, what was considered untreatable will be shown to be preventable.

CANCER

"Childhood cancer": few phrases evoke a greater level of concern and apprehension in a parent. Parents are understandably frustrated when scientists do not and cannot provide rapid, unequivocal answers to what seem to be the simplest questions. Are there toxins in my water? Is there something in the air or soil in my neighborhood that will affect *my* family? Another child in my child's school has cancer; will my child get cancer? There seems to be a lot of cancer in my neighborhood: should I move?

In this chapter, we hope to give you some perspectives on what childhood cancer is, how prevalent it is, what causes it (or, more correctly, what causes the many diseases we call "cancer"), what science can tell us about environmental cancer (and what it still doesn't know), and what you as parents can do to assess and minimize the chance that your child will develop cancer.

First, a word about risk perception: psychologists tell us that people are more willing to accept risks over which they have direct and personal control (such as smoking, eating or drinking to excess, and driving too fast). But most people are not at all willing to accept risks that are "invisible" or beyond their control, such as dangers from radioactive materials; X rays, electromagnetic radiation (EMF), and toxins in their water, air, or food. This seems to hold true, even if the risks that people voluntarily choose are many times greater than those over which they have no control.

The level of concern and anger expressed over a risk is often related to the level of control people have over it.

For many people, "childhood cancer" and "cancer clusters" seem to fall into the category of "things over which they have little control." It is easy to see why parents express alarm, anger, and agitation to their pediatrician and to public health officials when a child develops cancer or when a "cancer cluster" is perceived in their environment. With the tools and information contained in this chapter, we hope to give you as parents some control over these things. We hope to help you develop a realistic assessment of the cancer risk and to bring your level of concern to an appropriate intensity. Then we hope to give you some practical guidance about what to do.

Unfortunately, cancer is not a rare disease among children. Each year in the United States, approximately 6,500 new cases of cancer are diagnosed among children under the age of 15 years, and each year approximately 2,200 children die of cancer. On average, an American child has one chance in 600 of developing cancer before the age of 15. Cancer rates are slightly higher in Caucasian than in African-American children and somewhat higher in boys than in girls. Cancer is second only to trauma as a cause of death for American children beyond the newborn age group.

The good news is that over the past twenty years there has been a most impressive decline in the death rate from childhood cancer. Remarkable advances in cancer treatment have resulted in substantial reductions in the death rate for several forms of childhood cancer.

There are two extremely important facts that you need to know about cancer:

- *A substantial fraction of cancers may ultimately be preventable.* Scientists estimate that only 10 to 20 percent of cancer is due to a person's genetic inheritance. The rest is due to our environment—including what we eat, breathe, drink, smoke, or are exposed to during the course of our lives. Because many cancers are caused by exposure to toxic factors in the environment, these cancers can be avoided by preventing children's exposure to environmental toxins.
- *Childhood cancer, although always a terrifying disease, is highly treatable.* Children can be cured. Today more than 60 percent of children who develop cancer can be expected to survive their illness. Major advances have been made in the treatment of

leukemia, Hodgkin's disease, and non-Hodgkin's lymphoma. Given the treatability of childhood cancer, it is important that each case of cancer in a child be evaluated thoroughly, that treatment be begun promptly, and that state-of-the-art therapy be pursued aggressively.

THE NATURE OF CANCER

■ ■ ■

Cancer is characterized by uncontrolled growth and chaotic multiplication of cells. Cancerous cells have lost their normal ability to stop growing and dividing. They do not mature and become stable or respond to messages from other cells and organs.

Each case of cancer is now believed by medical scientists to originate from a single cell. The many billions of cells that comprise a fully developed cancer descend from a single cell that has gone awry and undergone malignant transformation.

The creation of a cancerous cell is a slow stepwise process, a transformation that usually requires many years or even decades. The first stage is a change in the genetic material, the DNA, in one of the body's many cells. This change in DNA is termed a mutation.

Many factors can trigger the initial mutation. These include physical agents such as radiation and chemical toxins. In some cases the initial mutation appears to arise spontaneously, perhaps because of an inherited predisposition. Some people are more sensitive than others to carcinogens in the environment. The initial mutation is a necessary step on the pathway to cancer, but by itself it is not sufficient to cause cancer. A series of additional changes are required before the initiated cell and its descendants actually become cancerous.

The subsequent steps in the formation of cancer consist of a series of further mutations. These additional mutations make the cell and its descendants more and more unstable, and they bring about further increases in the rate of cell growth. A common sequence is that the initial mutation activates a type of gene called an oncogene. Activation of the oncogene results in increased production of cellular growth factors that cause the cell to grow at a rapid rate. When the cell is growing too rapidly and undergoing division at an accelerated pace, the likelihood of a second mutation increases. This second mutation frequently consists of the deactivation of a tumor suppressor gene, a gene that normally slows the growth of cells. When an oncogene has been activated and a suppressor gene turned off, the effect is similar to that of a car running downhill without its brakes and with the accelerator held down by a brick.

At this point, with the affected cells multiplying much too rapidly and in a poorly controlled fashion, the cells become highly susceptible to still further changes in their genetic material. Chromosomes may be mistakenly transcribed or chromosomal breaks may occur. The cell becomes more and more independent and no longer responds to messages that it receives from the cells around it. Finally, the evolving cancer cell becomes totally independent and fully capable of multiplying chaotically. At this point, a true cancer exists. The cells have become malignant.

Once a true cancer has developed, the malignant cells can metastasize—that is, they can develop the ability to migrate from the initial site of the cancer to other areas of the body, where they may cause secondary cancers. For example, cancers of the intestine frequently metastasize to the liver. Cancers of the lung may metastasize to the brain. Usually, when cancer has become metastatic it responds poorly to treatment.

In recent years, enormous amounts of new information on malignant transformation and on the processes involved in the development of cancer have been provided by the tools of molecular biology. We now understand a great deal more about the steps in the evolution of human cancer than we did even five or ten years ago. The prospects are very real that it will be possible in the not too distant future to identify human cancer before it has become fully malignant. Such early identification could lead to early treatment, successful cure, and effective preventive action.

THE ENVIRONMENT AND CANCER

■ ■ ■

For centuries cancer was considered by doctors as well as by the general public to be mysterious, unpredictable, and inevitable.

Cancer was perceived as an occasional dark visitor in childhood or as a consequence of aging. That view is no longer accurate. Cancer is neither inevitable nor unpreventable. We now know the causes of a substantial fraction of cases of cancer, and because we know some of the causes of cancer, we are beginning to prevent and to cure the disease.

In the broadest terms, there are two types of causes of cancer —genetic causes and environmental causes.

Genetic causes are predispositions that we inherit from our parents. They include certain syndromes that predispose members of some families to cancer. For example, there are inherited syndromes that predispose to skin cancer and to cancer of the colon. Some families have a predisposition to cancer at many different sites within the body because of an inherited fragility of their chromosomes that leads to frequent mutations. For example, families with the Fraumeni-Li syndrome have a genetic rearrangement of their chromosomes associated with an increased frequency of many tumors. Screening tests are being developed that make it possible to identify individuals and families at high risk of cancer and to take appropriate preventive action.

Environmental factors are a major cause of human cancer. Chemical and physical factors in the environment that can cause cancer are termed *environmental carcinogens*. An estimated 80 to 90 percent of all human cancer is thought by medical scientists to be caused by exposure to carcinogens encountered in the environment. In this definition, the term "environment" is used broadly. It includes not only air pollutants, chemical toxins, asbestos, and other obvious environmental hazards but also carcinogens in the diet, toxic agents in drinking water, drugs, alcohol, and cigarette smoke. Another way to express this concept is to say that only 10 to 20 percent of cancer is an inevitable consequence of a person's genetic inheritance.

Because a very high proportion of human cancer is caused by environmental carcinogens, it should be possible to prevent many cases of cancer by avoiding toxic environmental exposures.

Tobacco is the single most important cause of cancer in the United States today. Tobacco is responsible for at least 40 percent of all cases of cancer. Lung cancer is the principal carcinogenic consequence of smoking. Smoking also causes cancer of the bladder, cancer of the esophagus, and cancers of other organs. Snuff

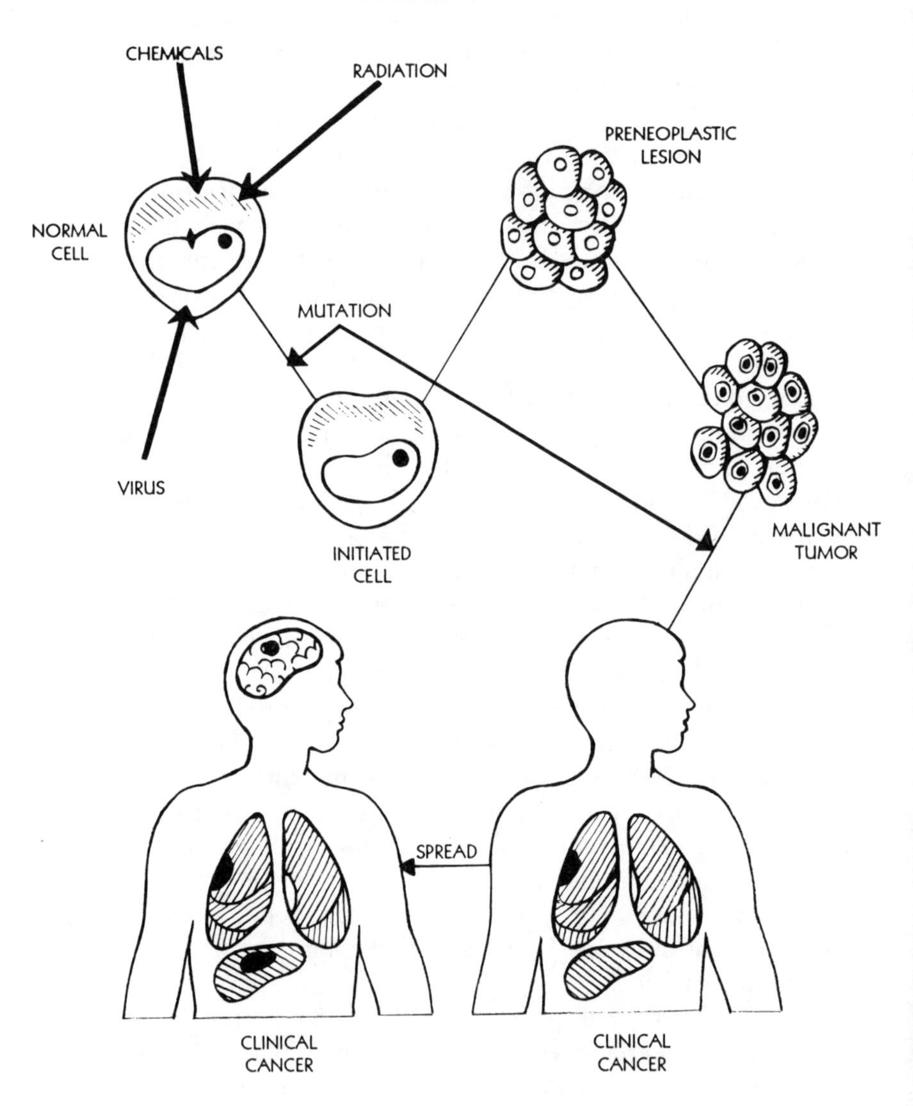
THE MULTIPLE STAGES OF CANCER DEVELOPMENT IN NORMAL CELLS
CHEMICALS
RADIATION
PRENEOPLASTIC LESION
NORMAL CELL
MUTATION
VIRUS
INITIATED CELL
MALIGNANT TUMOR
SPREAD
CLINICAL CANCER
CLINICAL CANCER

causes oral cancer. One of the most important steps in cancer prevention is to keep your children from smoking. (See Chapter 9 for a full discussion of tobacco and its hazards.)

Radiation was shown to cause cancer among children who were exposed to the atomic bombings in Hiroshima and Nagasaki. Leukemia was seen in these children as early as two to three years after the bombings, and later an increased incidence of tumors in many other organs, including brain, breast, and lung cancer, was observed. Radiation-induced leukemia and other radiation cancers have been seen in children who were exposed to high doses of X rays for the treatment of ringworm of the scalp. Thyroid cancer has occurred in children given X rays for treatment of an enlarged thymus gland. Radon causes lung cancer. Radiation therapy of childhood cancer has proven to be a two-edged sword. While radiation therapy can cure a child's initial cancer, it can itself cause later, so-called secondary cancers. Thus, bone cancers and cancers of the skin and breast have been seen as secondary cancers in children given radiation therapy for treatment of cancers earlier in their lives. In light of this new knowledge, radiation therapy is administered much more carefully today than in the past. (See Chapter 8.)

Asbestos has been shown to cause lung cancer and malignant mesothelioma in the children of asbestos workers. These children were exposed to asbestos-contaminated dust that was brought home from work on their fathers' shoes and clothing. Asbestos in homes, schools, and other buildings is also a hazard for children. Some researchers have estimated that at least 1,000 cases of cancer, principally lung cancer and malignant mesothelioma, will develop over the next thirty years among children who are exposed to asbestos in schools today. (See Chapter 6.)

Pesticides in food and drink pose a risk of cancer to children. Permissible levels of pesticides in foods, termed pesticide residue levels, are established by the Environmental Protection Agency. These permissible levels are based on the adult diet. These legally permissible levels do not at present recognize the fact that children's diets are very different from those of adults. The National Academy of Sciences has recently issued a report concluding that American children are overexposed to pesticide residues in their diets (see page 114).

The pesticide DDT may pose a particular hazard to children. Preliminary results from recently conducted medical studies indicate that DDT exposures may be associated with an increased risk of breast cancer. This may reflect the fact that DDT in the fatty tissue of the breast possesses certain estrogenic properties. (See Chapter 7.)

Benzene is a proven cause of leukemia and lymphoma. The major route of children's exposure to this solvent is through handling unleaded gasoline. Unleaded gasoline contains about 5 percent benzene, which is highly volatile and can easily vaporize. Children can be exposed to benzene by inhalation while pumping gas in self-service stations or when fueling small engines such as those of lawn mowers. Benzene can also be absorbed into the body through the skin (see Chapter 10). Exposure of children to solvents and to gasoline should be prevented whenever possible.

Formaldehyde is an irritating gas and a proven carcinogen. It has been shown to be capable of causing lung cancer and cancer of the nasal sinuses. In the 1970s and early 1980s, urea-formaldehyde foam, a form of insulation that was blown in between the inner and outer walls of homes, was a major source of formaldehyde exposure for children and parents. Formaldehyde gas is also released from new plywood furniture, carpets, and curtains. It is wise to air these products out of doors before use or to put them in a room with open windows and away from children for a few days when they are first unwrapped.

Steroids, particularly anabolic androgenic steroids used illegally by some athletes to enhance muscle bulk and improve performance, are carcinogenic. They have been shown to cause cancer of the liver. They should never be used for any purpose having to do with athletics by persons of any age. The short-term gains are dubious, and the long-term dangers are great.

Polychlorinated biphenyls (PCBs) are a family of synthetic chemicals that were used widely from the 1950s until the 1970s as liquid insulators in the manufacture of electrical equipment such as transformers, compressors, and the ballasts that are used in fluorescent fixtures. PCBs are now known to cause liver cancer.

Children's exposure to the liquid insulating material in electrical equipment should be prevented. If a transformer spill occurs, or if a fluorescent ballast explodes and sprays its liquid material into the environment, children should not be allowed to come into contact with the material. The area where the spill occurred must be properly cleaned by a hazardous-materials team from the local fire department or the EPA.

Air pollution. Concern is widespread among medical scientists that chronic exposure to air pollution, either by itself or in combination with cigarette smoking, may cause cancer, especially lung cancer. Children are at particular risk of cancer caused by air pollution because they have many years of life ahead of them in which to develop malignancy.

Toxic materials emitted into the environment by industrial plants are hazardous to children. Arsenic emitted by copper smelters can cause lung cancer. Benzene and 1,3-butadiene from oil refineries, chemical plants, and rubber plants can cause leukemia and lymphoma. If you live near major industrial plants, you should examine the EPA's Toxic Release Inventory to learn which types of toxic material the plants in your neighborhood may emit. Information on how to access the Toxic Release Inventory is provided in Chapter 11.

Indoor air pollution can also pose cancer hazards to your children. Perchloroethylene, a solvent commonly used for dry cleaning, can vaporize in your home from newly cleaned clothes and can pose a risk of liver cancer. Exposure to perchloroethylene vapor is most easily prevented by airing freshly cleaned clothes out of doors or in an area away from children for the first several days after they have been returned from the dry-cleaning shop.

Glues and solvents. Airplane glues, epoxies, instant glue, and other glues and adhesives that children may use in home hobbies can be very toxic. Exposures to glues containing benzene and related compounds carry a risk of leukemia. Never let your children use these glues in an inadequately ventilated room. Preferably they should be used out of doors. Better yet, encourage your child to use only those glues that contain no benzene.

It is also wise to beware of the hazard of glue sniffing in children who may use glues for hobbies. Vapors of these chemicals are intoxicating and addictive, and young children are at particular risk of this addiction. Prudent avoidance is clearly the best policy.

Municipal incinerators. There is an increasing trend in the United States to burn municipal waste as a means of reducing pressure on overcrowded dumps and landfills. Incineration does not solve the problem of waste. It only transfers the problem to another arena. With waste incineration, the consequence is air pollution instead of brimming landfills. Waste incinerators can emit carcinogenic compounds such as dioxins and furans. They can also disperse into the air other toxic materials, such as lead and mercury, which may be present in municipal waste. The only rational approach to preventing the formation of carcinogenic materials through waste incineration is to reduce waste at its source.

Toxic waste dumps. Hazardous waste disposal sites dot the landscape of the United States and other industrialized countries around the world. In many cases, local and state authorities as well as the EPA have only fragmentary knowledge of the contents of these dumps, because materials were placed there over many years and no records were kept of their disposal. To deal with the most serious of these sites in the United States, the EPA has designated a list of so-called superfund sites. These are the hazardous waste sites that have been deemed the most toxic in the nation, and monies for their remediation are made available under the federal superfund legislation.

Many of the materials in toxic waste sites are known carcinogens. The risk exists that these materials may escape from the waste site and either vaporize into the air or pass through groundwater into community drinking water supplies.

No general rules apply to toxic waste dumps. Each has different contents in a unique location. Therefore each dump must be evaluated individually to assess the possible risk that it may pose to you, your neighbors, and your children. To learn whether you are at risk of exposure to materials from a toxic waste site, you are advised to contact the environmental authorities in your city or state or the regional office of the EPA (see page 244).

Electromagnetic fields (EMFs). Concern has increased over the past decade that children's exposures to electromagnetic fields may increase their risk of cancer. Fortunately, the strength of an EMF decreases rapidly with distance from its source. Therefore, a policy of prudent avoidance suggests that you should carefully consider your options before you buy a house directly under or within a hundred feet of a power line. (See Chapter 8.)

Diet and cancer. Much has been written about the possible carcinogenic hazards of the American diet. Full information on this contentious topic is not yet available. A high-fat diet may be associated with increases in breast and colon cancer as well as with increased rates of heart disease. Major international studies have shown that the nations of the world that have the highest content of fat in the diet, such as the United States, most Western European nations, New Zealand, and Australia, also have the highest incidence of breast cancer and colon cancer and of heart disease. Persons whose diets are rich in yellow and green vegetables and rich in fiber have been found to have a lower incidence of cancer.

We strongly advise that you establish wise dietary habits in your child in early childhood. Limit your children's exposure to fat in the diet and increase the amount of green and yellow vegetables and fiber in their diet. If your children learn from an early age to reach for a carrot instead of a sweet, they can only be healthier in the years ahead.

EXPOSURES TO CARCINOGENS IN THE WOMB

■ ■ ■

Prenatal and preconception exposures to carcinogens are a potential source of childhood cancer. Pediatricians and medical researchers have been concerned that exposures of either mothers or fathers to certain carcinogenic pesticides and solvents prior to conception may increase the risk of cancer in their children. An increased rate of leukemia and brain cancer has been seen in the children of parents exposed to chemicals, paints, and solvents in their workplace.

Exposure of the fetus and newborn child to radiation is also hazardous. The fetus appears to be more sensitive to radiation than older children. An increased rate of leukemia has been observed among children exposed prenatally to X rays. Pregnant women should avoid X rays unless they are absolutely necessary. Ultrasound examinations are a safe alternative.

EMFs should also be avoided during pregnancy. Although full data are not yet available, it is prudent for pregnant mothers to avoid spending significant amounts of time near high-tension power lines or under electric blankets.

Certain drugs taken during pregnancy have been shown to increase the risk of cancer. The best-known case is the increased risk of vaginal cancer in young women who were exposed in utero to diethylstilbestrol (DES). Young women who were exposed to DES in utero should have regular gynecologic examinations once they have passed puberty. Young men who were exposed in utero to DES may also be at an increased risk of reproductive abnormalities and may suffer from lowered fertility when they reach adult life.

Dilantin, used to treat epilepsy, has been shown to produce congenital malformations of the face in certain children. Some of these children have also been found to be at high risk to develop a particular form of brain tumor.

Use of medications and exposures to hazardous or potentially hazardous chemicals during pregnancy should be reduced to an essential minimum.

EXPOSURES OF CHILDREN TO CARCINOGENS CARRIED HOME FROM WORK

■ ■ ■

Pediatricians have long recognized that parents can carry hazardous materials home from work that can cause poisoning in their children. As a result, lead poisoning has been seen in the children of lead workers, and pesticide poisoning in the children of agricultural workers. Carcinogens can also be carried home from work on the clothing, shoes, skin, hair, and autos of working parents.

Asbestos is the best known example of a carcinogen carried home from work. Cases of malignant mesothelioma have been seen in young and middle-aged adults who were never occupationally exposed and whose only exposure was to asbestos dust carried home from work by their parents twenty-five or more years earlier.

Parents who work around carcinogenic or other hazardous substances should make every effort not to transport these materials home. The safest procedure is to shower before leaving work if that is possible and to leave soiled clothes at work in a locker that is separate from the locker used to hold the clean clothing that you wear home. If that is not possible, then a parent who works with hazardous material should, immediately upon returning home, remove his or her clothes in an area where children will not be exposed to any dust. These clothes should be laundered separately from other clothing.

THE SPECIAL VULNERABILITY OF CHILDREN TO ENVIRONMENTAL CARCINOGENS

■ ■ ■

Children are more vulnerable to carcinogens than are adults. Children have many more years of life ahead of them after a toxic exposure in which to develop a tumor. Malignant transformation is a slow process. Children's ability to detoxify environmental chemicals is not fully developed. They lack certain mechanisms possessed by adults that enhance the removal of toxic chemicals from the body. Thus children's exposures to environmental carcinogens must be minimized.

CANCER CLUSTERS

■ ■ ■

A cancer cluster is defined as a group of cancer cases of the same or similar type of cancer that occur together in the same place and at the same time. The first report of a cancer cluster appeared in 1963 in Niles, Illinois. There a series of acute leukemia cases were observed among children attending a single elementary school. Although no specific cause was ever found for this cluster even after several years of research, this event prompted a widespread search for viral and environmental causes of cancer.

Cancer clusters are not uncommon. Several hundred have occurred in areas throughout the United States over the past two decades. The central question that confronts pediatricians and medical scientists is whether the cluster is caused by a preventable environmental factor or whether it is simply the result of a statistical artifact. Is it triggered by a preventable cause or is it simply a matter of unfortunate coincidence?

Every cancer cluster requires evaluation. Investigations of cancer clusters have provided the initial clues needed to solve several major problems in environmental health. For example, the hazards of asbestos were first recognized through evaluation of a cluster of cases of malignant mesothelioma. A cluster of liver cancer cases in Louisville, Kentucky, in 1974 led to the discovery that the chemical vinyl chloride monomer could cause angiosarcoma of the liver, and a cluster of lung cancers in young chemical workers in Philadelphia in the early 1970s demonstrated that the chemical bischloromethylether could cause lung cancer. In many cases even the most thorough evaluation of a cluster will find no obvious environmental cause.

The likelihood that a cancer cluster is caused by an environmental factor becomes much greater when all of the cancers in the cluster are of the same type or are closely related types of cancer.

If you suspect that a cancer cluster is occurring in your neighborhood, in your child's school, or in your parish, it is important that you discuss the problem with your pediatrician and with local public health authorities.

The first step that your pediatrician and the public health authorities will take in evaluating the cluster will be to compile a complete list of all cases of cancer that have occurred in the area. They will obtain information on the date of onset and on the type of each cancer. The likelihood of a common environmental factor is increased if several cancers of the same type are found. Also it is important to determine how long affected children have lived in the area. If cancer develops in a child who has moved into a community only recently, the likelihood of a local environmental cause is less.

The investigation of cancer clusters must be conducted in an open manner so that all people who may be concerned about the cluster are given full information about the study. Major problems have developed in communities where public health authorities have attempted to conduct the investigation in a secretive fashion.

If a true association is found between an environmental factor and a cancer cluster, then a special cancer registry must be established immediately. Any new cases of cancer that develop in the area must promptly be brought to the attention of public health authorities. Preventive measures must also be taken. The precise nature of those preventive measures will depend, of course, on the type of carcinogen detected.

Even if no identifiable cause for a cancer cluster is detected, it is still advisable that a special registry be established and that this registry be maintained for several years by the local public health authorities. These would include the city or county health department or the state epidemiology department. In this way, no possibility of environmental cancer will be overlooked. Parents, teachers, pediatricians, and other members of the community will be reassured that everything possible is being done to monitor and protect the health of their children.

INCREASING RATES OF CHILDHOOD CANCER

■ ■ ■

Although the death rate from childhood cancer has declined in recent years, the occurrence of new cases of cancer among children—the incidence rate—has been increasing. This upward trend has been most strongly evident for acute lymphocytic leukemia and brain cancer, two of the most common forms of cancer in childhood.

For acute lymphocytic leukemia, the most common childhood cancer, the rate of increase over the past fifteen years has been 10.7 percent. For brain tumors, the incidence has increased by 30.5 percent. As frightening as those figures are, the actual numbers are small. In the case of leukemia, the incidence rate rose from 2.4 cases for every 100,000 children in 1973 to 3.2 cases per 100,000 in 1988. For brain cancer, the incidence rate increased from 2.3 per 100,000 in 1973 to 3.4 per 100,000 children in 1988.

These increases have not been explained. In part they may reflect better diagnostic detection of new cases, especially with brain cancer. However, the strong possibility also exists that environmental factors may be playing a role. Continued research to identify the environmental causes of childhood cancer is therefore essential.

What might be some of the environmental factors responsible for these increasing rates of cancer incidence? One possibility is increased exposure to synthetic chemicals. Since World War II, the number of new synthetic chemicals that have been released into the environment has increased almost astronomically. Today there are approximately 70,000 unique chemical substances in use in the United States, and there are almost 7 million commercial chemical products. Production levels of synthetic chemicals have doubled every seven to eight years since the 1930s, and total production is now in excess of 200 billion pounds per year. Although it is difficult to know precisely how much human exposure has resulted from these increasing rates of chemical production, it is clear that children's exposures to synthetic chemicals have become much more extensive.

Increasing exposure to electromagnetic fields constitutes a second possible explanation for the observed increase in brain cancer and leukemia among children. These specific types of childhood cancer have been shown in several well-conducted recent studies to be associated with residence near high-tension power lines.

Melanoma, a particularly aggressive form of skin cancer, is also on the rise in the United States. This is almost certainly due to increased exposure to the sun. Rates are higher in the southern United States than in the north. Melanoma rates are much higher in persons who had repeated sunburns in childhood than in people who were not burned. Melanoma rates are much higher in people with light complexions, particularly redheads, than in persons with darker complexions. This cancer is almost unknown among African-Americans. Melanoma can largely be prevented by minimizing children's exposure to the sun. In particular, it is important to prevent blistering sunburns in childhood. Shirts, hats, and ultraviolet blocking creams are essential for children who spend substantial amounts of time out of doors.

Breast cancer is increasing in the United States among adult women. The causes of this increase are unknown. Chemicals, pesticides, industrial chemicals, and electromagnetic fields have all been suggested as possible factors, but detailed investigations into the causes of the current increases in female breast cancer are only beginning. Past exposures to the pesticide DDT may be a risk factor. Recent epidemiologic studies have suggested a link between DDT and breast cancer.

We suggest that to reduce the risk of future breast cancer you encourage your children to eat a diet relatively low in fats and high in vegetables and fiber. This approach will reduce exposure to DDT, which is concentrated in fatty foods. Although the association between dietary fat and breast cancer is by no means proven, enough information is already in hand to warrant prudent avoidance of a high-fat diet.

WHAT CAN PARENTS AND PEDIATRICIANS DO?

■ ■ ■

Except for those few children who have clearly defined cancer syndromes, it is impossible for you or your pediatrician to determine whether your child is susceptible or resistant to cancer. There is no way at present to detect the early changes, the early mutations, that may precede the later development of cancer. The only prudent approach is to minimize your child's exposures and your own exposures to environmental carcinogens whenever possible.

The following is a list of suggested approaches to cancer prevention. Some of the cancers that will be prevented are childhood cancers. However, the majority of the cancers prevented are those that could develop in your children after they have grown into adulthood.

CIGARETTE SMOKING

Cigarettes and other forms of tobacco are the major causes of cancer in the United States. You must take every possible measure to prevent the initiation of tobacco use by your children. (See Chapter 9.)

RADIATION

Prevent unnecessary exposure of your children to radiation. (See Chapter 8.)

ELECTROMAGNETIC FIELDS (EMFS)

See Chapter 8.

DIET

Carefully watch the foods that your children eat. Whenever possible purchase foods that are grown without pesticides or with only minimal pesticide applications. Encourage your child to eat a diet low in fats and high in vegetables, fiber, and calcium.

Pediatricians must work through the American Academy of Pediatrics to persuade the EPA that the present approach to the setting of pesticide residue levels in foods makes no sense for the protection of the health of children.

ASBESTOS

The argument that asbestos in schools and homes is not hazardous is false. The guidelines developed by the EPA and the American Academy of Pediatrics for the assessment and management of asbestos in schools must be followed closely. (See Chapter 6.)

BENZENE AND OTHER SOLVENTS

Minimize your children's exposure to benzene and other solvents in drinking water, in airplane glues, and in other settings. When glues must be used, use them out of doors.

SUNLIGHT

Sunlight is a proven cause of skin cancer. Blistering sunburns are particularly dangerous. Children with light complexions, fair or red hair, and blue eyes are at particular risk. It is essential to minimize the exposure of your children to direct sunlight from the earliest age. We strongly recommend the use of hats, long-sleeved shirts, and ultraviolet blocking creams, especially among light-complexioned children.

HOUSEHOLD CHEMICALS

Formaldehyde from furniture and carpets, and perchloroethylene from dry-cleaned clothing can vaporize into the home environment. To minimize your children's exposure to these chemicals, we suggest that dry-cleaned clothes be aired for a few days out of doors or in an area where children will have no contact with the vapors. New furniture and new carpeting should, if possible, also be aired out in an area where children will not have contact with vapors.

RECOMMENDATIONS TO PEDIATRICIANS

■ ■ ■

It is critical that pediatricians understand the importance of counseling parents and prospective parents about reducing their own exposure and the exposure of their children to environmental carcinogens. Parents should be encouraged to stop smoking, to eat a healthy diet, and to minimize their use of alcohol. The benefits from these healthy behaviors will be manifold. Children of parents who pursue healthy lifestyles will have good role models and positive examples.

Pediatricians also need to be aware of the health hazards of specific exposures, such as to asbestos, radiation, and industrial releases and pesticides. When counseling new parents, ask about the presence of toxic chemicals in the home and suggest appropriate approaches to reducing children's exposure.

Cancer clusters pose a difficult dilemma for pediatricians and public health authorities, because they know in advance that the majority of cluster investigations will not identify a specific environmental cause. Yet it is essential that the pediatrician and public health authorities investigate every cluster. The possibility of a preventable environmental cause always exists, and it would be tragic to overlook such a cause. The approach that is suggested in this chapter represents a reasonable introduction to the subject. Pediatricians who wish to read further are referred to a special supplement to the *American Journal of Epidemiology* (132: July, 1990) on cancer clusters.

NORMAL CELLS

Every organ is made up of millions of cells. Each of these cells has the same general structure. Surrounding the cell is a tough outer layer, the *cell membrane*. It receives and transmits messages from other cells and organs, and regulates the flow of materials into and out of the cell.

At the core of each cell is the *nucleus*. The nucleus contains 46 chromosomes, 23 derived from the mother and 23 from the father. These chromosomes came together at the moment of conception with the joining of sperm and egg to form your child's first cell. As this original cell grew and divided to form all of the cells and organs in your child's body, the chromosomes were also replicated, so that a complete copy is present in each and every cell.

The chromosomes contain *deoxyribonucleic acid (DNA)*. DNA is the fundamental human genetic material. It contains the genetic code, handed down from generation to generation, that directs the construction and the functioning of every cell and every organ in your child's body. It is the inherited information in DNA that determines the sex, the color of the skin and eyes, the proper functioning of the liver, the shape of the blood cells, and the susceptibility or resistance to environmental cancer. The DNA is organized into message units termed *genes*.

The *cytoplasm* lies between the nucleus and the cell membrane. It contains all of the enzymes, mitochondria, and other structures that are responsible for the day-to-day metabolism and operation of each cell. The activities of most of the cytoplasmic components are directed and controlled by messages sent from the nuclear DNA.

DIAGRAM OF A CELL

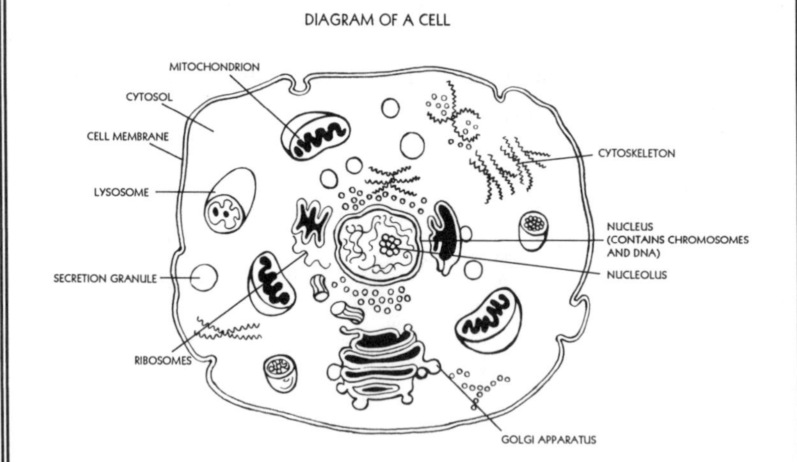

Every organ in the human body is made up of millions of cells. Each cell is surrounded by an outer coat, the plasma membrane, and contains numerous internal structures, called organelles.

WHAT IS THE EVIDENCE THAT ENVIRONMENTAL FACTORS CAN CAUSE CANCER?

Four types of study have provided data on the role of environmental factors in cancer:

1. Studies of geographic variation

There is an enormous variation in the incidence of cancer from one nation to another. Esophageal cancer occurs 300 times more frequently in northeastern Iran than in Nigeria. Stomach cancer is approximately 25 times more frequent in Japan than in Uganda. Skin cancer is more than 200 times more frequent among Australians than among Indians who live in Bombay.

Within nations great regional variation is also evident in mortality from certain cancers. In the 1950s mortality from cancer of the lung and bronchi among white males in the United States was much higher in the port cities of the east, south, and west coasts than it was in most of the nation. Heavy smoking in those urban environments and exposure to asbestos in the wartime shipyards appear to have accounted for most of the excess. Counties with excess lung cancer mortality were noted in the Rocky Mountains; most of those excesses were found to have occurred in communities surrounding arsenic-emitting copper smelters. Bladder cancer in males was found to be heavily concentrated in the Middle Atlantic States, particularly in New Jersey. Further analysis indicated that most of that excess mortality was centered in counties with a concentration of chemical industries.

2. Migrant studies

Evaluation of migrant populations provides a second technique for separating environmental from genetic factors in cancer causation. Migrant studies compare persons of identical genetic stock living in differing environments.

In these studies, the incidence of cancer has tended to change within one to two generations from that observed in the home country to that of the new land. In Japanese immigrants to the United States, the rate of stomach cancer fell within two generations from the high incidence found in Japan to a much lower rate approaching that of United States Caucasians. Over the same generations, the incidence rates for cancers of the breast and colon increased approximately fourfold among Japanese migrants to the United States. Among Polish immigrants to Australia, the high rate of carcinoma of the stomach practically disappears within one generation, and among British immigrants to the tropics, the incidence of skin cancer is much higher than among Britons in Britain.

WHAT IS THE EVIDENCE THAT ENVIRONMENTAL FACTORS CAN CAUSE CANCER? *(cont.)*

3. Trends over time

Incidence rates of several cancers have changed markedly over time. Lung cancer among white males in the United States rose sharply in the years following World War II. This epidemic appears to have reflected increased cigarette smoking, which became widespread during the war years, as well as extensive exposure to asbestos. More recently mortality rates for lung cancer in white males in the United States have begun to decline, while those in black males have increased rapidly, particularly in the younger age groups. Those changes may reflect recent alterations in smoking behavior. Finally, lung cancer mortality rates in the past decade have risen alarmingly in American women as sexual equality has become the norm in the consumption of tobacco.

4. Identification of specific causes

The strongest confirmation of the role of environmental factors in the causation of cancer comes from studies which have identified specific chemicals as the cause of particular types of cancer. More than 30 human carcinogens have been so identified either through testing in animals or through studies of exposed response. Among the more well known are radiation, benzene, vinyl chloride, and benzidine.

Many specific chemicals with which we and our children come into regular contact have never been properly tested for their cancer-causing potential. Federal regulations to require the testing of new chemical compounds for their human health hazards have long been weak.

ENVIRONMENTAL SOURCES OF SOME CARCINOGENS

CARCINOGEN	ENVIRONMENTAL SOURCES OF CARCINOGENS	POSSIBLE CANCER RISKS
Ionizing radiation	X rays Radiation therapy Nuclear explosions	Leukemia Thyroid cancer Cancer of other organs
Asbestos	Insulation in schools and other buildings Dust on parents' clothing	Lung cancer Malignant mesothelioma
Pesticides	Food and drinking water Lawn care Home application against termites and cockroaches	Leukemia Cancer of various organs
Benzene	Unleaded gasoline (by both inhalation and skin contact)	Leukemia Lymphoma
Formaldehyde	Urea-formaldehyde foam insulation (UFFI) Pressed-wood furniture Carpeting and other fabrics	Nasal sinus cancer Lung cancer
Polychlorinated biphenyls (PCBs)	Ballasts for fluorescent lights Electrical equipment—transformers and capacitors Toxic waste sites	Liver cancer
Steroids (androgens)	Drugs	Liver cancer
Toxic air pollutants	Industrial releases Toxic waste sites	Lung cancer Leukemia Cancer of other organs
Electromagnetic fields	High-tension electric lines Step-down transformers Electric blankets (possible)	Leukemia Brain cancer

ENVIRONMENTAL SOURCES OF SOME CARCINOGENS (*cont.*)

CARCINOGEN	ENVIRONMENTAL SOURCES OF CARCINOGENS	POSSIBLE CANCER RISKS
Tobacco	Cigarettes Cigars Pipes Smokeless tobacco (snuff)	Lung cancer Oral cancer Cancer of the bladder Esophageal cancer Cancer of the larynx
Alcohol	Beer, wine, and spirits	Liver cancer Esophageal cancer

THE MOST COMMON ENVIRONMENTAL TOXINS

LEAD

Jason was 6 years old when the local lead-screening program reached his neighborhood. His parents, both primary school teachers, had him tested, even though they did not think that he had been exposed. His blood-lead level was found to be elevated to 38 μg/dl (micrograms per deciliter). Both Jason's parents and their pediatrician were puzzled; they had believed that lead poisoning was a disease associated exclusively with deteriorating housing, and they lived in a well-preserved hundred-year-old Victorian house. His father recalled that he had refinished Jason's bedroom six months earlier. On closer questioning, Jason's mother said that she had noticed that he was more irritable and aggressive with friends in the past month. His teacher reported that he had recently become restless and fidgety.

Rashena, a 5-year-old African-American from the inner city, had been born at term and was a precocious baby. At 2 years of age she was said to be bright and active. She liked to sing along with phonograph records and talked in short sentences. One day in the summer when Rashena was 2½, her mother noticed flecks of paint on her lips. At about the same time, she began to appear irritable and listless. She vomited occasionally and was taken to the emergency ward of the local children's hospital. There she was given a drug to stop her vomiting and sent home. Over the next three days her mother noticed that she was "wobbly" when she walked and then became extremely sleepy. She was admitted to the hospital, where she was difficult to awaken. Her blood-lead level was 100 μg/dl. She was treated four times with drugs to reduce her lead level. Now, at six years of age, her IQ score is 74, she is sluggish, distractible, and she is not able to identify letters.

Deon, a 4-year-old African-American, was in a special nursery for developmentally handicapped children because of his rocking behavior and because his speech was limited to repeating over and over what other people said to him. After a thorough evaluation at the local children's hospital, he was given a provisional diagnosis of infantile autism. Members of a new lead-screening program in the community visited his nursery school and tested his blood. His lead level was 80 μg/dl. He received five courses of drug therapy to lower his blood level. Over the next two years, he gradually began to speak in a more communicative fashion, but he continued to be slower than his age-mates.

These three children's stories portray some of the different outcomes that can follow exposure to lead and the types of children who are affected. Lead is both a useful metal and a pervasive danger. Its menace to children has been known for over a hundred years. High doses of lead affect many organ systems, but the most serious effect is clearly seen in the child's brain. At high doses, children can get brain swelling (edema) and have changes of consciousness and seizures. Severe lead poisoning is now rare, but when it occurs it is frequently followed by severe mental retardation.

HOW MUCH LEAD IS DANGEROUS?

■ ■ ■

Until relatively recently, it was generally thought that if a child did not die during the acute phase of lead poisoning, he or she was left with no traces of the disease. But when children who recovered from acute lead poisoning were followed up, it was seen that many had mental retardation, hyperactivity, and aggressive behavior. A few pediatricians wondered what happened to those children who had excessive lead in their bodies but showed no obvious symptoms. The notion that silent exposure to a toxin could have lasting effects was a radical idea when it was first raised in the mid-1940s. It is now a central principle of modern toxicology, brought to light by the study of lead in children.

In the 1970s, there were hints that silent doses of lead produced lower IQ scores and behavior problems. Parents of children who recovered from high-dose lead poisoning often reported that their children became restless, impulsive, and aggressive toward other children. More attention disorder and more school failure were found in areas where lead exposure was known to be common.

MODERN STUDIES OF LEAD IN CHILDREN

■ ■ ■

In the 1970s and 1980s, children from the United States, Western Europe, and Scandinavia who had slightly elevated amounts of lead in the blood or teeth, but no symptoms of lead poisoning, were reported to have lower IQ scores and to show attentional and language changes. In a large study of Massachusetts first and second graders, IQ scores of two groups of children, neither of whom had symptoms of lead intoxication but who had different amounts of lead in their shed baby teeth, differed significantly. In this study, as in most others, other variables, such as family income and parental intelligence and education, were measured and their effects taken into consideration.

THE EFFECTS OF LEAD IN THE CLASSROOM

■ ■ ■

To see if the effects of lead intruded into the classroom, teachers were also asked to rank these children on their behavior. Each child was evaluated on eleven "yes or no" questions dealing with classroom disabilities. The teachers knew their students for at least two months but did not know their lead levels. Figure I shows that as the tooth-lead level rose, teachers reported an increasing proportion of children with bad grades on each measure. This is what is known as a dose-response relationship. The IQ findings and the effects of lead on attention and classroom behavior have subsequently been found in similar studies from around the world, in Western Europe, Scandinavia, China, and New Zealand.

HOW IMPORTANT ARE THE EFFECTS OF LEAD?

■ ■ ■

The difference in mean IQ scores between high- and low-lead groups is about 6 points in many of the studies from around the world. But, as Figure II shows, a small shift in the curves is associated with a huge difference at both extremes of the groups. The proportion of low-lead children with IQ scores below 80 is 4 percent, but for the high-lead group the proportion is 16 percent. This means that shifting the curve this "small" amount increases the rate of severe deficit by 400 percent. Probably just as important is the effect of lead at the top of the distribution. Five percent of the low-lead group had IQ scores above 125, some reaching as high as 143. No high-lead subject exceeded 125. One of the costs of lead exposure is that it prevents a certain number of children from reaching their peak superior function. Although these children appear to be doing well, they are not operating at their full potential.

The U.S. government's definition of what level of lead is toxic has changed dramatically over a relatively short time span. In the 1960s, children with blood-lead levels below 60 μg/dl were considered normal. Recent statements by the EPA and the Agency for Toxic Substances and Disease Registry (ATSDR) have asserted that toxicity in children begins somewhere between 10 and 15 μg/dl. The definition of toxic level continues to change as new data come in; a safe level of lead for children has yet to be found.

HOW MANY CHILDREN ARE AFFECTED?

■ ■ ■

A report by the Agency for Toxic Substances and Disease Registry in 1989 estimated that 3 to 4 million children in the United States had blood-lead levels above the defined toxic level of 15 μg/dl. The same report stated that 17 percent of *all* children, without

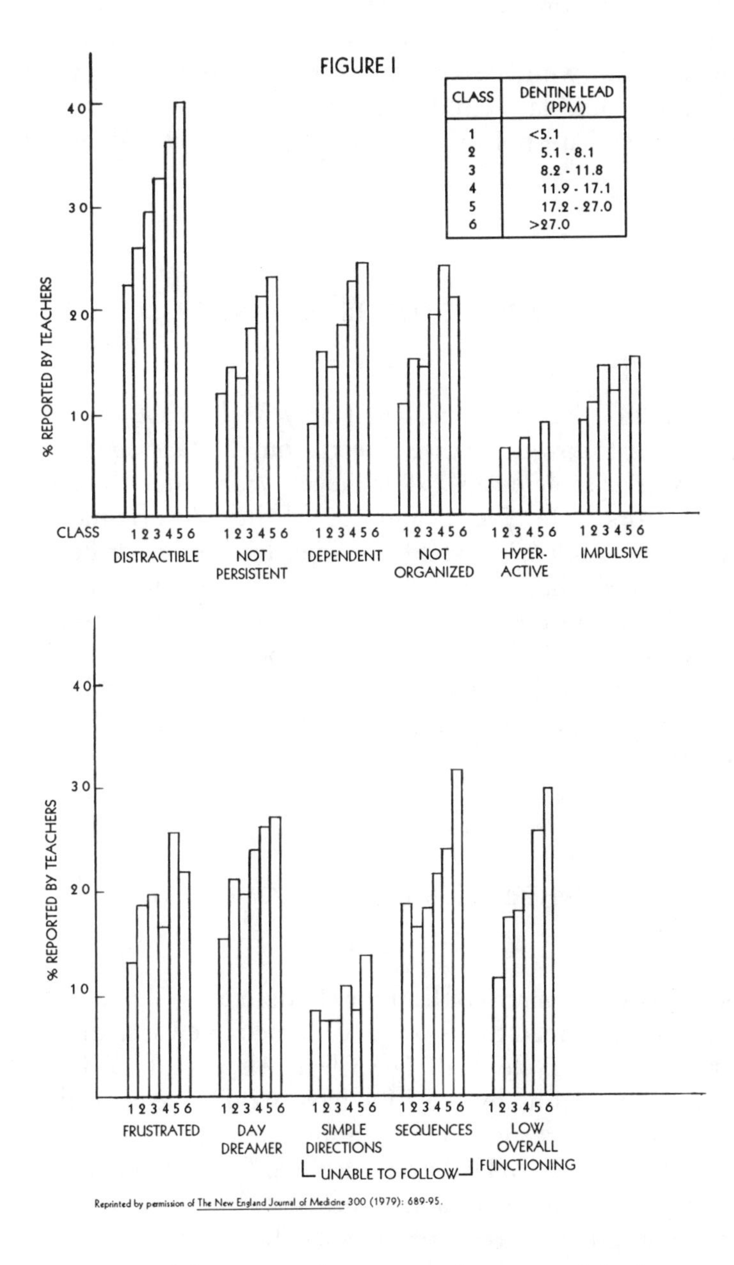

Teachers' reports of classroom behavior according to tooth-lead concentration. The proportion of bad reports in each group, from 1 to 6, is shown. As tooth-lead level rises, the rate of negative behavior in each category increases.

regard to race or family income, exceeded this toxic threshold. There is, however, a clear increase in risk attached to being poor or black. Poor white children had a rate of 26 percent over 15 μg/dl, but for poor black children the rate was 55 percent. These data clearly place lead poisoning at the top of the list of preventable diseases.

ARE THE EFFECTS PERMANENT?

■ ■ ■

This question has been answered only in the past few years. An eleven-year follow-up of the subjects from the Massachusetts tooth study was completed in 1989. Eleven years after the study, the investigators were able to find 132 of the 270 original subjects, now young adults. If a child had high lead in his or her teeth in 1978, he or she had a much higher rate of failure to graduate from high school, more reading disabilities, greater absenteeism in the final year of high school, and a number of other impairments. Figure III shows that as tooth-lead levels obtained when the subjects were 7 years old increased, the rate of high school failure rose strikingly.

WHERE DOES THE LEAD COME FROM?

■ ■ ■

The important sources of lead for children are old paint, dust, tap water, some canned foods, some ceramic tableware, and factories that smelt or recycle lead. The Clean Air Act of 1970 and subsequent regulations by the EPA have reduced lead in the atmosphere by 90 percent. The single most important action was the successful removal of lead from gasoline. The Lead Paint Poisoning Prevention Act of 1971 banned the use of lead in household paint, but as many as 50 percent of American houses have lead in interior paint. It is clear that household paint is the most important threat. Almost all houses built before 1960 have leaded paint, and of those houses built between 1960 and 1974, 20 percent have leaded paint.

FIGURE II

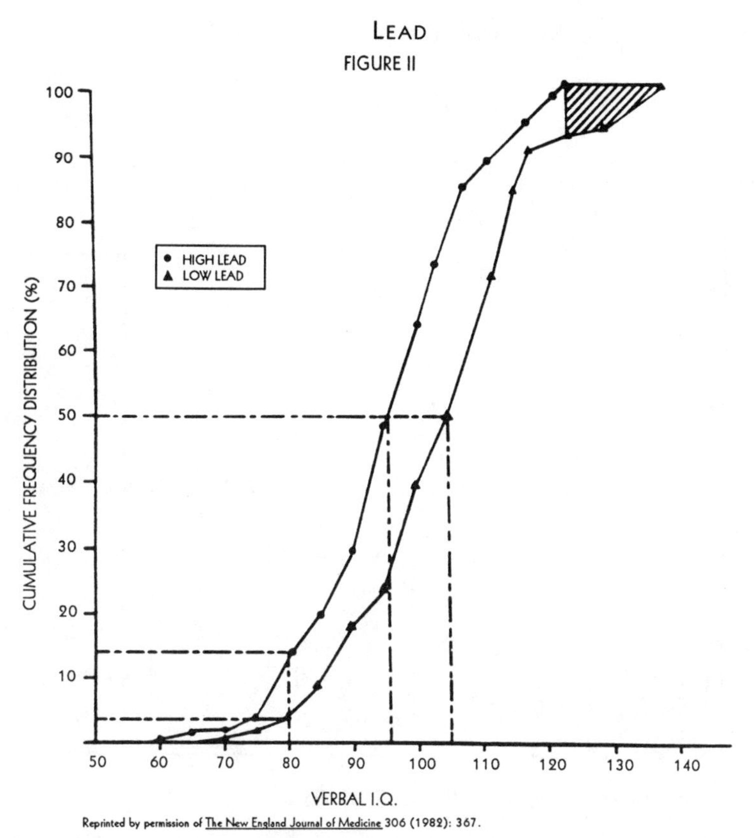

Reprinted by permission of The New England Journal of Medicine 306 (1982): 367.

The importance of a "small" shift in the mean or median IQ scores in high- and low-lead groups. Shifting the curve a small increment to the left increases the rate of severe deficit (defined as IQ score of less than 80) from 4 percent to 16 percent. It also truncates the top of the distribution, so that 5 percent of the children are prevented from achieving superior function.

Peeling paint is a serious health hazard, and this is one of the reasons that poor children, in the oldest, most deteriorated houses, are at greatest risk. There are about 2 million houses in the United States with peeling paint in which children live. These need the most urgent attention. But paint removal, if done without great care, can be dangerous to the worker and to any residents, as the anecdote about Jason illustrates. A number of middle-class families have been sickened in this manner. Deleading a part or all of a house requires experience, great care not to distribute the lead more widely in the dust, and careful cleanup at the conclusion. If the area under renovation cannot be isolated, all residents should be moved out until the project is complete and the area has been thoroughly cleaned up.

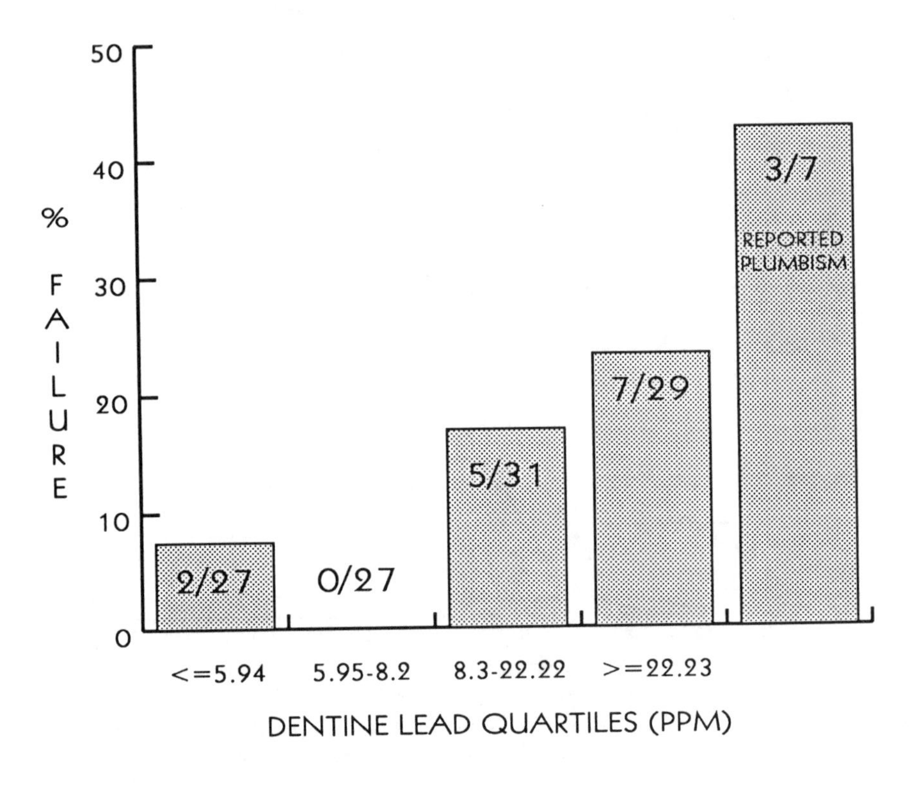

Reprinted by permission of The New England Journal of Medicine 322 (1990): 83-88.

The effect on school success of early exposure to lead. As the tooth-lead level in 1976 rises, the rate of failure to graduate from high school also rises. Having a high tooth-lead level is associated with a sevenfold increased risk for failure to graduate. This number is adjusted for other factors.

In some areas, household drinking water may contain excessive amounts of lead. This rarely originates at the source; water in reservoirs generally has very low concentrations of lead. Lead enters the drinking water from the connection between the street main and the home, from the pipes themselves if they are made of lead, from lead solder, and in some circumstances from certain brass fixtures that can introduce lead into the water supply. Some older water coolers used leaded storage tanks or soldered joints with lead. Water that is soft, that contains low amounts of minerals, is more likely to leach lead from pipes. Minerals from hard water tend to form a coating that has protective properties. This coating takes some time to develop, and new homes, for that reason, are more likely to have lead in their drinking water.

Ceramic dinnerware, if improperly fired and if the clay or the glazes contain lead, can be dangerous. A generally safe rule is not to use any ceramic dinnerware that comes from outside of the United States. Ceramic dinnerware from the United States should have a written statement that it is lead-free.

Certain cans may contribute lead to food. Any can with a seam is suspect. We believe that it is wise to purchase canned food or beverages only if they are in seamless aluminum cans.

Some hair dyes contain lead, which can be transferred to children who touch their parents' hair. Examine the labels on hair dyes carefully. Similarly, certain cosmetics used by Muslims (kohl) and Hindus (surma) have high concentrations of lead.

Some natural calcium preparations made from pulverized animal bones have been found to contain high concentrations of lead. This source of calcium should be avoided.

The Household Inventory (Appendix 1) contains a structured questionnaire that will assist you in surveying your home for hazardous substances. One section is devoted to evaluating the risks to your child from lead in the home from paint, soil, water, and other sources.

WHAT CAN BE DONE TO PREVENT LEAD POISONING?

■ ■ ■

SCREENING FOR LEAD

Every child under six years of age should have a blood-lead test once a year beginning at 9 months of age. If a child has normal blood-lead levels at 9 months to 1 year, and a second normal level at 2 years, he or she is probably not at risk. If a child should start eating nonfood substances, or be moved to a lead-containing environment, screening should be more frequent. This is the recommendation of the U.S. government, but it is frequently ignored by public health departments and pediatricians. A blood-lead test requires a finger prick. It should be done by a licensed laboratory and should cost about $15. It may be necessary to convince some pediatricians to order this. It is common belief that being middle-class means that lead exposure cannot be a problem. This is not true. The estimates of the Agency for Toxic Substances and Disease Registry shows that one American child in seven has an elevated blood-lead level. The current definition of an elevated blood-lead level is above 10 μg/dl. At this level, children do not require treatment, but should be followed.

Reducing Absorption

Here are some general rules to reduce lead absorption: First, old tales to the contrary, it is not healthy for a child to eat dirt. Gently correct your child if he or she does this. Lead is only one of the nasty things in soil. There are also many pesticides, other pollutants, and frequently eggs of parasites. Playing in dirt or sand is great fun for kids. A clean sandbox is the safest medium. But be sure that it is filled with beach sand and not crushed stone. (See Chapter 6.) If your child wants to play in dirt, be sure that the soil is not lead-contaminated. Relevant questions to ask are: "Is this near an old smelter site?" "Is there a heavily traveled highway within a hundred yards of the play site?" "Is the soil on a plot where old houses stood and were demolished?" Your local health department can advise you about where to have soil tested for lead. If the soil is risky, use a sandbox. If this is impractical, consider importing agricultural topsoil for the play site.

Nail biting and thumb sucking are habits that transfer lead from the hands to the digestive system. Children who indulge should have their blood lead tested at frequent intervals—about three times a year. Frequent hand washing and keeping fingernails short are helpful steps. Children should be taught to wash before eating anything.

FOOD, TABLEWARE, AND CRYSTAL

Ceramic tableware, some of the decorations on chinaware, and leaded crystal can introduce lead into food or beverages. Do not drink hot beverages from ceramic mugs. These can leach lead into the beverage. Do not feed your baby from a crystal nursing bottle. Do not store brandy or wine in leaded-crystal decanters. Avoid wines with a metal capsule. If you open such a bottle, wipe the rim carefully with a damp cloth before removing the cork. Cans with soldered seams can introduce lead into food. Most cans in the United States have been seamless since 1991. Some restaurant-size cans still have soldered seams. They should be avoided, as should cans from foreign countries that have seams.

WATER

A recent survey by Consumers Union showed that many communities had lead in the water over the EPA standard. There are a number of companies that will test your water supply for a reasonable fee. Most of the lead is introduced into the water while it is standing in the pipes overnight. You should run the water from the kitchen tap each morning until the temperature changes—about ninety seconds. This will, in most circumstances reduce the concentration of lead. Never use water from the hot tap for cooking purposes.

LEAD PAINT, THE GREATEST HAZARD

If you live in a house built before 1950, it is almost certain to have old paint. Almost all paint used before 1950 contained lead. If you live in a house built before 1970, it may well contain old paint. The next things to determine are whether the paint is intact and whether your child has pica—a tendency to eat foreign substances. If your paint is peeling and your child has pica, this should be attended to immediately. Obtain a blood-lead test and consult with your pediatrician.

If you suspect that your house has risky lead paint in it, the next step is to bring in a trained expert to verify it and if lead is present to remove it. (Qualified contractors are at present a minority of those who represent themselves as lead abaters. Listings may be obtained from the EPA.) If you are determined to do it yourself, you should understand that this is potentially dangerous work. Lead removers and residents have themselves been made sick by this activity. The Department of Housing and Urban Development has published Interim Guidelines for Hazard Identification and Abatement in Public and Indian Housing. These are not perfect, but they represent the only published guidelines in existence at present. Here are some important things to consider:

- Sloppy deleading can put more lead into the dust and air, and people can get sick.
- The work site should be sealed off from the rest of the house, and rugs, clothing, and furniture should be protected from lead dust.
- Using open flame is unacceptable practice. It can vaporize lead, causing severe poisoning.
- The residents should be relocated until the deleading is complete and the site cleaned up and the dust retested.
- The deleader can carry lead in the dust in his clothing and hair. Work clothes should not leave the work site and should be laundered separately.
- Workers who sand and scrape paint should wear OSHA-approved, positive-pressure respirators and should have their blood-lead levels measured at the conclusion of the job.

Title X of the 1992 Housing Act requires states to establish training programs and licensing for lead contractors. This should radically change the picture of lead abatement and increase the number of competent contractors. If you are going to hire a contractor, find out about his methods. Where has he been trained? Will he adhere to the points listed above? How will he clean up? What are his costs? Some contractors, recognizing the risks outlined above, have begun to treat lead as though it were asbestos, and have attempted to get the last lead particle out of the home. This has skyrocketed the costs for removing lead from houses. Deleading a small (two-bedroom) house should not cost more than $5,000–$8,000.

WILL WE ALWAYS HAVE THIS DISEASE?

■ ■ ■

The authors of this book believe that lead poisoning is one of the most important pediatric diseases and that it is a major cause of behavior disorders and school failure. There is considerable evidence that the costs to our society for remedial education, decreased earning power, and disordered behavior are in the billions of dollars per year. There is a greater irony surrounding this disease: lead poisoning is completely preventable. We believe that this disease can be eradicated, not simply controlled or reduced, in a reasonable time period.

There are a number of reasons why the epidemic of lead poisoning has received so little attention over the past fifteen years. First is the belief that this is a problem solved long ago. Another reason is that pediatricians and others believe that the disease was eradicated with the passage of legislation banning the use of lead in paint and with the removal of lead from gasoline. Many otherwise knowledgeable officials believe that there is no problem. Of course, banning lead from paint did nothing to take it off walls. The lead industry must also accept some of the blame for obscuring the effects of lead at low doses. The International Lead Zinc Research Organization, for example, steadily maintains that there is no proof that lead at low doses is brain-damaging. In this activity, they resemble no one so much as the tobacco industry. Pediatricians and academics in medicine, who should be active in preventing this disease, regard lead toxicity as a rather uninteresting problem; it doesn't have the technological glamour of organ transplants or molecular biology. And finally, the U.S. government, with a few exceptions, has turned its back on the problem by inadequately funding lead-poisoning research and abatement.

But there is reason for optimism. In 1990, the Senate Subcommittee on the Environment, spearheaded by Senators Harry M. Reid and Joseph Lieberman, proposed a bill that represents a good beginning in reducing the amount of lead entering the human environment. In the House of Representatives, Congressman Henry Waxman proposed a bill that would advance the preventive measures substantially. In the last minutes of the legislative session of 1992, a major bill, Title X of the Housing Act, was passed that established the first steps to removing paint from houses on more than a token basis. Another bill put before the House of Representatives in 1993 by Congressman Benjamin Cardin would introduce a tax on lead at its origin. The proceeds from this, estimated to be $1 billion per year, would be put into a trust fund for cleanup of inner-city homes.

The most significant source of lead poisoning for children is old lead paint. Lead in paint is relatively easy to identify and to remove. If one were to map where lead is found in superabundance, and then to map where decent housing was needed and where jobs were short, the three maps would be virtually identical. A simple, uncluttered approach to this problem would be to train the unemployed in safe deleading and pay them for it. Certain major labor unions have, in fact, already begun such programs. For the same expenditure, we could get three benefits: jobs where they are most needed, the return of houses to decency, and the eradication of one of the most serious public health problems. If this sounds utopian, one should be reminded that the cost for care and remedial education of a single case of lead toxicity is conservatively estimated at $4,600 and there may be as many as 3 to 4 million such children.

5

MERCURY

Robert, a healthy and agreeable young child, lived in suburban Detroit in 1989. One day his parents noticed a sudden change in his disposition. Abruptly he became irritable and withdrawn. Then he began to tremble. With each day he became progressively weaker, until he was unable to walk. Then the skin of his hands and feet reddened and began to peel. An alert clinician made a diagnosis of acrodynia, a rare condition. Acrodynia is one form of toxicity from mercury exposure. The medical history revealed that a few days before, the family had painted the interior of the house and used sixteen gallons of mercury-containing paint. Other homes that had used the paint were identified. Two of three households had children with elevated urinary mercury levels.

Mercury is a heavy metal with a unique and fascinating property; it is a liquid at room temperature. Because of this, it possesses a strong attraction for children. Mercury has been widely used since antiquity; Aristotle named it "quicksilver." Cinnabar, or mercuric sulfide, has been mined in Spain since the fourth century B.C. Mercury has been used in the purification of gold, in making mirrors, and in the manufacture of felt hats and paper. Because it has strong germ-killing properties, it has been widely used as a fungicide and disinfectant. It is used in making batteries, thermometers, and fluorescent light bulbs, and is an important part of dental amalgam.

The metal exists in three forms: in the pure uncombined state, which is liquid at room temperature, as inorganic salts, and combined with organic molecules to form organic salts. Each form has different risks.

METALLIC MERCURY

High levels of metallic mercury can be found in dentists' offices. An average dentist uses about two pounds of mercury each year. Mercury readily vaporizes, and elevated levels of mercury in the air have been measured in about one in ten dental offices. Irving Shapiro, a dentist and biochemist, compared dentists who had over 20 parts per million (ppm) of mercury in their bones with those with lesser amounts. Dentists with higher mercury levels had slower nerve conduction time and poorer visuomotor performance. They also had a greater incidence of carpal tunnel dysfunction. Exposure through this route is a risk for dental technicians and dentists; it is not for patients who are exposed for only relatively short periods of time.

On occasion, a child having his or her temperature taken will break the thermometer while it is in the body. This is no cause for alarm. Liquid mercury is very poorly absorbed and will be excreted in the child's stool. If, however, liquid mercury spills in the house, this must be treated seriously. Mercury vaporizes readily and then is easily absorbed through the lung. Chronic exposure to low levels of mercury vapor have been associated with tremor, irritability, impulsiveness, drowsiness, impaired memory, and sleep disturbances.

Spilled mercury must not be picked up by a home vacuum sweeper; this will only disperse the particles widely in small droplets. The local health department should be notified immediately and a trained cleanup crew used to collect the metal and clean the site. Needless to say, children should never be allowed to play with mercury.

INORGANIC MERCURY COMPOUNDS

Most uses of mercury salts have been abandoned. Mercury was once used as a teething powder, and as a treatment for worms. Exposure to these salts resulted in a condition in children known as "pink disease," or acrodynia, because of reddening of the palms and the soles of the feet. Although a rarity in modern society, an occasional case of this disease is reported.

ORGANIC MERCURY

When a mercury molecule is attached to an organic molecule, its physical and toxic properties are radically changed. Organic mercury molecules are much more soluble in fatty tissue. Because of this, they cross membranes and enter cells more readily. Methylmercury, which has found wide use as a mold killer, penetrates the brain and is a potent neurotoxin. Methylmercury is a man-made molecule, synthesized for commercial purposes. It is also made by certain bacteria.

Two large-scale epidemics have demonstrated the intense toxicity of organic mercury. In the Minamata Bay in Japan, a chemical plant discharged large amounts of methylmercury into the water in the 1950s, and it was taken up by the aquatic life. Residents who lived on the shore fished the waters, and many became stricken with severe neurological damage. Methylmercury crosses the placenta. As a result, large numbers of pregnant women who were exposed bore severely brain-damaged children.

Another series of disasters occurred in Iraq in 1956, 1960, and 1971. As part of its international aid program, the United States shipped large amounts of seed grain there. This was seed grain, intended to be planted, not eaten. The grain was coated with methylmercury to prevent fungal infestation and dyed red as a warning. Starving Iraqi farmers, instead of planting the seeds, washed the dye off and baked bread with it. Huge numbers of Iraqi peasants became ill, some fatally. Once again infants exposed during pregnancy were the most severely affected.

LATEX PAINT

Until recently, some paint manufacturers added phenylmercury to latex paint to inhibit the growth of mold in the can. This was brought to light through the case of the Detroit family described earlier. The EPA has secured a voluntary agreement from paint manufacturers to discontinue the addition of mercury to paint. But no recall of already manufactured paint was conducted. There may indeed still be cans of interior household paint on shelves with mercury in them. If you are considering painting the interior of your house with latex paint, there is only one way to be sure that the paint that you purchase is mercury-free. The National Pesticide Telecommunications Center (phone 1-800-858-7358) has a listing of 1,600 paints and their reported mercury content. Check with them. Only buy a paint that you are certain does not contain mercury.

ARE DENTAL FILLINGS HAZARDOUS?

Recently, considerable attention has been given to the possibility that mercury in dental amalgam gets into the general circulation and affects the health of the individual. The response of the American Dental Association has been to categorically deny that there is any possibility of risk to individuals from the mercury in their teeth. This is a difficult issue. Some investigators have shown that mercury levels in the breath of individuals with dental fillings rose after chewing, while those from patients without amalgam fillings did not. This is not the same as showing that fillings increase the amount of mercury in critical tissues. One careful study done by dental scientists at the University of Iowa showed that when mercury fillings were removed from ten volunteers, blood-mercury levels fell over time. These concentrations were extremely small to begin with and may not be biologically important.

The question of dental amalgam is a subject that bears watching. Because of recent publicity, more research on the health significance of low-dose mercury is being conducted and may change the picture. We do not recommend removal of amalgam fillings. The procedure is uncomfortable at best, always expensive, may in itself present some health risks, and is at this time of unproven merit. The authors of this book, it should be mentioned, have mouths replete with mercury fillings. This may or may not be comforting to the reader.

ASBESTOS

In September 1976, students in a northern New Jersey suburban elementary school returned to classes from their summer vacation to find their desks covered by a fine powder and the classroom air filled with dust. The school, a low-lying, one-story structure, had been built in 1954, at the peak of the postwar baby boom. Asbestos had been sprayed on the ceilings of the classrooms and hallways as fireproofing and acoustic insulation, a common practice at the time. Over the summer, the roof had leaked, the ceiling insulation had cracked and deteriorated, and the dust had drifted down. In some areas, strands of insulation hung from the ceiling. Some of the older boys began to make balls from clumps of asbestos that had fallen to the floor.

When word of the situation reached the children's parents, the reaction was intense. Some parents had worked with asbestos, and others had relatives in the industry. They were deeply worried about their children's health and held a series of urgent meetings. Parents talked with teachers and with the principal. The school board was consulted. Nothing happened. There was delay after delay. Tension, impatience, and a sense of powerlessness spread.

On a Saturday morning in early December, a group of frustrated parents broke into the school and began to remove the asbestos. The results were horrendous. The parents were heavily exposed during their work, a situation that endangered their own lives. They were not able to clean up all of the material that they dislodged from the ceilings, and a thicker layer of asbestos dust was left lying on the floor. The school had to be closed for several months for proper cleaning, and the children's education was seriously disrupted.

Deteriorating asbestos in a school can be hazardous for children's health; it should never be removed by amateurs. Asbestos abatement is dangerous work. It must always be left to trained professionals.

As a consequence of this and other episodes, the public and the government became acutely aware of the problem of asbestos in schools. New legislation was passed, and a logical framework for dealing with asbestos was put into place.

WHAT IS ASBESTOS?

■ ■ ■

Asbestos is the name given to a group of six naturally occurring fibrous minerals. It is mined in many nations, particularly in Canada, Russia, and South Africa. When pulverized and milled, rocks containing asbestos release thin, virtually indestructible fibers. These fibers can be carded, woven, and spun into cloth. They can be used in bulk or mixed with materials such as asphalt or cement.

Asbestos fibers resist heat, acid, and fire. As a result, asbestos has been used extensively in consumer goods, in industry, and in construction, wherever temperature control was needed, heat loss had to be prevented, or fire was a danger. Since the 1920s, and especially in the 1950s and 1960s, billions of tons of asbestos were used in homes, schools, and public buildings in this country and around the world. It found wide application in insulation, fireproofing, pipe wrapping, boiler lagging, ceiling tiles, floor coating, and spray-on wall and beam coverings.

Today, in the United States, the use of asbestos has virtually ceased. This decline began during the 1970s after the industry belatedly disclosed the hazards of asbestos.* Most recently, a ban on all new use of asbestos has been proposed by the EPA. This will take effect in 1997, if it is not blocked in the federal courts.

* For a detailed description of the long suppression by the asbestos industry of information on the health hazards of asbestos, see Paul Brodeur's book *Outrageous Misconduct*.

TABLE 1. FACTS ABOUT ASBESTOS

- Asbestos is a naturally occurring fibrous mineral. It does not burn and provides excellent thermal insulation. Because of these properties, it was used widely in building construction in the United States, especially in the 1950s and 1960s.
- All new use of asbestos is banned in the United States. Millions of tons of asbestos are present today in schools, homes, and other buildings—a legacy of the past. New use of asbestos continues in many nations outside of the United States.
- Lung cancer and malignant mesothelioma are the two principal adverse consequences of asbestos inhalation by children. Lung cancer can result after a latency period of 10 to 30 years from first exposure. The latency period for mesothelioma ranges from 20 to 50 years.
- The Asbestos Hazard Emergency Response Act (AHERA), passed by Congress in 1984, provides a detailed blueprint for achieving control of exposure to asbestos. Visual and microscopic inspection of every surface in every room of every building where children spend time is the essential first step in controlling asbestos exposure. Inspection must be performed by a qualified certified inspector. Parents, teachers, and other interested persons must be fully informed of the results of inspection.
- If asbestos is found, three options exist for dealing with it: (1) observation and maintenance (O&M), (2) containment, and (3) removal (abatement). The EPA has issued guidelines to help school officials and homeowners choose from among these options. Often, observation and maintenance or containment may be as effective as abatement and much less costly. Removal is not required in most cases and should be considered the remedy of last resort.

It will end all manufacture, importing, and processing of asbestos-containing materials in the United States. Overseas, asbestos continues to be used widely, particularly in the nations of the Third World.

Despite the recent decline in new use, enormous amounts of asbestos remain in place in buildings throughout the United States, a future hazard of great proportions. Public health officials have been challenged to develop a systematic approach to asbestos removal that enables parents, pediatricians, and school officials to take control of the problem in a sensible manner.

DETERMINING THE EXTENT OF THE PROBLEM

■ ■ ■

The first step in coming to grips with the problem is to determine its extent. In 1988, the EPA surveyed public and commercial buildings. Asbestos-containing materials were present in at least 700,000 public and commercial buildings in all areas of the United States. About 500,000 of these buildings contain at least some damaged asbestos.

In New York State, where the Department of Education conducted a statewide survey in 1989, 252 million square feet of asbestos was found to be present in public and private schools. Approximately 10 percent (23 million square feet) was in deteriorated condition. Despite the recent upheaval in the New York City schools asbestos program, the federal standards in New York remain sound. In New York City, two-thirds of public and commercial buildings contained asbestos. High-rise structures were most commonly involved. Private homes were not included in the study. Asbestos was in poor condition in 19 percent of the buildings examined.

Clearly asbestos in American schools and other buildings is a major environmental hazard. As building materials containing asbestos age, they become increasingly fragile and friable and release fibers into the air. These microscopic airborne fibers can remain suspended in the air for hours or even days and are readily inhaled. Spray-on asbestos that was applied as insulation to ceilings and beams is the form most likely to become friable.

Any disturbance will increase the release of asbestos fibers. This can be caused by routine building maintenance, bouncing a basketball off an asbestos-containing ceiling, water damage, renovation, reconstruction, or demolition. Today, as tens of thousands of buildings in the United States containing asbestos age, and as plans are made for their renovation and demolition, grave potential exists for the widespread exposure of children and adults.

FIGURE I

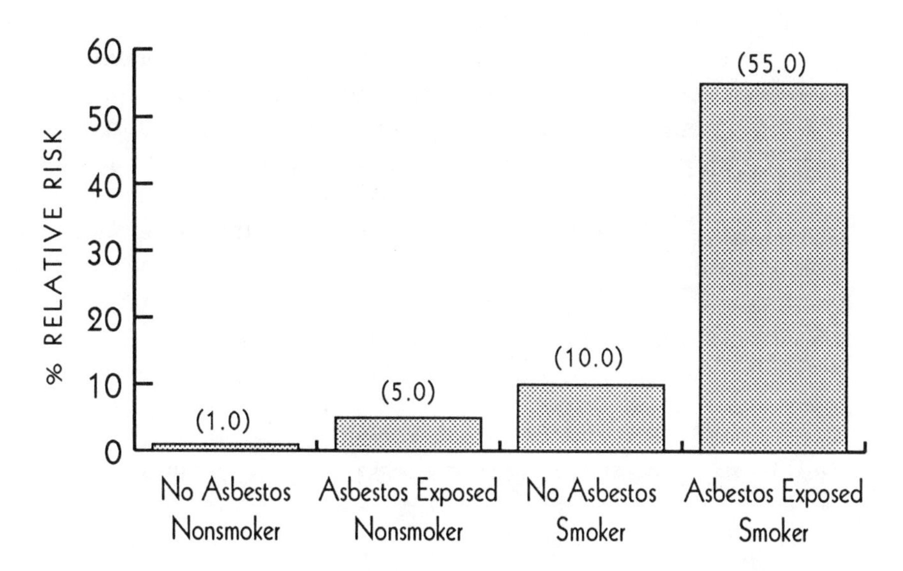

Risk of Lung Cancer in Relation to Asbestos Exposure and Cigarette Smoking: An Example of Interaction

THE HEALTH HAZARDS OF ASBESTOS

■ ■ ■

A proven human carcinogen, asbestos can cause a number of different types of cancer. Any exposure involves some risk; no safe threshold level of exposure has been established. However, parents can derive reassurance from the fact that the degree of risk increases with the degree of exposure. The risk associated with low levels of exposure or with brief, one-time encounters is much less than that resulting from regular exposure.

The two most important cancers caused by asbestos are (1) malignant mesothelioma, a cancer of the inner lining of the chest or abdomen, and (2) lung cancer. Asbestos can also cause cancer of the throat, larynx, and gastrointestinal tract.

The relationship between mesothelioma and asbestos was first recognized among workers who had been exposed occupationally as miners, shipbuilders, and insulation workers. Among workers exposed to asbestos, thousands of cases of mesothelioma have occurred, and cases resulting from past exposures will continue to occur well into the twenty-first century. It has been estimated that at least 300,000 American workers will eventually die of mesothelioma and other asbestos-related diseases. Cases of mesothelioma have been seen as long as fifty years after first exposure.

A strong interaction has been found between asbestos and cigarette smoking in the causation of lung cancer. Persons who are exposed to asbestos and who do not smoke have five times the rate of lung cancer. By contrast, people who are exposed to asbestos and who also smoke have more than fifty times the rate of lung cancer (see Figure I). This powerful interaction is another reason why children and adolescents should not begin to smoke cigarettes.

THE SPECIAL HAZARD OF ASBESTOS FOR CHILDREN

■ ■ ■

Several factors increase the risk for children. Because of their long life expectancy they have many years in which to develop cancers triggered by early exposures. They tend to be much more physically active than adults, and breathe at higher rates and more often by mouth. They spend much of their time close to the floor, where dust and fibers accumulate.

EXTENT OF EXPOSURE

■ ■ ■

In 1980, the EPA estimated that more than 8,500 schools nationwide had friable, deteriorated asbestos and that approximately 3 million students (and also more than 250,000 teachers, maintenance workers, and other adults) were potentially exposed. The EPA concluded:

> A total of between 100 and 7,000 premature deaths are anticipated to occur over the next 30 years as a result of exposure to asbestos in schools. The most reasonable estimate is that there will be approximately 1,000 premature deaths. About 90% of these deaths are expected to occur among persons exposed as schoolchildren.

The American Academy of Pediatrics has concurred in this assessment, and noted that virtually all of these preventable deaths will be caused by either lung cancer or malignant mesothelioma.

IDENTIFICATION AND CONTROL OF ASBESTOS HAZARDS

■ ■ ■

How does a parent determine whether a building contains asbestos? How do you ascertain whether the asbestos in a building poses a hazard to your children? And if asbestos is found, what can parents, school officials, and pediatricians do to minimize the risk to children?

The first point to bear in mind is that you are not alone. The medical community across the United States, the EPA, state health departments, and Congress have directed enormously detailed attention to the problem of asbestos in schools and other buildings. They have considered the risks most carefully, and they have developed blueprints for assessing and then minimizing the hazard.

The strategy that has been put in place for dealing with asbestos in buildings rests on two principles:

1. Medical screening of children who have been exposed to asbestos in schools and other buildings is *not* recommended, because asbestos exposure (except for very heavy exposure in an occupational setting) does not produce any detectable physical damage or X-ray changes until twenty, thirty, forty, or more years after exposure.
2. Because no worthwhile medical screening exists, all efforts should focus on the prevention of exposure.

THE ASBESTOS HAZARD EMERGENCY RESPONSE ACT

■ ■ ■

In 1984, acting on this strategy, Congress passed the Asbestos Hazard Emergency Response Act (AHERA). AHERA is one of the most enlightened and far-reaching pieces of environmental legislation to have been enacted by Congress in recent years. This

TABLE 2.
SOURCES OF ASBESTOS EXPOSURE IN SCHOOLS, PUBLIC BUILDINGS, AND HOMES*

USES IN SCHOOLS AND PUBLIC BUILDINGS	RESIDENTIAL USES
Boilers and heating vessels	Duct insulation
Cement pipe	Fire-protection panels
Clutch, brake, and transmission components	Artificial logs or ashes for fireplaces
Conduits for electrical wire	Furnace-insulating pads
Corrosive chemical containers	Fuse-box liners
Electrical motor components	Heat-register tape and insulation
Heat-protective pads	Joint compounds
Laboratory furniture	Patching plaster
Paper products	Pipe or boiler insulation
Pipe covering	Sheet vinyl or floor tiles
Roofing products	Shingles
Sealants and coatings	Textured acoustical ceiling
Textiles	Underlayment for sheet flooring
Theater curtains	

* Data from the Agency for Toxic Substances and Disease Registry, U.S. Public Health Service, 1990.

legislation codified the preventive approaches to the control of asbestos that are now used by the EPA and that must be followed by school districts. AHERA makes federal monies available to school districts with limited financial resources to assist with asbestos control. The act requires the governor's office in each state to develop a priority list of schools in need of funds (see box).

The AHERA legislation and the national program for asbestos control require that the following actions be taken in every school in the United States:

▪ Every room and every surface of every school—public, private, and parochial—must be systematically inspected for the presence of asbestos. Visual inspections followed by microscopic examination of suspect samples are required. Construction records must be reviewed to determine, to the extent possible, how much asbestos was used and where it was utilized. As of this writing, the EPA estimates that more than 99 percent of all school districts have complied with this aspect of the law.

▪ All inspection and abatement of asbestos must be undertaken by properly qualified professional inspectors and contractors. The legislation lays down specific requirements for the training and

ASBESTOS GRANTS FOR LOCAL SCHOOL DISTRICTS

In 1984, Congress passed the Asbestos Hazard Emergency Response Act (AHERA) to protect children and school employees from the hazards of asbestos in schools. At the same time, Congress passed legislation authorizing that federal funds be provided to financially needy school districts to enable them to deal with asbestos hazards.

In 1992, Congress appropriated approximately $52 million for this program nationwide. Funds are disbursed by the EPA, and school districts that wish to receive funding must apply to the EPA.

To obtain an application package, a school district must contact the EPA Asbestos Coordination Center: 1-800-462-6706, or write: EPA Asbestos Coordination Center, ATLIS Federal Service, Inc., 6011 Executive Blvd., Rockville, MD 20852.

Parents and teachers should check to make certain that their school district has applied for appropriate federal assistance.

certification of a range of qualified persons, including project designers, program managers, contractors, and asbestos workers.

- Parents, teachers, and other relevant groups must be fully informed as to the findings of each school survey.

This extensive series of legal protections should be a source of considerable security to parents, pediatricians, and school officials. Unquestionably, the work that has been undertaken in the United States under AHERA has already reduced the hazard of asbestos to our children. Nevertheless, there have been and will continue to be gaps in implementation and enforcement of the law. The recent scandal in the New York City school system is an unfortunate but instructive example. It is important, therefore, that parents, school officials, and pediatricians be aware of the options that exist for dealing with asbestos.

Caution. Parents should be aware that the steps discussed here for dealing with asbestos are required by federal law *only for schools*. For other buildings, such as apartment and commercial buildings, these steps are recommended by federal law but are not required. Also, federal asbestos grants are available only for schools, and not for other buildings. Certain states, however, have developed strong regulations that go beyond the federal laws and that apply to commercial and apartment buildings.

Parents can obtain up-to-date information on regulations in their state from their state's asbestos program office or from EPA regional offices (see Appendix 3).

DEALING WITH ASBESTOS STEP BY STEP

■ ■ ■

ASBESTOS PROGRAM MANAGER

Under AHERA, every school district in the United States must appoint an Asbestos Program Manager. This manager is frequently the building engineer, superintendent, or facility manager. It is essential that this person be properly qualified and that he or she has taken an EPA-approved training course. If any questions arise as to the qualifications of the Asbestos Program Manager, parents, school officials, or building occupants should request to see copies of the appropriate diplomas certifying that the manager has indeed successfully completed the necessary EPA- or state-approved training. This is a reasonable request, and one with which a properly certified manager should readily comply.

BUILDING INSPECTION

The Asbestos Program Manager, or a properly certified person acting under his or her supervision, is required by law to conduct a systematic inspection of every school building in which children study and play. Every room, every wall, every floor, and every ceiling must be examined. This also applies to the structural components of the building, such as the air-handling system, the boiler room, and the plumbing.

The inspection of a building must proceed in two steps. The first step is a visual inspection. All surfaces are examined. Areas that are suspected of containing asbestos are identified. The physical condition of any asbestos-containing material is noted. Note is also made of the potential for disturbance of asbestos-containing areas and of the accessibility of these areas to children. All of these findings are recorded systematically in a log. In most school districts, this log is maintained in a computer, and a computer-based inventory of all asbestos-containing material in the school is periodically updated. Additionally, AHERA requires that school officials report their findings to the EPA. Parents have the right to examine this information, and school officials should be willing to provide it upon request. If there is a problem with access, a parent or pediatrician can contact the appropriate regional office of the EPA (see Appendix 3) or telephone the EPA directly.

MICROSCOPIC ANALYSIS

If the visual inspection identifies materials that are suspected of containing asbestos, microscopic analysis of samples is required. Visual inspection alone and a review of labeling information is not sufficient to make a definitive determination of whether asbestos is present. The EPA has developed detailed procedures for collecting samples of suspected asbestos materials and for performing microscopic analyses.

School officials and parents should ascertain that any laboratory performing microscopic analysis is properly certified by the EPA or by state authorities. The laboratory should be required to present credentials proving its up-to-date certification.

The following is a checklist of items that should be included in the report from the asbestos laboratory on each specimen:

- The sample identification number
- The analytical method used
- A description of the appearance of the sample
- An analysis of the percentage of each type of asbestos
- Analysis of other fibrous materials
- Description of the laboratory's quality-control program

To ascertain the qualifications of asbestos laboratories, parents and school officials can contact the Asbestos Program Manager in their regional EPA office to obtain a listing of certified laboratories in their region. Any difficulty or questions should be referred to the regional office with a demand for immediate federal inspection.

HAZARD ASSESSMENT

When the presence of asbestos in a school or other building has been confirmed by visual inspection and corroborated by microscopic analysis, the actual degree of hazard must be determined on a case-by-case basis. The EPA has developed a checklist of quite reasonable criteria to use in assessing asbestos hazards:

- Is there evidence of deterioration?
- Is there evidence of physical damage?
- Is there evidence of water damage?
- Is the asbestos near the air ducts?
- Is the asbestos accessible to children and other building occupants?
- Is there any pending change in building use (e.g., construction or renovation)?

On the basis of these criteria, the Asbestos Program Manager classifies asbestos as undamaged, damaged, or potentially damageable. Potentially damageable materials are those in an area regularly used by children or other building occupants and potentially subject to damage.

LOG

All findings in every building survey must be carefully recorded in a log (preferably a computerized log) that is available for inspection by parents, physicians, and local authorities. In this log it is important to record (1) the location and presence of all asbestos-containing materials; (2) their condition; (3) their accessibility to children and others; and (4) the total number of square feet of asbestos-containing materials in the school or home.

AIR SAMPLING

Levels of asbestos in the air are not usually measured in the initial assessment of asbestos in a building. Air sampling provides only a transitory and sometimes unreliable estimate of potential asbestos exposures. The release of asbestos fibers from walls and ceilings is usually intermittent, not constant. It occurs only when children hit the asbestos with their hands or bounce a basketball off the ceiling, or when vibration or building maintenance takes place. Air sampling is typically performed at night and on weekends, and misses these episodic releases of asbestos fibers. Thus it tends to provide falsely reassuring data on the degree of hazard.

COMPREHENSIVE ASBESTOS-CONTROL PROGRAMS

■ ■ ■

If asbestos is found in a building, AHERA requires that a written policy be developed for dealing with it. The Asbestos Program Manager or a qualified consultant is responsible for developing this policy. The goal of the policy is to prevent *any* asbestos exposure. The policy must be a written document, and this document must be available to parents, school officials, and building occupants. A comprehensive asbestos-control program will systematically consider three options for dealing with asbestos in every location in which it is found:

- Removal
- Enclosure
- Operations and maintenance (O&M). In an operations and maintenance program, the asbestos is left in place, its condition is carefully monitored, and a detailed series of procedures is developed for dealing with the material. Immediate action is deferred.

Frequently in large buildings, a combination of all three approaches will be used.

REMOVAL

This is the most obvious and direct approach for dealing with asbestos in buildings. When correctly done, removal provides a permanent solution. It is important to emphasize that removal is often *not* the appropriate course of action. Not all asbestos needs to be immediately removed. If removal is not done properly, it can result in the wide dispersal of asbestos fibers that previously were contained, producing a significant hazard to the workers carrying out the remediation and also to children and other building occupants. *Asbestos removal, if not properly performed, can do more harm than good.*

Because of the potential hazards of asbestos removal, an individual decision must be made in regard to abating each room and each surface. It is always cheaper and better to use approaches other than removal when they can be achieved safely.

If asbestos removal must be undertaken, because asbestos-containing materials are friable, easily accessible, or about to be disturbed, then it is essential that the removal be done by a properly certified contractor under the direction of a certified Asbestos Program Manager.

The procedure for performing asbestos removal is complex and has been addressed in detailed regulations produced by the EPA. Before the work can begin, the area to be abated must be completely sealed off by barriers of plastic or other impregnable material. All workers who enter the area must wear proper respiratory protection and protective clothing, and they must shower each time they leave the area. All asbestos that is removed during abatement must be treated as hazardous waste, must be properly placed in bags or drums, and must be discarded safely in a hazardous materials landfill. Every worker and supervisor on the job must be fully certified by the EPA or state authorities. Asbestos removal is extremely hazardous work. If not performed correctly, it can result in disease and death among abatement workers.

At the conclusion of the removal operation, air samples must be collected using the technique of "aggressive" air sampling. In aggressive air sampling, an air blower is operated for several minutes in the area that has been abated to disturb any asbestos fibers that may still be present. This operation is performed before the plastic barriers are taken down. Then air samples are taken in the area that has been abated, and fans are run during the air sampling to keep any asbestos fibers suspended in the air. This technique assures that the environment has not been contaminated with asbestos fibers in the course of the removal operation and that no residual asbestos fibers are left behind. If residual asbestos is found during the aggressive sampling, then abatement and cleanup must be repeated until an asbestos-free environment is achieved.

ENCLOSURE

Enclosure of asbestos in a building involves the construction of airtight walls or drop ceilings over asbestos surfaces. All enclosure of asbestos-containing materials must proceed under the strict supervision of the Asbestos Program Manager. It is important that the performance of enclosure work be noted in the building log, so that in the future, workers and school officials will know that asbestos is present beneath the barrier.

OPERATIONS AND MAINTENANCE (O&M)

An operations and maintenance program is used to manage asbestos that does not pose an immediate hazard. In such a program, immediate action is deferred, and the asbestos is carefully monitored.

In-place management in an O&M program requires action as well. This involves having a program to ensure that the day-to-day management of the building is carried out in a manner that minimizes release of asbestos fibers into the air. It ensures that when asbestos fibers are released, either accidentally or intentionally, proper control and cleanup procedures are implemented.

An O&M program requires an accredited inspector to reexamine asbestos-containing material at least every three years. The inspector must be certified by the EPA or by state authorities. Proper records of every inspection must be maintained in the log and must be made available by school authorities to parents immediately upon request.

The EPA has developed strict guidelines for O&M programs. These guidelines apply to the cleaning, maintenance, renovation, and general operation of buildings containing asbestos. The goal of these regulations is to maintain a building environment that is free of asbestos contamination. All custodial and maintenance personnel who work in a building that contains asbestos must have at least two hours of training in asbestos recognition, log keeping, and notification. An additional two-day training program is required for persons who actually handle asbestos. All training must be done by appropriately accredited organizations. According to EPA regulations, an O&M program should include the following elements:

▪ *Notification.* A program must be developed to let parents, teachers, tenants, and other building occupants know where asbestos-containing materials are located and how to avoid disturbing them. It is essential that this information be presented in clear language, that it be specific, and that it be understood by building occupants.

▪ *Monitoring.* Regular visual inspection and monitoring of asbestos-containing materials by certified individuals is required to document any changes in the condition of the materials.

▪ *Control system.* A work permit system must be in place to control any activities that might disturb asbestos-containing materials. Custodians, craftpersons, persons installing telephone or computer cables, and other workers must not be allowed into these areas without written permission of the Asbestos Program Manager.

▪ *Work practices.* All work conducted in the vicinity of the asbestos-containing materials must proceed under the direction of the Asbestos Program Manager. It must comply with all relevant regulations of the Occupational Safety and Health Administration. Asbestos-containing materials that are removed must be discarded as hazardous waste in a safe landfill.

▪ *Periodic reinspection.* According to EPA regulations, an EPA-accredited inspector must reinspect school buildings containing asbestos at least once every three years to reassess the condition of asbestos-containing materials.

The table below summarizes the advantages and disadvantages of the three principal options for asbestos control.

THERE IS NO SUCH THING AS "HARMLESS ASBESTOS"

▪ ▪ ▪

Over the past several years, the asbestos industry and its consultants have mounted an extensive and highly misleading campaign that attempts to minimize the hazards of asbestos to children and other building occupants. Articles placed in *Reader's Digest*, *Forbes*, and scientific journals have received much attention and caused confusion. This campaign is an effort to reduce the industry's future liability in the United States and also to protect its

THREE OPTIONS FOR ASBESTOS CONTROL

METHOD	ADVANTAGES	DISADVANTAGES
Removal	Eliminates asbestos source; eliminates need for operations and maintenance program; ends exposure.	Most costly in the short run; replacement with substitute material may be necessary; improper removal may increase fiber levels; high potential for worker exposure.
Enclosure	Reduces exposure; initial cost may be less than removal unless utilities need to be relocated or other major changes need to be made; usually does not require replacement of material.	Asbestos source remains and must be removed eventually; fibers continue to be released behind enclosure (and during construction of enclosure); operations and maintenance program is required to control access to enclosure for maintenance and renovation; periodic reinspection is required to check for and repair damage; long-term cost could be more than removal.
Operations and maintenance	Lowest initial cost.	Asbestos source remains; special operations program is required for maintenance or renovation procedures; periodic reinspection is required.

strong market overseas. The central theme of this industry campaign is that the health risk to children posed by asbestos in buildings is "very small."

You should be aware that two false claims run through this industry-sponsored campaign:

- Different types of asbestos vary in their hazards, and the hazards associated with the most widely used form of asbestos (Canadian chrysotile asbestos) are minimal.
- Initial assessment of the risk posed by asbestos in buildings should be based on air sampling.

Both of these claims are highly inaccurate. Moreover, they are directly dangerous to children's health because they are falsely reassuring. The claim that different types of asbestos fibers vary in their hazard is particularly insidious and it is absolutely untrue. It is put forth by the manufacturers of Canadian chrysotile, the type of asbestos most widely used throughout the United States. The central claim of the industry is that the Canadian product is relatively harmless. That claim, however, is not supported by the results of extensive epidemiological and toxicological studies. These studies have shown repeatedly that all types of asbestos, including Canadian chrysotile, are fully capable of producing the complete spectrum of asbestos-related diseases, including asbestosis, malignant mesothelioma, and lung cancer. Parents should make sure that these false claims do not lull school administrators into an inappropriate sense of security. Economic interests cannot be allowed to dictate decisions that are intended to protect the present and future health of our children.

The industry's claim that air sampling provides the most accurate initial assessment of the hazards of asbestos in buildings is also false. It too is intended to minimize the hazard. This claim ignores the fundamental fact that asbestos in buildings is released into the air only intermittently—usually only when it is disturbed. Air sampling, which typically is conducted on only one or a few nights and on weekends, can very easily miss such episodic releases. In such a case, air sampling will provide an apparently negative and thus falsely reassuring result. By contrast, schoolchildren who are present in a building with asbestos for five to eight hours every day will be exposed to airborne asbestos whenever a release occurs. This release may not occur on a sampling day under "best case" conditions. The actual exposure of children and other building occupants may not be accurately reflected by the results of occasional air sampling. A much more accurate assessment of risks to children from asbestos in a building is provided by periodic visual inspection of all buildings containing asbestos. Moreover, visual inspection is the approach that is mandated under federal law.

WHAT CAN PARENTS DO?

■ ■ ■

The most important responsibility of parents in dealing with asbestos in schools and other buildings is to ensure that school authorities act properly to protect their children. This means that school officials and other authorities must comply fully with the legal procedures that have been established under the AHERA law.

Parents must recognize that the AHERA legislation is only as good as its enforcement. This principle is clearly illustrated by a recent series of disclosures in New York City in which a number of inspectors employed by the city were discovered to be falsifying data instead of inspecting schools.

Specifically parents should:

- Ensure that the legally mandated inspection of the school has been completed. Parents are fully entitled under federal law to request and examine school records. As of this writing, all school buildings in the United States should already have been inspected for asbestos; any school district (public, private, or parochial) that has not conducted an inspection is in violation of federal law.
- Ensure that proper remedial action has occurred. Removal, enclosure, and operations and maintenance procedures should by now be in place in all school buildings known to contain asbestos. Periodic inspections and reinspections should be proceeding. Parents can monitor these activities by reviewing school records.
- Ensure that all persons responsible for directing the operations and maintenance programs are properly trained and certified.
- Ascertain that custodians, janitors, and contract repair persons who might be working around asbestos have been properly trained and certified.
- Ensure that any removal is undertaken by properly certified, bonded contractors in a way that is entirely consistent with the law and that all removal operations are followed by aggressive air sampling.

To obtain information on any of these points, parents can write to the school administrator (with a copy to their state and federal representatives and the nearest EPA regional office). If a response is not forthcoming or appears to be inadequate, you can then report it to the EPA regional office or state authority (see Appendix 3).

Asbestos should be removed only when it needs to be removed. It is most important that parents make sure that school administrators are not pressed by unscrupulous contractors into believing that all asbestos must immediately be removed from schools. In most cases it is not necessary to remove asbestos.

WHAT CAN PEDIATRICIANS DO?

■ ■ ■

Pediatricians usually become involved with asbestos problems in schools and other buildings when they are called upon to advise parents, school boards, health departments, and other citizens groups. Because of their knowledge, their status in the community, and their role as advocates for children, pediatricians are in an excellent position to provide reasoned and influential advice. To do this effectively, pediatricians need to understand and communicate the long-term health concerns about asbestos. Pediatricians should emphasize that each situation needs to be evaluated and judged according to its individual severity and according to the potential it poses for exposure to children.

Pediatricians should caution against unnecessary removal of asbestos, but they should also caution against unwarranted complacency. Pediatricians can help school officials and parents to steer a safe course around the sometimes alarmist claims of unscrupulous removal contractors. At the same time they can provide sober caution against the rash claims of the asbestos industry. When appropriate, pediatricians should work with parents' groups and local authorities to ensure that cleanup and remedial actions are timely and effective and that children as well as workers are fully protected during and after remedial operations.

Pediatricians can obtain additional guidance and consultation on the asbestos issue from several sources:

- The American Academy of Pediatrics. In 1987, the Academy issued a position paper, "Asbestos Exposure in Schools," *Pediatrics*, February 1987, 79:301–305; this document is still quite valid and up-to-date. Also, for many years, the Academy has sponsored a national Committee on Environmental Hazards, and the members and staff of this committee constitute a resource for pediatricians. The committee can be contacted through the Academy's headquarters: P.O. Box 927, Elk Grove Village, IL 60009.

▪ The U.S. Environmental Protective Agency. The asbestos program in each of the regional offices of the EPA (see Appendix 3) has available extensive materials on asbestos—on its hazards, proper approaches for dealing with it, and relevant statutes and regulations. An additional resource is the EPA's Office of Toxic Substances, 401 M Street SW, Washington, DC 20460.

▪ The Centers for Disease Control. The Agency for Toxic Substances and Disease Registry within the CDC has developed consumer guides to asbestos and other environmental health hazards. Contact address: 1600 Clifton Road NE, Atlanta, GA 30333.

▪ The New Jersey Environmental and Occupational Health Sciences Institute. This Institute is jointly sponsored by the University of Medicine and Dentistry of New Jersey (UMDNJ)–Robert Wood Johnson Medical School, and Rutgers, The State University of New Jersey. It provides reliable information about the environment and about occupational health and safety. A wide variety of material is distributed to workers, educators, and consumers. Contact address: 45 Knightbridge Road, Piscataway, NJ 08854.

▪ State and local health departments. With increasing frequency, health departments now employ physicians and other experts knowledgeable about environmental health hazards, including asbestos (see Appendix 3).

ASBESTOS IN THE HOME

▪ ▪ ▪

Asbestos is not found as commonly in private homes in the United States as it is in schools, apartment buildings, and public buildings. Nevertheless, asbestos is present in many homes in the United States as a legacy of the past.

The following are locations in homes where asbestos may be found:

- Insulation around pipes, stoves, and furnaces
- Insulation on walls and ceilings, especially as sprayed-on or troweled-on material
- Vinyl floor tiles and sheet coverings

- Patching and spackling compounds and textured paint
- Roofing shingles and siding
- Door gaskets
- Older appliances such as washers and dryers

In the past, asbestos was used in electrical appliances such as hair dryers and washing machines. Hair dryers containing asbestos were recalled by the Consumer Products Safety Commission more than a decade ago, and currently no household appliance in the United States is allowed to contain asbestos.

To determine if a home contains asbestos, a parent can take the following steps:

- To evaluate appliances and other consumer products, examine the label or the invoices to obtain the product name, model number, and year of manufacture. If this information is available, the manufacturer ought to be able to inform you whether the product contains asbestos.
- To evaluate building materials, a parent may wish to hire a professional asbestos manager with qualifications similar to those of managers employed in school districts. This person can inspect the home using both visual and microscopic approaches.
- State and local health departments as well as regional offices of the EPA will have available lists of individuals and laboratories certified to analyze a home for asbestos (see Appendix 3).
- If asbestos-containing materials are found in a home, precisely the same options exist for dealing with these materials as for dealing with those in the schools. In most cases, asbestos-containing materials in the home are best left alone. If materials such as insulation, tiling, and flooring are in good condition, there is no need to worry about them. However, if materials containing asbestos are deteriorating, or if you are planning renovations and the materials will be disturbed, it is wise to find out if they contain asbestos and to have them properly removed.

Parents should *never* undertake asbestos-removal work themselves. The work creates considerable hazards. Additionally, improper do-it-yourself removal of asbestos can cause serious contamination. Any asbestos work in a home should be performed only by properly accredited and certified contractors. Information on certified contractors in your area may be obtained from state or local health departments or from the regional office of the EPA. Parents should be aware that many contractors who advertise themselves as asbestos experts have, in actuality, never been trained properly (or at all). Parents should hire only those contractors who have been certified by the EPA or by a state-approved training school. Parents should ask to see written proof of up-to-date certification.

Children should never play in areas where there are friable asbestos-containing materials.

ASBESTOS IN PLAY SAND

Certain play-sand products that are sold for use in sandboxes are very dangerous, because they are made from rock containing asbestos. Sand that is taken from a beach poses no hazard. However, crushed stone, which may be either white or tan-colored, may contain tremolite, an asbestos-like fiber that is known to cause lung cancer and malignant mesothelioma. A child playing in sand that contains tremolite may create a cloud of tremolite-containing dust that can be inhaled into the lungs, putting the child at future risk.

A fundamental problem is that the Consumer Products Safety Commission has no requirement that sand be labeled as containing tremolite. Although pediatricians and other groups have been attempting for many years to persuade the CPSC to label sand, the agency has resisted such requests.

Parents should, therefore, not buy any sand for use in a sandbox unless the merchant can certify that the sand comes from a beach and contains no tremolite. Also, parents should ascertain whether any sand possibly containing tremolite is present in sandboxes at nurseries, day-care centers, or schools. When in doubt, two options exist:

- Do not purchase the sand or get rid of it if it is already in place.
- Have a certified laboratory examine several samples of the sand microscopically to determine whether asbestos-like fibers are present. The procedures used here are identical to those used in the microscopic examination of building materials.

To obtain additional information about asbestos in the home, a parent can write for the EPA's booklet *Asbestos in Your Home*. This can be obtained from the EPA Public Information Center, 401 M Street SW, Washington, DC 20460. Your state or local health department will have additional information about asbestos in your area.

Two other sources of asbestos need to be considered, because they represent potential hazards to children. They are: (1) asbestos in drinking water and (2) asbestos carried home from work.

ASBESTOS IN DRINKING WATER

■ ■ ■

Approximately 10 percent of all public drinking water supplies in the United States are contaminated with asbestos. Most commonly, asbestos in water comes from asbestos-cement pipes. Asbestos-cement pipes are used to transport water in many systems, and when acidic drinking water comes into contact with these pipes, fibers can be dissolved from the walls. In addition, natural sources account for asbestos in drinking water in some areas of the United States, particularly in the San Francisco Bay area, where some naturally occurring rock formations contain asbestos minerals and are known to release fibers. In certain areas where mining operations exist now or existed previously, old mine tailings are a source of asbestos fibers in drinking water.

To evaluate whether asbestos fibers in drinking water represent a hazard to health, extensive toxicological and epidemiological studies have been conducted. These studies have sought to determine whether asbestos in drinking water causes cancer of the gastrointestinal tract—of the esophagus, stomach, small intestine, or colon.

These studies indicate that if asbestos in drinking water has any harmful effect on humans, the effect is small. Some of the better-conducted epidemiological studies have, however, suggested that asbestos in drinking water may be related to cancer of the stomach, the small intestine, and the pancreas. To reduce the health hazards that may be associated with asbestos in drinking water, even though those hazards are substantially less than the risks of asbestos in buildings, it would appear prudent to minimize exposure. Your local health department is the best source of information on asbestos levels in water in your area.

The most effective way to reduce asbestos levels in drinking water is to add small amounts of lime to drinking water supplies in order to make the water less acidic. When drinking water is less acidic, it will be less likely to dissolve asbestos fibers from pipes. Also, the addition of lime to drinking water will produce a limestone precipitate on the inside of pipes; this precipitate will tend to seal in any asbestos fibers. An additional benefit of the addition of lime is that it will reduce the leaching of lead from lead pipes or lead solder. Therefore, it may be recommended that in any acidic drinking water supply where either asbestos or lead is present, the careful addition of lime is an option deserving of serious study. This addition is not done in the home. It needs to be systemwide.

Parents can take a series of steps:

- Contact your state or local health department (see Appendix 3) to determine whether your drinking water supply contains asbestos fibers.
- If fibers are present at levels that exceed federal guidelines, write to state health authorities, with a copy to the EPA regional office, to request that state authorities spell out their plans for dealing with the asbestos in drinking water.
- If state or federal officials do not provide adequate answers to your inquiries, make contact with national, nongovernmental environmental groups who have guided other communities in similar situations. These groups will be able to provide guidance and assistance (see Appendix 2).

ASBESTOS CARRIED HOME FROM THE WORKPLACE

■ ■ ■

Many jobs involve occupational exposure to asbestos. These include:

- Asbestos mining and milling
- Asbestos product manufacture

- All of the construction trades, including sheet-metal work, carpentry, plumbing, insulation work, air conditioning, rewiring, cable installation, spackling, and dry-wall work
- All shipyard work
- Any form of asbestos removal
- Firefighting
- Demolition work
- Custodial and janitorial work

Parents who work in any occupation potentially involving contact with asbestos are at risk of bringing asbestos fibers home on their clothing, shoes, hair, skin, and cars. These fibers can contaminate the home and become a source of exposure for children and spouses.

Studies conducted in the homes of asbestos workers have shown that dust can be contaminated by high levels of asbestos fibers. Cases of mesothelioma, lung cancer, and asbestosis have been observed in the family members of asbestos workers. All parents who work with asbestos in any occupation must scrupulously shower, change their clothing, and change their shoes before they get into their cars and go home. These procedures are mandated by federal OSHA law, but are frequently not enforced, especially in the construction trades, and workers are often not alerted to their exposure. Only if contaminated shoes and clothing are left at the workplace and only if no contaminated clothing is brought into cars and into homes can the exposure of children to asbestos fibers from the workplace be prevented.

Parents who work in any of the jobs and trades listed above should ascertain from their employer or union whether their work involves exposure to asbestos. Working parents are legally entitled under federal "right-to-know" and "hazard communication" standards to be informed by their employer of any toxic materials with which they work.

The problem of asbestos in schools and other buildings in the United States is enormous, but it is not unconquerable. Reasonable action by thoughtful people in all sectors of our society will, however, be required to meet this challenge. Neither the false claims of the asbestos industry nor the false alarms of certain unscrupulous contractors can be allowed to determine the course of action. Action must be based on concern for children coupled with careful evaluation of asbestos in each building where it is found. The goal must always be the prevention of children's exposure.

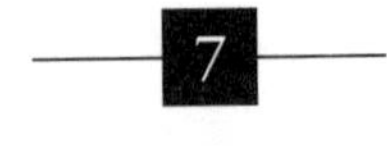

PESTICIDES

THE STORY OF AN EPIDEMIC*

■ ■ ■

At 4 a.m. on the Fourth of July 1985, a 62-year-old woman was admitted to a hospital emergency room in Lake County, California, in shock. She was salivating and sweating profusely, her heartbeat was irregular, and all of her muscles were twitching. With difficulty she told her doctors that she had been well until thirty minutes earlier, when she had eaten her traditional Fourth of July breakfast, a quarter of a watermelon.

Two other members of the woman's family had similar, although milder symptoms. They had also eaten watermelon.

The alert emergency room physicians suspected pesticide poisoning. Because pesticides are used extensively by farmers in that region of California, the doctors recognized the symptoms and administered atropine, a pesticide antidote. The woman's symptoms immediately disappeared. The cases were reported within the hour to the California Department of Health Services.

Because more watermelons are eaten on July 4 than on any other day in the year, the California Department of Health Services took the report from Lake County seriously. They immediately con-

* This account is taken from a report entitled "Pesticide Food Poisoning from Contaminated Watermelons in California, 1985," by Lynn R. Goldman, M.D., and the staff of the California Department of Health Services, published in *Archives of Environmental Health*, 1990, 45:229–236.

tacted local health departments, poison-control centers, and emergency rooms across the state.

One day earlier Oregon health officials had notified the CDHS of several cases of possible pesticide poisoning from watermelons. Late in the morning of July 4, the Oregon officials informed the CDHS that they had found traces of the pesticide aldicarb in several watermelons and that the melons had been traced to California.

By noon, California health officials had learned of twelve more presumed cases of acute poisoning across the state, each due to eating watermelon. Urgently, the CDHS issued a statewide advisory, warning all citizens against eating watermelons and embargoing the fruit throughout California. By late afternoon a melon shipper in Kern County was identified as the source of several, though not all, of the episodes. The melons from Lake County also had detectable amounts of aldicarb.

Aldicarb is the most toxic pesticide registered for use in the United States today. It is a member of the carbamate family of insecticides, and is widely used on citrus crops, cotton, potatoes, peanuts, and soybeans. Using it on watermelons is illegal. The CDHS determined that the epidemic had been caused by the illegal or accidental use of aldicarb by a small group of melon farmers.

In the summer of 1985, over 1,000 cases of probable and possible pesticide poisoning were ultimately reported in watermelon eaters in California. In nearly 700 of these cases, traces of aldicarb were documented. Most people had relatively short-term illnesses. But 17 persons required admission to hospitals. Of 47 reports of suspected pesticide poisoning in pregnant women, two women subsequently had stillbirths.

On July 7, three days after the first case, all watermelons in the state were destroyed. A regulatory program to prevent the future occurrence of similar episodes was installed.

WHAT ARE PESTICIDES?

■ ■ ■

Pesticides are chemicals, most of them synthesized from petroleum and some of natural origin, that are used for the control of insects, unwanted plants, fungi, rodents, and other pests. Pesticides are used in an extraordinarily wide range of settings in industrialized societies. By controlling agricultural pests, they have contributed to dramatic increases in crop yields and in the quantity and variety of our diet. In the home, they control termites, mice, and other rodents. In gardens and lawns as well as along highways and under power line right-of-ways, pesticides control the growth of unwanted plants.

Although specifically designed to kill insects, unwanted plants, and fungi, many pesticides are also highly toxic to the environment, to humans and particularly to children. They can cause cancer, damage the nervous system, the lungs, and the reproductive, immune, and endocrine systems.

More than 1,500 different pesticides are currently in use in the United States. These are blended together to produce more than 50,000 commercial pesticide products. The toxicity of these materials varies widely. Some, like aldicarb, can cause massive acute poisoning. Others have no obvious acute effects, but years or decades after exposure can lead to cancer, neurological injury, or damage to the immune system. Some have no known toxicity.

Pesticide products also contain so-called inert ingredients. The term "inert" means only that these materials have no toxic effect on insects. Many of these inert materials such as diesel fuel, solvents, or other petroleum products can be quite toxic to children. At present, these inert ingredients are not required to be listed on the pesticide label.

Legally, pesticides must be registered with the EPA. However, this is *not* a certificate of their safety. The registration merely certifies under the Federal Insecticide, Fungicide, and Rodenticide Act (FIFRA) that, in the EPA's opinion, the use of the pesticide presents no "unreasonable risk to man or the environment, taking into account the economic, social and environmental costs and benefits of the use of any pesticide." Registration involves many considerations in addition to an evaluation of health risks. In no way can registration of a pesticide by the EPA be taken as a guarantee of the safety of these chemicals for children.

A recent report from the National Academy of Sciences has thoroughly documented the extent of the problem of children's exposure to pesticides in food. The committee responsible for the report (chaired by one of the authors of this book, Philip Landrigan) criticized as inadequate the current EPA standards that ignore the critical differences in the diet and physiology of children. The report, which was three years in the making, calls for new standards that take these differences into account, allow for an adequate margin of safety, and make risk assessments on the basis of health alone. This document may mark the beginning of a new approach to the judicious use of pesticides.

THE MANY TYPES OF PESTICIDES

■ ■ ■

About 600 different pesticides are registered with the EPA. These include *insecticides*, chemicals designed to kill insects; *fungicides*, chemicals designed to kill molds and fungi; and *herbicides*, chemicals designed to kill unwanted plants and weeds. In 1991, an estimated 817 million pounds of active pesticide ingredients were used in agriculture in the United States. This included 495 million pounds of herbicides, 175 million pounds of insecticides, and 72 million pounds of other pesticides.

ORGANOCHLORINE INSECTICIDES

This class includes DDT, chlordane, heptachlor, and dieldrin. DDT is the best known and most widely used member of this group. It was first developed during the 1930s for the control of mosquitoes and was enormously effective. During World War II, and throughout the 1940s and 1950s, DDT was widely used around the world to control the insects that spread malaria and other serious diseases. The success of the organochlorine compounds in controlling insects, pests, and disease vectors during that era was truly unparalleled in human history.

A great advantage of DDT is that it has very low acute toxicity. Persons can work and live around DDT and show no obvious signs of any toxicity, at least not until many years later. Because of this low acute toxicity, DDT and the other chlorinated hydrocarbon insecticides replaced most of the toxic arsenic-containing pesticides that had been in use since the early years of this century. By 1955, more than 90 percent of all pest-control chemicals used in the United States were chlorinated hydrocarbon compounds.

Questions about the safety of DDT began to be raised in the 1960s. A major turning point was the publication in 1962 by Rachel Carson of her landmark book, *Silent Spring*. For the first time this book put before the public evidence that DDT and other chlorinated pesticides had serious toxic effects. In particular, Carson documented that DDT could cause destruction of the eggs of eagles, ospreys, and other large birds and showed that these chemicals were toxic to reproduction. She raised the possibility that reproductive and other effects might also occur in humans. The publication of *Silent Spring* is considered by many to mark the beginning of the environmental movement in the United States.

DDT and other chlorinated hydrocarbons can last in the biosphere for centuries. As it moves up the food chain, because it is stored in fatty tissue, it increases in concentration. The low concentrations of DDT that are found on the bottoms of rivers and lakes are concentrated in plankton, concentrated again in mussels and other shellfish that feed on plankton, concentrated further in game fish such as salmon and striped bass that feed on the little fish. Eagles, bears, and ospreys, the predators who live at the top of the food chain, have extraordinarily high levels in their tissues and are the most seriously affected. Because humans live high on the food chain, and eat game fish and other animals that have high concentrations of DDT and other chlorinated pesticides, we too are threatened.

Concern about DDT was a major force in the creation of the Environmental Protection Agency. Two years after it was established in 1970, the EPA banned the use of DDT on all food crops. By the end of the 1980s most other uses of chlorinated compounds were also discontinued in this country.

High concentrations of DDT have been found in the fatty tissue of people from around the world. Especially high levels are seen in breast milk, because of its very high fat content. The highest breast milk levels of DDT are seen in agricultural regions, especially in developing nations, where DDT is still used extensively. In most areas of this country, breast milk levels of DDT have been declining steadily since the chemical was banned.

Despite its ban in the United States, DDT continues to be widely used elsewhere. Because most imported foods are not closely monitored for pesticides by federal agencies, imports into the United States from other countries may still contain high levels of DDT.

Chlorinated hydrocarbons and cancer. Cancers have been seen in laboratory animals treated with chlorinated hydrocarbon pesticides. Virtually all of these chemicals are now regulated by the EPA as likely human carcinogens, and their use is strictly limited.

Medical scientists have become concerned in recent years that DDT may be linked to female breast cancer. A study conducted in New York State has found that women with breast cancer have higher body levels of DDT than women of the same age without cancer. DDT is known to be able to mimic certain actions of the hormone estrogen, and elevated estrogen levels are known to be a risk factor for breast cancer. This, in fact, is the suspected mechanism by which DDT is thought to damage the eggs of eagles. Further studies of this important issue are currently under way.

ORGANOPHOSPHATE INSECTICIDES

The organophosphates were first developed in the 1930s. As the use of the organochlorines declined, the organophosphates came to replace them. They are now the most common type of pesticides in use. They include such well-known chemicals as parathion, malathion, and Diazinon.

The organophosphate pesticides are extremely toxic to both insects and humans. Indeed, many members of this family were developed for use as war gases during World War II and are still in the armories of many nations.

Organophosphates cause prompt and severe damage to the nervous system. Acute exposure can produce illness within minutes, particularly in children. The typical symptoms include pinpoint pupils, nausea, vomiting, abdominal pain, diarrhea, profuse sweating, and muscle twitching. In severe cases, respiratory paralysis can develop, and this can be fatal. All of these effects are brought about by the actions of the organophosphates on the nervous system.

Chronic exposure to the organophosphates can also damage the nervous system, but in a different fashion. People who are chronically exposed to these chemicals develop damage in the peripheral nerves, the long nerve fibers that control the arms and legs. Tingling, numbness, and weakness of the hands and feet can result. Farmworkers, pesticide applicators, and people who spend extended periods of time around pets that have been treated with organophosphate-containing flea powders are the usual victims.

Emergency room physicians and EMT teams, especially in agricultural areas, know the symptoms of acute pesticide poisoning and are trained in the use of specific antidotes. This saved lives in Lake County, California, during the aldicarb epidemic.

THE CARBAMATE INSECTICIDES

Carbamates have toxic actions very similar to those of the organophosphates. Like organophosphates, they are acutely toxic, and their toxicity is directed principally at the nervous system.

Carbamate pesticides in common use today include aldicarb, the compound responsible for the epidemic in California, and carbaryl.

A major advantage of the organophosphates and the carbamates over the organochlorine pesticides is that these chemicals break down rapidly in the environment. They do not persist or accumulate in living organisms.

PYRETHROID INSECTICIDES

Pyrethroid pesticides were originally produced from the dried flowers of the chrysanthemum plant. Today, synthetic pyrethroid compounds are widely available. These compounds are effective against a wide range of insect pests. They have low acute toxicity, although some persons become allergic to them and can develop acute allergic reactions upon repeated exposure.

HERBICIDES

Herbicides are chemicals used to kill unwanted plants. They are employed on lawns, in home gardens, along highways and railways, under power lines, and in the forest beneath the tree canopy. The use of herbicides has increased dramatically in the United States. In 1955, only 3 percent of all acreage planted with corn and soybeans was treated with herbicides. By 1985, that figure had increased to more than 95 percent. Each year in the United States approximately $2.5 billion is spent on herbicides.

Herbicides have been associated with cancer. Dioxin, the most toxic synthetic chemical known, is frequently a contaminant of the herbicide 2,4,5-T used in Vietnam as Agent Orange. Exposure to 2,4,5-T contaminated with dioxin has been linked to the development of two types of human cancer—soft tissue sarcoma and non-Hodgkin's lymphoma. These particular types of cancer have been seen in excess among persons employed in the manufacture of these herbicides. There is concern that these same tumors may exist among Vietnam veterans who were exposed during their military service.

Groundwater in many areas of the country, particularly in the midwestern states, is contaminated with triazine herbicides such as atrazine. As a result, persons of all ages, including children, can be exposed to these chemicals in their drinking water.

FUNGICIDES

Fungicides are compounds used to control molds and other plant diseases. These compounds tend to be extremely toxic and virtually all of them have been shown to be capable of causing cancer. They include compounds such as maneb, captan, and benomyl.

Although fungicides account for less than 10 percent of annual pesticide sales in the United States, they have the potential for extensive human exposure, especially through the diet. They are applied throughout the growing season to a large variety of fruits and vegetables, many of which are eaten in large quantities by our children.

Other pesticides used in American agriculture include the following:

- *Chlordimeform* is a relatively recently developed pesticide. It has been found to be very toxic to the bladder. High-dose exposure can cause damage to the lining of the bladder which results in the occurrence of blood in the urine. Chronic exposure can cause cancer of the bladder.
- *Paraquat* is used as a defoliant and herbicide. It is toxic to the lungs. If even a tiny amount of paraquat is taken into the human body either by inhalation or by accidental swallowing, it can cause severe damage to the lungs which results in widespread scarring and frequently leads to death.
- *Alar* is a compound that until a few years ago was widely applied to apples and other fruit crops to slow the development of these fruits and to prolong their shelf life in grocery stores. Extensive animal testing has confirmed that a major metabolic breakdown product of Alar is a potent cause of cancer. Alar was widely used on apples and other fruits consumed in large quantities by young children. After intense controversy, Alar was removed from the market because of its cancer hazard.

In general, the amounts and variety of pesticides used in American agriculture have increased rapidly since World War II. The greatest increases occurred during the 1960s and 1970s. In 1982, 880 million pounds of active pesticides were applied to crops in the United States. This represented an increase from 320 million pounds in 1964.

The good news is that in the past ten years pesticide use, except for herbicides, has begun to decline. Increasingly, the Department of Agriculture, the EPA, and farmers have come to recognize that more effective control of insects and other pests can be achieved through integrated pest management systems which avoid heavy pesticide use. In these programs, pesticides are used less often than in the past and in smaller amounts. Also, they are combined with other, more environmentally friendly means of pest control such as crop rotation, crop separation, and the use of plants which contain natural pesticides. These alternative programs have achieved substantial cost savings for farmers. They have also contributed to the more and more frequent appearance in our market of foods that are certified "organic."

HOW ARE CHILDREN EXPOSED TO PESTICIDES?

■ ■ ■

The most common route of our children's exposure to pesticides is through eating pesticide residues that are present in their food. They can also be exposed to pesticides in their homes, in their yards, in their schools and playgrounds, and through consumer products.

DIETARY EXPOSURE

Infants and children are regularly exposed in their diets to trace amounts of pesticides that are applied to food crops. These traces are termed *residues*. They include DDT and other organochlorines, herbicides, fungicides, organophosphates, and carbamates.

Levels of pesticide residues in foods are regulated by the EPA. The EPA regulates concentrations of pesticide residues through a system of standards called *food tolerances*. A tolerance is a legal limit that the concentration of a pesticide in a particular food must not exceed.

Although the food tolerance system is in theory a good approach to limiting children's exposures, in practice it presents a number of problems. Tolerances are based on the diet of the general American population and on the susceptibility of adults. No consideration is given to the fact that children consume a diet considerably different from that of adults, a diet that contains much higher quantities of milk, applesauce, and orange juice. Nor is consideration given to the fact that babies and children may be more susceptible than adults to certain pesticides that injure the developing nervous system, the immune system, and the reproductive organs. Because of these deficiencies in the present regulatory system, children may be exposed to substantial concentrations of pesticide residues in their diet. The present regulatory system also considers the effects of each pesticide in isolation and fails to recognize that in the real world children are frequently exposed to many pesticide residues at once.

High-dose exposure to acutely toxic pesticides such as aldicarb, other carbamates, and organophosphates can cause acute neurologic disease. This has been reported in children who have eaten contaminated fruits and vegetables. Repeated exposure of children to pesticides that are carcinogens, neurotoxins, or toxins to other organs can result in delayed disease that appears years or decades after exposure.

PESTICIDES IN BREAST MILK

Certain pesticides, especially DDT and the other fat-soluble organochlorine pesticides, may be highly concentrated in breast milk. In certain areas of the United States, breast milk DDT levels are substantially above the permissible standards for DDT in dairy products.

Women who have worked around pesticides should have their breast milk tested for DDT content. In some cases when breast milk DDT levels are very high, pediatricians may recommend that mothers pump their breasts to remove the toxin from their bodies, but not feed it to their babies. Usually, however, levels are not too high, and mothers can safely breast-feed their infants. When in doubt, consult your pediatrician.

EXPOSURE VIA PARENTS

Children can be exposed to pesticides if their parents work in agriculture or with pesticides. After work, unless they take appropriate precautions, they may bring home chemically soaked clothing and contaminate the home environment.

If you work around pesticides regularly or even only occasionally, it is very important that you remove your contaminated shoes and clothing before you get into your car or go into your home.

AIRBORNE EXPOSURE

In farm country, children can be exposed to pesticides in the air. This is especially likely to happen if there has been aerial spraying and the chemicals drift into residential areas. Many of the pesticides in common use are volatile and can evaporate into the community air to cause high levels of exposure in neighborhoods close to farmlands or in communities near pesticide manufacturing facilities. When urban and suburban developments are interspersed with agricultural lands, as sometimes happens on the fringes of our cities, airborne exposure to pesticides presents a serious health threat to nearby children and adults. Episodes of illnesses in communities near farms have been reported following pesticide applications in California, Arizona, and other states. The application of defoliants to cotton crops has been associated with high rates of respiratory complaints among persons living near cotton fields.

SKIN EXPOSURE

Many pesticides are readily absorbed into the body through the skin. These chemicals therefore represent more of a hazard to children because of their relatively large skin surface area, the delicacy of children's skin, and their extensive contact with lawn areas, flowers, and gardens.

PESTICIDES IN THE HOME

■ ■ ■

The widespread use of pesticides such as flea bombs, insecticide sprays, and foggers in homes exposes children to these toxic chemicals in their indoor environments. Most home-use products contain either organophosphate or carbamate pesticides, acute nervous system toxins.

The last national survey to assess home applications of pesticides was conducted by the EPA in 1976–77. This survey estimated that 84 percent (61 million) of American households used pesticides, about 22 percent (16 million) in the garden, 39 percent (28 million) in the yard. About half of these pesticides were applied by the homeowner.

Many pesticide labels say that people may return to an area where pesticide has been used one to two hours after application. Often, those recommended intervals are too short. To protect your children against recently applied pesticides, keep your children from going into the sprayed area until at least twice the recommended "reentry period" has passed.

FLEA BOMBS

The pesticide chloropyrifos (Dursban) is widely used to treat pets and carpets for fleas. Scientists at Johns Hopkins University measured concentrations of chloropyrifos in a baby's room shortly after the application of the material. They found high concentrations of the chemical in the baby's living area. Also, they noted that concentrations were much higher one foot above the floor, where the baby played, than six feet above the floor, where adults breathe. The scientists concluded that the treated carpet was a reservoir of chloropyrifos, which then contaminated the entire room, and particularly the area where the baby played. They recommended extensive ventilation before children and infants be allowed to reenter the room.

Pesticides are used extensively in homes, apartments, schools, day-care centers, and public buildings for the control of cockroaches and other insect pests. Outbreaks of pesticide poisoning have been reported among the pupils and employees of treated schools and houses. Typically, the treatment takes place over a weekend or on a holiday. The building is then sealed for several days. On the Monday morning or after the holiday, when the pupils and teachers reenter the building, they encounter a very high level of pesticide vapor that can cause acute illness. Levels decrease over time with ventilation.

TERMITE CONTROL

The pesticide chlordane is particularly insidious. It is used widely for the treatment of basements and foundations for termites. The problem with chlordane is that, like DDT, it is extraordinarily persistent in the environment and can last for decades. Some homes that were treated with chlordane in the 1950s still have high levels today. Chlordane is a cause of cancer in humans. For that reason it has been banned by the EPA for use as a termite-control agent. However, there are reports that unscrupulous pest-control operators are still occasionally using chlordane.

WOOD PRESERVATIVES

Pentachlorophenol (PCP) is a commonly used wood preservative. It is the second most heavily used pesticide in the United States. It is used widely in wooden homes, such as log cabins, and on playground equipment. Children can get PCP on their skins and then absorb it. Doctors in Arkansas found high concentrations of PCP in the urine of children who lived in log homes. Cases of PCP poisoning have been reported in children who spent many hours around playground equipment that had been treated with this chemical. It is extremely dangerous to burn PCP-treated wood in the fireplace, because smoke rich in PCP can be released into the air.

LAWN-CARE PESTICIDES

■ ■ ■

Lawn care pesticides present a serious threat to the health of children. These chemicals are very widely used in the United States. Annual sales are over $700 million.

Case report. A six-week-old infant was sleeping in her crib on the porch of her parents' garden apartment while a lawn-care product containing organophosphate was applied to the yard. The family was not warned of the pesticide application, and there was no notification sign indicating that a toxic product was being used.

Within an hour, the infant was noted by the mother to have

excessive sweating and salivation. She called the local poison-control center, which advised her to take the baby to the hospital immediately. The baby was diagnosed as having pesticide poisoning, and she received the antidotes atropine and pralidoxamine for twenty-four hours. She recovered fully.

Follow-up growth and development of the child had been normal. On two occasions she has had febrile convulsions.

PROBLEMS WITH LAWN-CARE PESTICIDES

Some ingredients of lawn pesticides are highly toxic. The herbicide 2,4-D (2,4-dichlorophenoxyacetic acid) is an active component in such common products as Weed-B-Gon, Weedone, and 1,500 other lawn-care products. Some common fungicides (maneb, zineb, mancozeb, and metriram) are ethylene bisdithiocarbamates (EBDC) and are metabolized to ethylenethiourea (ETU), a compound that causes birth defects, cancer, and thyroid disorders in rats and mice.

Diazinon (Spectocide), the most widely used pesticide, is an organophosphate compound. According to EPA estimates, about 6 million pounds are used annually on home lawns and commercial turf. This agent may cause congenital malformations in humans and is acutely toxic to birds. The EPA has banned Diazinon use on golf courses, sod farms, and corn and alfalfa fields, but this restriction does not apply to commercial lawn-care companies and homeowners.

Lawn-care companies frequently use inexperienced, improperly protected personnel, especially during the busy summer months. Many of these summer workers are teenagers with only minimal training. This causes a problem of exposure both for the applicators and for the consumer.

ADVERTISING CLAIMS

The U.S. Government Accounting Office has expressed concerns about protecting the public from exposure to the risks of lawn-care pesticides. They found that the lawn pesticide industry continued to make illegal claims that their products are "safe and nontoxic." Misleading language is frequently used in advertisements by these firms. On the basis of these concerns, the attorney general of the state of New York brought legal action against the

Chemlawn Company for false advertising. This case was settled on June 29, 1990, in a landmark agreement forbidding Chemlawn from advertising its lawn-care applications as "safe" or "nontoxic" and ordering Chemlawn to pay the state $100,000 in fines.

MEDICATIONS AND PERSONAL PRODUCTS

■ ■ ■

Another important route of exposure involves the direct application of insect repellents to children's skin.

N,N-Diethyl-m-toluamide, commonly called DEET, is the active ingredient in numerous commercially available insect repellents. Since 1961, at least six cases of toxic reactions from repeated exposure to DEET have been reported. Six girls, ranging in age from 17 months to 8 years, developed behavioral changes, ataxia, encephalopathy, seizures, and coma after repeated exposure to DEET; three died.

In August 1989 the New York State Department of Health investigated five reports of generalized seizures associated with topical use of DEET. Four of the patients were boys aged 3 to 7 years.

Lindane shampoo. For almost thirty years the pesticide lindane (a chlorinated hydrocarbon) has been used in a shampoo for the treatment of head lice. Lindane is toxic to the nervous system, and concern has been raised about the possibility of neurological damage from children's exposure.

Lanolin, a derivative of sheep wool, is commonly used as an ointment to treat sore, cracked skin. Mothers who breast-feed frequently use it on their nipples, and it is sometimes applied directly to children's skin. Diazinon and chloropyrifos as well as several organochlorine pesticides have been found at measurable levels in lanolin. The Food and Drug Administration identified sixteen pesticides in samples of lanolin it sampled in 1988. The principal source of these residues is the wool from sheep treated with a pesticide dip to control parasite infestations in the fleece. Do not use lanolin around babies.

ACCIDENTAL INGESTION

■ ■ ■

Accidental pesticide poisonings are all too common among young children. In one study of thirty-seven children who had been hospitalized at Children's Medical Center in Dallas as a result of organophosphate or carbamate pesticide poisoning, ingestion of a liquid was the most common mechanism (73 percent) of exposure. Most of these poisonings took place in the home and were the result of careless storage of the original container or putting the pesticide in unmarked or uncovered containers. *You must never, not even "temporarily," put a pesticide in a container that might be attractive or tempting to your child, such as a soda bottle.* It is never too early to begin to educate your children about the dangers of putting strange objects in the mouth.

One of the most dangerous times for ingestion by young children is when the family is moving. When you are moving from one house or apartment to another, you are distracted; containers of pesticides, drain cleaners, paints, solvents, and other dangerous materials are taken out of their usual safe hiding places and set in the open; and children are relatively unguarded. This is a clear prescription for disaster. Moving day is a good time to spend a few dollars on a babysitter.

PESTICIDES IN THE SCHOOLS

■ ■ ■

Because of concern about the health hazards of pesticides, particularly to children, efforts have been made in the past several years to reduce pesticide use. Local school boards across the United States have been in the forefront of these efforts, and they have been energized by the realization that schools use a wide variety of pesticides in very substantial amounts. For example, of the 47 pesticides in use in the Los Angeles School District in 1991, 11 are carcinogens, 12 can damage the nervous system, 15 are mutagens (chemicals capable of causing mutations), and 3 can cause birth defects. The high costs of pesticides, many of which are petroleum-based chemicals, and the fact that more and more pests are developing resistance to the most widely used pesticides have also stimulated efforts to reduce the use of these chemicals.

INTEGRATED PEST MANAGEMENT

■ ■ ■

The most effective approach to minimizing pesticide use while still providing excellent long-term control of pests is called *integrated pest management (IPM)*. IPM is a logical approach that takes advantage of all appropriate pest-control options—nonchemical as well as chemical. At the heart of IPM is an orderly decision-making process that contains the following elements:

▪ First, a pest management policy is established from the site—be it a school, a school district, a neighborhood, a community, or a farm. The policy states that the overall goals of the IPM will be to minimize pesticide use, to choose those pesticides that are least toxic to people and the environment, and to utilize nonchemical approaches like good housekeeping, preventive maintenance, and staff training wherever possible. This policy statement acts as a guide in the specific decisions that follow. It is most effective when it has the clear and committed support of the people in charge—the school board, the principal, the mayors, or the farm manager.

▪ Next, the site is thoroughly inspected, and all pest problems are noted.

▪ Then action thresholds are set. These are the levels at which pest populations or environmental conditions require remedial action.

▪ Programs are then put in place that utilize all available nonchemical options, such as pheromone traps, caulking the cracks around plumbing, weeding the lawns instead of treating them chemically, and emphasizing food sanitation in dining areas and kitchens.

▪ Finally, written records need to be kept and there should be periodic evaluation to ensure that the program's objectives have been met.

IPM programs have been successfully adopted by school districts across the United States—in Montgomery County, Maryland; San Diego, California; Wheaton/Warrenville, Illinois; Ann Arbor, Michigan; and Plum Borough, Pennsylvania. The National Parent-

Teacher Association recently passed a resolution to work toward the elimination of pesticides in schools. In addition to reducing the use of hazardous pesticides, these programs have also achieved substantial cost savings for schools.

To guide parents and school officials in their transition from chemical pest control to IPM, the EPA has issued a booklet, *Pest Control in Schools: Adopting Integrated Pest Management*. It is available from the Field Operations Division, Office of Pesticide Programs (H7506C), U.S. EPA, Washington, DC 20460.

Additional information may be obtained from NCAP, the Northwest Coalition for Alternatives to Pesticides, P.O. Box 1393, Eugene, OR 97440. Telephone 503-344-5044.

WHAT CAN PARENTS DO?

■ ■ ■

In the long run, the most effective way to reduce your children's exposure to pesticides is to reduce the use of pesticides. Pesticide use needs to be minimized in all sectors of our society—in agriculture, in the home, on lawns, in gardens, and in schools and playgrounds.

In agriculture, work conducted in recent years by the EPA and the Department of Agriculture has shown that currently available methods of pesticide reduction could cut pesticide use by between 25 and 75 percent. In more and more areas of the United States, food retailers have come to realize that parents are willing to pay slightly higher prices for foods that have been grown without pesticides or with only minimal levels of pesticide application. These "organic" foods are becoming increasingly available in grocery stores. We encourage you whenever possible to investigate the possibility of purchasing organic foods. You should understand that foods labeled "organic" are not necessarily pesticide-free, but that less pesticide than usual has been applied in their production.

Pesticide exposure in the home is something you can control directly. There is simply no need to employ chemical companies to produce manicured green lawns. Such lawns may look beautiful. In fact, however, they are toxic chemical dump sites, not fit for children's play.

SUGGESTIONS FOR THE SAFE USE OF PESTICIDES IN THE HOME

No use of pesticides is completely safe. Infants and children are especially vulnerable to certain pesticides. Therefore, whenever possible, do not use pesticides at all. However, if you must use pesticides, follow these common-sense rules.

- *Purchase.* Find out about the substance before purchase. Is it approved by the EPA? Is the EPA reviewing it for health risks? Is it legal to apply the pesticide in the desired area? Are there other alternatives? Are there other formulations? Is it a fire hazard? How long is it effective? Is the pesticide suitable for the pest you want destroyed? To avoid storage health hazards, purchase only the amount you need to do the job.
- *Directions.* Read the directions on the container carefully *before purchasing*, again before using, and follow them, especially the safety precautions. If directions call for rubber gloves, masks, protective clothing, or goggles, leave this application to certified experts or use a less potent substance.
- *Spraying.* A 48-hour prenotification should be given prior to pesticide application to multiple-family dwellings. Inform your neighbors when you plan to use lawn-care pesticides or to treat for termites or roaches. Avoid spraying into the wind so that you do not inhale the sprays and dust. It is best to stay out of sprayed areas for at least the rest of the day. Work in well-ventilated areas. If spraying outdoors, close windows and keep children and pets indoors. Chemicals sprayed into the air or onto the ground can drift or wash into nontargeted areas.
- *Smoking.* Do not smoke while spraying or dusting. Some of the chemicals are flammable and you may inhale poisons along with the smoke or your hands may carry the pesticide to your mouth.
- *Play areas.* Children should not be allowed on a lawn or in a garden after the use of pesticides until the area has been watered and all residues washed into the ground and dried. All odor of pesticide should have disappeared before children are allowed to return. The usual instructions permitting reentry into the area one to two hours after spraying are inappropriate especially for crawling infants and toddlers.
- *Pregnant women.* Pregnant women should leave any area where a pesticide is being used and should not return until the chemical has dried completely and there is no odor remaining (usually at least eight hours).
- *Health problems.* Chemically hypersensitive individuals should be forewarned about the use of pesticides. Persons with known diseases of organs such as the kidneys or liver should be excluded from exposure to pesticides that affect those organs. The package directions should list the symptoms of an adverse effect of the pesticide.

SUGGESTIONS FOR THE SAFE USE OF PESTICIDES IN THE HOME (*cont.*)

- *Furniture.* Cover furniture and wading pools. Cover or remove birdbaths, dog dishes, and fish pools before spraying.
- *Fruits and vegetables.* Avoid spraying fruits and vegetables ready for harvest and allow the full time recommended between spraying and picking for consumption. Wash, scrape, and peel appropriate vegetables and fruits before eating them.
- *Wash hands.* Wash your hands and those of your children thoroughly after using pesticide and especially before eating or smoking.
- *Contamination of skin and clothes.* Avoid getting pesticides on your skin or your child's skin. If they are spilled on the skin, wash off immediately and thoroughly for at least fifteen minutes and change clothing. Change clothing and bathe thoroughly at the end of each operation involving pesticides. If clothing becomes contaminated, wash and launder the contaminated clothes before wearing. Do not wear contaminated clothing into your home. Avoid wearing leather when using pesticides, because exposed leather is impossible to decontaminate and must be discarded.
- *Storage.* Store the pesticide in its original container, with the original intact label, in a safe locked compartment, away from children and pets. *Never* transfer containers. Containers used for mixing are considered contaminated.
- *Disposal.* "Empty" containers are never completely empty. Contact the Department of Health or the EPA about proper method of disposal. Destroy empty containers immediately. Wash out the container twice before placing it in the trash and punch holes in the top and bottom.

RECOMMENDATIONS WHEN PURCHASING CHEMICAL LAWN-CARE SERVICES

We strongly advise that you and your neighbors *not* use chemical lawn services. The immaculate, perfectly green lawn is not a necessary component of human existence, and the chemicals used to achieve it are extremely toxic to you and your children. But if you must . . .

- Written contracts should be obtained with written notice prior to spraying in subsequent seasons, if an automatic renewal policy exists. Oral agreements are not sufficient or valid. Prior notification is important to allow time to remove toys, cover lawn furniture, pet-food dishes, and wading pools, and warn individuals with chemical hypersensitivity.
- Obtain information before application of lawn-care substances: names of pesticides to be applied, precautions to be taken to ensure safety for family members, pets, label warning, time and date of spraying. Many companies provide Pesticide Fact Sheets. Are there nontoxic alternatives without pesticides?
- Give advance notice to neighbors, including all the information you have received, and post warnings on treated lawns. This is particularly important if neighbors are chemically sensitive individuals.
- Pesticides should not be applied under adverse conditions—for example, during high winds.
- Check if the applicators are trained and certified.
- Know the potential acute and chronic health effects of the pesticides to be used.
- Is the EPA presently testing the product for any health risks?
- How long should residents wait after pesticide application before using the premises? Are there specific recommendations for the reentry of children and pregnant women to the premises?
- Does the lawn-care service company carry liability insurance to cover claims for personal injury? Check your homeowner's insurance for "pollution exclusion" clause which excludes coverage for environmental damage.
- Outdoor lawn pesticide applications should have signs indicating "pesticide treated area" with international "Do Not Walk on the Grass" symbol for at least 24 hours. Notices should be placed 24 to 48 hours in advance of spraying. They should contain the date of the aplication, the name(s) of active pesticide ingredient(s), the name and phone number of applicator, and proposed date of the next application.

STEPS PARENTS (AND TEACHERS) CAN TAKE TO REDUCE SCHOOL PESTICIDE USE*

- Meet with your school principal and grounds maintenance personnel. Ask about current pesticide use practices:
  - Which weed and insect pests are present (if any)?
  - What chemicals or other means are used to control them?
  - When and how often are pesticide applications done (on a schedule or only when a pest problem is present)?
  - Who makes the decision about whether to use pesticides?
  - Who does the actual application (school personnel or outside contractors)?
  - Is there a written record of reasons and justification for pesticide use?
  - Are alternatives considered?
  - Is advance notice given of treatment? To parents? To teachers?
  - Is there an appeals process if parents wish to challenge a proposed use of a pesticide?
  - Are treated areas posted?
  - Are adequate records kept of pesticide application?
  - Is the school nurse trained to recognize pesticide poisonings?
- If you are not satisfied with the answers you receive, express your concerns to the school superintendent, school board, and school district management. Raise your concerns to the Parent-Teacher Association, and find other allies among the parents and teachers. NCAP can help you with information about the particular pesticides being used.
- Do your research, and go to meetings prepared to suggest a nonchemical policy alternative. Read NCAP's *Planning for Nonchemical School Ground Maintenance* (see page 129 for ordering information). Alternative controls are available for most weed and insect problems. Preventing the conditions that lead to pest problems is often the most successful (and least toxic) way to get rid of a pest problem.
- Work to get a standing citizens committee set up to oversee the development and implementation of the new policy. Involve as many interested parties as possible, and be sure that the committee meets regularly to review the progress and setbacks as the new policy is carried out.
- It may be desirable to consult (or even hire) an integrated pest management specialist when developing a policy for your district. Such a specialist can tailor a grounds or interior maintenance plan to the specific needs and conditions of your area. If your school district is small, consider getting several districts to jointly sponsor the visit of such an expert, to help defray costs.

* This list is produced with the permission of NCAP, the Northwest Coalition for Alternatives to Pesticides.

STEPS PARENTS (AND TEACHERS) CAN TAKE TO REDUCE SCHOOL PESTICIDE USE (*cont.*)

- Remember that your school grounds and maintenance staff must be involved in the development of any new policy. They are the ones who will have to make the policy work, and they will work harder for the success of a program if they have a sense of participation in it. Otherwise, they may feel that the new policy is unnecessary, impractical, or forced on them by others. After the policy is developed, make sure all existing and new staff are trained in its principles. Encourage ongoing training and celebrate program milestones.
- Don't forget to involve the teachers and students. Helping implement a grounds design and school maintenance policy can be a rewarding educational experience. Students can be involved in digging weeds and beds, planting trees and shrubs, etc., for a low-maintenance landscaping project, while learning about insects and natural predators, the toxic effects of chemicals, and environmentally sound ways of managing our natural resources.
- There are many other products used in schools that are, or may contain, hazardous materials. These include plywood and particle board (containing formaldehyde), asbestos, wood preservatives (especially those containing TBT or PCP), paints and additives, urethane, etc. Working with your school's PTA, principal, maintenance staff, and district purchasing department, take inventory of these items, and then research less toxic alternatives. You may want to ask your school district to do air testing for formaldehyde levels.

The application of pesticides to control termites is an inherently dangerous procedure. We realize that in some areas of the country, particularly in the southern states, it is absolutely necessary to control termites in order to keep houses from collapsing. However, the procedure must always be carried out with great care and only by licensed applicators. Parents should make sure that no chlordane is used for termite control and that the chemicals being used are not carcinogenic for their children. The only effective way to obtain this information is to actually examine the labels on the chemicals that are to be used and, when in doubt, check these labels with the EPA.

Parents who live in agricultural areas and near farmlands should pay close attention to scheduled pesticide flyovers. Children should be kept indoors whenever possible during such spraying.

If you live in an agricultural area, particularly in the Midwest, it would be wise to check with your state health department or with the regional office of the EPA to obtain information on herbicide levels in your water supply. When in doubt, take a water sample, usually the first sample obtained in the early morning, and send it to the state laboratory for herbicide testing. We advise that you not use herbicide-contaminated water to make formula, juice, and other drinks for your children. Moreover, boiling is not guaranteed to destroy these chemicals.

Parents should recognize that the Delaney Clause, a piece of federal pesticide legislation that has been on the books for many decades, is a very powerful weapon in the war to protect their children against pesticides. The Delaney Clause is a simple statement in the law that no carcinogenic pesticides should be added to the food that children eat. In recent years, the chemical industry has invested millions of dollars in advertising propaganda which claims that the Delaney Clause is not necessary. This is foolish. What could be better for our children than prevention of their exposure to carcinogenic pesticides? Fight to keep the Delaney Clause. You may wish to write to your congressman or senator.

RECOMMENDATIONS FOR PEDIATRICIANS

■ ■ ■

Pediatricians are an important source of health information for parents, and they are likely to be asked by parents about the toxicity of pesticides.

Pediatricians need to be aware of the major categories of pesticides listed in this chapter and their hazards. We suggest that during routine examinations pediatricians ask about the use of pesticides in the home and on the lawn in order to provide anticipatory guidance. As an "alert clinician," the pediatrician should be aware that subtle and confusing clinical presentations may be associated with exposure to pesticides in the environment. As an advocate of child health, the pediatrician should inform local health authorities when there is concern about unnecessary application of pesticides.

Pediatricians must work with the American Academy of Pediatrics to persuade the EPA to improve the present antiquated approach to the setting of pesticide residue levels in foods. The current approach makes no sense from the perspective of protecting the health of children.

8

RADIATION

Radiation is a dread word for most parents. It conjures up pictures of mushroom clouds, Hiroshima, Nagasaki, Chernobyl, and Three Mile Island. Recently this concern has spread to include radon, electric power lines, and electromagnetic fields (EMFs).

Much of the information available on radiation is confusing, and parents are besieged by conflicting advice. Should your children receive dental X rays and chest X rays or not? How often? For what indications? Is radon in your home a hazard? Does the risk of radon differ across the country from region to region? How can you tell if your home contains dangerous levels of radon? And finally, what about EMFs? Should you and your children avoid power lines? Transformer stations? Electric blankets? Home computers? Color TV? Cellular telephones?

A fundamental problem with radiation is that we cannot sense it. We cannot see, feel, or smell X rays, radon, or EMFs. Except at very high levels of exposure, the effects of radiation are silent, subtle, and delayed. For this reason, it is very important that both individually and as a society we take carefully considered actions to minimize our exposures and those of our children to all forms of radiation.

The encouraging news is that despite the current welter of confusing information, the fundamental base of scientific knowledge about most forms of radiation is very good and getting better. We know much more about the health hazards of X rays, radioisotopes, and radon than we do about most other environmental hazards. The challenge therefore is to convey this information in a clear and straightforward way that will cut through the confusion and enable you to take reasonable actions to protect yourself and your children against the hazards of radiation.

WHAT IS RADIATION AND HOW DOES IT CAUSE INJURY?

■ ■ ■

Radiation is energy. Each kind of radiation contains a specific amount and type of energy. The many forms of radiation differ from one another in the ways that they can deliver their energy to the human body and in the types of damage that they produce.

All forms of radiation cause injury to the human body by transferring energy to the cells through which they pass. Different forms of radiation behave in very different ways, are found in different environmental settings, and can cause quite different types of injury. However, energy transfer is always the fundamental mechanism of radiation injury.

The transfer of energy that is produced by radiation is similar to that caused by other forms of acute injury such as an automobile crash or a bullet wound. A bullet, when it is fired from a gun, contains a very high level of energy. When this bullet enters the human body, it rapidly loses its energy as it collides with tissues, tears them apart, and is slowed down. This is a crude form of energy transfer. The difference between a bullet and an X ray lies principally in the size of the particle. While a bullet destroys tissues and entire organs, a particle of radiation collides with single atoms or molecules deep within cells.

TYPES OF INJURY CAUSED BY RADIATION

■ ■ ■

ACUTE POISONING

High doses of radiation can kill the cells with which they collide. Deep burns, eye injury, and death from radiation sickness are the results. Destruction of the bone marrow can occur. With the destruction of the marrow, the body loses its ability to make new red cells and white cells for the blood. Anemia and an impaired ability to fight off infections result. Destruction of the cells lining the gastrointestinal tract is another feature of acute radiation sickness. Intractable, bloody diarrhea results and can soon lead to death.

MUTATION AND CANCER

Lower-dose exposure to radiation causes more subtle effects, which may not appear for many years. At lower doses, radiation can alter and distort molecular structures within the cells of the human body. Deoxyribonucleic acid (DNA), the fundamental human genetic material, is the most vulnerable target. When radiation strikes the nucleus of a cell, it can alter the structure of DNA within the nucleus. This change is termed a mutation. Mutations caused by radiation can transform cells, lead to their becoming malignant, and result eventually in the development of cancer.

In general, the higher the radiation dose, the more severe the effects on human health, the greater the likelihood of mutation and of eventually developing cancer.

HERITABLE MUTATIONS

When radiation strikes the human reproductive organs, it can cause mutations in the DNA of human sperm or ova. Some of these mutations have the potential to be passed on from generation to generation, to the children and the grandchildren of an affected parent. These are termed heritable mutations. Heritable mutations can produce a wide range of effects. The most serious include death, mental retardation, and congenital malformations. An inherited mutation can also be silent, or recessive, and can be passed on from generation to generation without any noticeable consequence. Such a silent mutation may not cause a harmful effect until two persons who are both carriers of the same mutation come together and have children. Then the recessive trait can appear and cause disease or malformation many generations after the initial radiation injury.

IS THERE A SAFE DOSE OF RADIATION?

■ ■ ■

It is frequently asked, "Is there a safe threshold below which radiation does not cause mutations or cancer?" This question has been highly controversial. Most scientists have long believed that no safe thresholds exist for radiation exposure. However, some scientists, especially those employed by the atomic weapons and nuclear power industries, have argued that safe thresholds do exist below which radiation causes no cancer.

This question has been carefully reviewed by the National Academy of Sciences (NAS). In 1990, the NAS issued a definitive report in which they declared that there are no safe thresholds for exposure to radiation. The indications are very strong from many studies that even the smallest dose of radiation is capable of causing mutations within DNA and therefore capable of causing cancer. The evidence is also very strong from many studies that there exist positive dose-response relationships between radiation and cancer at even the lowest doses of radiation. In study after study, the greater the radiation dose, the greater the likelihood of cancer. In view of this evidence, it makes eminently good sense to reduce your children's exposure to radiation wherever possible.

X RAYS AND GAMMA RAYS

■ ■ ■

X rays are a man-made form of radiation. They were first discovered in 1895 by Wilhelm Roentgen, a scientist in Germany. They are produced by an electric current within a specially constructed vacuum tube. X rays are identical in their physical properties and health effects to naturally occurring gamma rays and cosmic rays.

Medical X rays are the most important man-made source of radiation to which we and our children are exposed. Children are exposed to X rays whenever they have their dental films or if they have to undergo special diagnostic procedures such as studies to evaluate their kidneys or gastrointestinal tract. All American children, and especially those who suffer from chronic illness, are at risk of accumulating substantial exposure to X rays.

The harmful effects of repeated exposure to X rays have been known for many years. The first realization that radiation could cause cancer and other forms of injury arose soon after the discovery of X rays in the 1890s. At that time a number of cases of severe skin burns followed by leukemia occurred among the early radiation scientists. These men and women did not understand the hazards of radiation and took few precautions against them. These scientific pioneers have come to be known as the "radiation martyrs."

Detailed information on the relationship between cancer and radiation has come from careful long-term follow-up studies of the children and adults who survived the atomic bombings in Hiroshima and Nagasaki. These groups experienced a very high incidence of leukemia. The highest incidence occurred just a few years after the bombing. There was a strong dose-response relationship between leukemia rates and radiation dose. Those persons who received the heaviest radiation doses had the highest incidence of leukemia.

Additional information on the ability of X rays to cause cancer has come from studies of groups who received heavy doses of medical radiation.

- Among men in Britain who were given high-dose radiation for the treatment of ankylosing spondylitis, a severe form of arthritis, a high incidence of leukemia was observed, related to the total radiation dose.
- Excess rates of thyroid cancer have been seen in people who as children in the 1930s and 1940s received X rays for treatment of an enlarged thymus gland.
- Excess brain cancer has occurred in children who received radiation to the head and neck to treat ringworm of the scalp.
- Excess rates of cancer have been seen among women who received pelvic radiation for treatment of menstrual difficulties.

X rays and gamma rays have been found to cause many other

types of cancer besides leukemia. In the atomic bomb survivors, many excess cancers, including lung cancer and cancer of the female breast, have been observed. Unlike the leukemias, most of which occurred within a few years of the bombings, these other cancers tend to develop only decades later.

X Rays During Pregnancy

The developing fetus is highly sensitive to X rays. Studies conducted in England have found that the children of women who received abdominal X rays during pregnancy had a greater chance of dying of leukemia in the first ten years of their lives than other children. This effect has been seen even at extremely low levels of radiation.

High doses of radiation during pregnancy, particularly during the first trimester, have been shown to result in mental retardation. Intense early radiation appears to interfere with the development of the brain and results in babies with small heads. The severity of this effect is also dose-related.

Clearly, exposure to X-rays should be kept to an absolute minimum during pregnancy. If an abdominal examination is needed, it is standard practice today to use ultrasonography of the abdomen rather than X rays. Ultrasonography (also called an echogram) involves no ionizing radiation.

The technology of X-ray machines has improved greatly over the past five decades. The amount of radiation to which you or your children are exposed today during a chest X ray or a dental film is far less than was the case forty or fifty years ago.

OTHER FORMS OF MEDICAL RADIATION

■ ■ ■

Radioactive iodine, a radioactive chemical that is concentrated in the thyroid gland, is used to treat an overactive thyroid. It is very effective therapy and reduces the need for thyroid surgery. However, radioactive iodine, also termed iodine 131, must be used with care. If too much is given, a long-term result can be cancer of the thyroid.

Other radioactive chemicals, such as radioactive gallium and technetium, are used in modern medicine for special scanning procedures to assess the functioning of the body's organs. Gallium scanning is used to assess cardiac function. Technetium scanning is used to measure the function of the liver.

All of these radioactive chemicals, which are termed *radioisotopes* or *radionuclides*, contribute to the total radiation that we and our children receive. Just as with diagnostic X rays, each medical use of a radioisotope should be carefully considered. When the test is clearly necessary and medically indicated, there should be no hesitation to proceed with it. However, when it is possible to defer, postpone, or cancel a test, that approach is always prudent.

Radiation is also used in the treatment of cancer. High doses of radiation therapy can kill cancer cells and stop the growth of cancer, sometimes permanently and sometimes temporarily. Cure or remission can result.

Radiation therapy for cancer can be a two-edged sword. With some children who received radiation therapy for successful treatment of a cancer, so-called secondary cancers have arisen years or decades later. Now that the hazards of therapeutic radiation are better understood, radiotherapy is administered much more carefully today than was the case in the past.

COSMIC RADIATION

■ ■ ■

All living things are constantly exposed to background radiation. This includes radiation emitted by the earth itself (terrestrial radiation) and gamma rays from outer space (cosmic radiation).

Cosmic rays and gamma rays are physically identical to X rays and have the same effects on human health. We can do nothing to shield ourselves and our children against cosmic radiation short of living inside lead boxes. We can do a great deal to protect ourselves against X rays by thoughtful action and prudent avoidance.

RADON

■ ■ ■

The single most important source of radiation for the American population is radon. It accounts for about 10 percent of the cases of lung cancer in the United States, ranking second only to smoking. This is a risk that can be substantially reduced.

Recognition of this hazard is quite new. In 1984, a construction engineer who lived in a small town in Pennsylvania entered the nuclear power plant at Limerick and triggered all the radiation monitors. His home in nearby Berks County was tested for radiation, and was found to have a level of radiation of 2,700 pCi/L due to radon. This is a level higher than had ever previously been measured in any home in the United States. The engineer and his family were advised to leave their home immediately. They had been exposed to more than fifty times the annual radiation permitted for uranium miners.

Radon levels in an adjacent home were found to be low, but levels were extremely high in other nearby houses. The region of the country in which the engineer lived is known as the Reading Prong, an area in the Appalachian Mountains that includes parts of Pennsylvania, New Jersey, and New York. The Reading Prong contains underground geologic deposits of low-grade uranium ore, the source of the radon that contaminated the engineer's home.

THE NATURE AND SOURCES OF RADON

Radon is a colorless gas. It is produced by the natural radioactive decay of uranium in the earth and it is found in small amounts in soil, rocks, water, and some building materials in all areas of the United States. Radon itself breaks down rather rapidly into four other radioactive products: two forms of polonium, bismuth, and lead. These products are called "radon daughters." Each daughter can damage cells, cause mutations, and thereby result in cancer.

While radon is a gas, its daughters are ionized atoms. Each polonium atom emits a hazardous form of radioactive energy called alpha radiation. Because they are ionized atoms, these ions may adhere to particles in the air. When inhaled, they do not migrate into the bloodstream. Instead they are trapped on the inner lining of the bronchial tree and the lungs. The radiation that they emit penetrates only a very short distance into the surrounding tissue. As a result, the dangerous properties of radon are limited to the bronchi and the lungs. Radon is estimated to cause over 10,000 lung cancer deaths in the United States each year.

Because it is a gas, radon moves readily through cracks or gaps in the soil and accumulates in underground air pockets. From there it seeps into houses, generally through cracks in the basement walls or floors, through gaps around service pipes, and through drinking water supplies that come from groundwater. If the air pressure within a basement is lower than the pressure outside, radon gas infiltrates easily. Older, leakier, less tightly sealed houses exchange more air with the outside. This dilutes the radon in these homes. But newer construction techniques, storm windows, and increased insulation reduce air turnover in houses. Radon daughters pile up as a result. Forced-air heat, exhaust fans, and other changes lower air pressure in homes and draw radon gas into the house from deep in the ground.

Although certain areas of the country, such as the Reading Prong and radium-rich areas in the West, are known to have high soil radon, radon can be found in all areas of North America. Within a given area, the level in each home differs, and large variations between adjacent dwellings are common because of differences in construction materials and in the tightness of insulation.

Water in private wells and in other underground water sources may contain radon, providing another route of entry. Most public water supplies do not have excess amounts of radon, and surface water supplies such as rivers and reservoirs contain no radon.

Recognition of the extraordinarily high rates of lung cancer in uranium miners brought the cancer-causing properties of radon to light. Then studies from Sweden showed that even household exposure could increase the lung cancer risk. In rare circumstances, some homes have concentrations of radon daughters that actually exceed those found in uranium mines.

Is There a Risk in Your Home?

The first step in answering this question is to measure the amount of radon-induced radiation in your home. This must be done on a home-by-home basis. A radon screening test should be done in every home. If the screening test shows elevated levels, the home should be thoroughly inspected by a professional.

There are two types of radon detectors available for purchase by homeowners: charcoal canisters and alpha track detectors. Both types of detectors can be obtained in many hardware stores. The state radon office can tell you where they can be purchased. Charcoal canisters measure levels over a short term, generally two to seven days. Alpha track detectors collect measurements over longer periods of time, as long as twelve months. Because radon levels in a house vary over time, a long-term measurement is generally a more accurate reflection of the exposure of the residents.

If a short-term charcoal canister test is used, it should be placed in the lowest living area of the home, usually the basement, during the winter, with doors and windows closed.

AT WHAT LEVEL SHOULD YOU ACT?

The EPA has constructed a set of guidelines that can assist you in determining the urgency of response to any radon found in your home. Levels of radon radiation are expressed in picocuries per liter of air (pCi/L).

- If the screening measurement shows a level greater than 200 pCi/L, follow-up measurements should be done immediately. You should use an alpha track detector for the follow-up. The detectors should be exposed for no longer than one week. If these results confirm the initial finding, you should take action as soon as possible. At these high levels of exposure, you may need to vacate your home until abatement has been successfully completed.
- If the level is between 20 and 200 pCi/L, rapid follow-up should be done. Exposure of the alpha track instrument should be no longer than three months.
- If the level is between 4 and 20 pCi/L, follow-up should be done. Exposure of the detector should last for one year. Many short-term tests tend to overestimate the true level. You may find, on long-term measurement, that radon control is unnecessary.
- If the level is less than 4 pCi/L, follow-up is not required. However, it is possible that in the future, as more is learned about the toxicity of radon at low doses, this action level may be reduced. This is something that you may wish to monitor.

If the follow-up test with the alpha track detector confirms that the level of radon is above the action level of 4 pCi/L, a contractor who specializes in ridding homes of radon should be consulted. Choosing a contractor is a critical process. You can obtain lists of radon contractors from the EPA regional office (Appendix 3), state or county health department or state radon office, and the Better Business Bureau.

Since there is no known safe level of radon, there will always be some risk. But the risk can be reduced by lowering the radon level in your home. Because the risk of cancer due to radon is amplified by tobacco, parents should not smoke in the home.

HOW DO YOU REDUCE THE RADON LEVEL?

This is a job for trained professionals. Interview a prospective contractor carefully. Before you sign a contract, he should survey the property and submit a detailed plan of action with an estimate. Ask him how many homes he has renovated, what method he uses, how he chooses the method, and whether the work is guaranteed. This will offer some insight into whether he is a knowledgeable craftsman. You should also obtain and contact references.

The steps involved in radon control include:

- First, identify the routes of entry. Drains, cracks in the basement floor or walls, gaps around pipe entries or at the top of the basement walls all can allow radon gas entry and permit accumulation. If the water supply comes from a deep well or other groundwater source, the radon level in the water supply should be checked.
- Second, identify those features of the house that contribute to depressurization. Heating the air in a house causes it to rise, and this lowers the air pressure in the basement. Some heaters draw in air from the basement, and this further lowers the pressure. Exhaust fans on upper floors also lower pressure.
- Short-term measures to reduce radon include:

Increase ventilation by opening windows on opposite sides of the house, particularly on the lower levels of the house.

Use a window fan to blow outdoor air into the house.

Vent the crawl space if one is present.

Cap sumps in the basement.

Fill trapped floor drains with water.

If segments of the cellar slab are cracked, fill them. If whole segments are missing, pour new slabs.

Seal voids in the top of the foundation walls.

- Longer-term measures include:

Change the pressure relationships in the basement. Low pressure in the basement draws radon gas from the soil into the space.

Air can be pumped into the basement to raise the pressure and reduce infiltration.

Seal radon entry routes.

Install soil ventilation.

Aerate the water supply if it contains radon.

Following abatement, retesting of the residence should be done to be sure that the abatement has succeeded.

The cost of making repairs to reduce radon depends on how your home was built and the extent of the problem. Most homes can be fixed for about the same cost as other common home repairs like painting or having a new hot-water heater installed. A contractor charges about $1,200 to fix the average house, although the price can range from about $500 to as much as $2,500.

RADON AND HOME RENOVATIONS

If you are planning any major structural renovation, such as converting an unfinished basement area into living space, it is especially important to test the area for radon before you begin the renovation. If your test results indicate a radon problem, radon-resistant techniques can be included as part of the renovation. Because major renovations can change the level of radon in any home, always test again after work is completed.

There are other factors to take into consideration when calculating the risk from radon. How much time do you and your children spend in the home? The longer the amount of time spent at home, the greater is the radon risk. How much time is spent in the basement? If there is a basement bedroom or recreational room that you or your children use on a regular basis, exposure will be increased. Does anyone smoke in the house? Smoking acts cooperatively with radon in the production of cancer—one more reason not to smoke.

RADON IN SCHOOLS

Schools may provide a significant source of radon exposure for children. Schools in Virginia, Maryland, Pennsylvania, New Jersey, Florida, Washington, New York, Maine, Ohio, Iowa, Colorado, Tennessee, and Illinois have had elevated radon concentrations measured. Those schools with heating or air-conditioning systems that lower the air pressure tend to have higher concentrations.

RECOMMENDATIONS ON RADON FOR PEDIATRICIANS*

- Pediatricians should be aware that radon exposures are greater in some geographic areas than others, but may be present in any home in any area of North America. Information about local radon levels can be obtained from state health departments, local environmental health authorities, or the EPA. Pediatricians should urge all families to test their home for radon, particularly basements.
- Pediatricians should be aware of, and warn their patients about, the multiplicative effects of radon and cigarette smoking on the risk of lung cancer. Pediatricians should urge parents not to smoke in a home where children are present. Because the major cause of lung cancer is cigarette smoking, pediatricians should also counsel children not to smoke cigarettes.
- Pediatricians should alert parents to the educational resources available about radon. These resources include a guide published by the EPA and the Centers for Disease Control entitled *Citizens' Guide to Radon*, available from the EPA's regional offices.
- Pediatricians should warn families living in homes with radon levels greater than 4 pCi/L that they should undertake actions to decrease the level of radon in their homes. In this work, parents should be guided by the booklet published by the EPA and the Centers for Disease Control entitled *Radon Reduction Methods: Homeowner's Guide.*

* Adapted from the American Academy of Pediatrics statement, "Radon Exposure: A Hazard for Children," *Pediatrics*, 1989, 83:799–802.

Some systems have positive air pressure; this lowers radon concentrations.

In schools, significant variations in radon concentrations between classrooms and over time are generally found.

You should contact your local school board and inquire about the radon testing that should have been done at your children's school and the results. At this point, there is no federal legislation requiring radon testing in schools, but individual school boards or communities may have adopted such policies.

RADIOACTIVE FALLOUT FROM WEAPONS TESTS

■ ■ ■

The term "fallout" has been used to describe radioactive contamination that was thrown into the atmosphere by aboveground testing of nuclear weapons. According to data from the United Nations' nuclear agency, there have been a total of 423 aboveground explosions of nuclear weapons. Fortunately, most atmospheric testing ended in the early 1960s and no aboveground tests have been conducted since 1980.

In the United States, fallout from nuclear explosions is especially concentrated in areas of Utah and Nevada that are downwind of the Nevada nuclear test site. A series of epidemiologic studies conducted in this area have shown that leukemia rates in southwestern Utah appear to be higher in areas downwind of the test site than in other parts of Utah. The scientists who conducted these studies stated that these excesses "may be attributable to fallout radiation."

We hope that aboveground testing of nuclear weapons will never be a problem again. However, it is wise to remember that testing was halted in the past by the concentrated actions of thousands of concerned citizens. If it becomes necessary, we and our children must be prepared to mobilize again.

NUCLEAR POWER PLANTS

■ ■ ■

In a typical nuclear power plant of the type most commonly used in the United States, heat is produced in the radioactive core by the controlled breakdown (fission) of uranium. The energy produced by uranium fission heats pressurized water in the cooling system to form steam. This generates energy through a turbine. After it passes through the turbine, the steam is condensed and collected and the cycle is repeated. Two main functions are involved in this process. The first is energy production. The second is the cooling of the reactor core to prevent its overheating.

Nuclear power plants are portrayed by the nuclear industry as a clean, safe, environmentally compatible form of energy generation. Unfortunately, this description is not entirely true. The generation of nuclear power is associated with several significant risks to human health.

An explosion is the greatest risk from nuclear power plants. This has happened in the Soviet Union at Chernobyl and almost happened at Three Mile Island in Pennsylvania.

Both of those episodes resulted from a combination of procedural violations and inadequate training of operators. Both were events that the public had been assured could never happen. At Three Mile Island there were two malfunctions. First, the feed water pump in the secondary cooling system closed down, and water stopped flowing in the secondary cooling system. Then a pressurizer valve stuck in the open position. This resulted in spillage of approximately 10,000 gallons of radioactive water onto the reactor floor. Throughout this sequence of events the reactor operators, who had been inadequately trained, made a series of mistakes that exacerbated the problem. Some radioactivity was released to the atmosphere, but the levels were low and the consequences were far less than they could have been.

The effects of an explosion of a nuclear power plant in a densely populated area would be unimaginably terrible. The consequences for human health would be devastating. They could include acute radiation poisoning, burns, and deaths. Persons at greater distances would suffer high doses of radiation exposure that could result eventually in cancer. All of this happened at Chernobyl and apparently happened also at another location in the former Soviet Union that until recently was kept secret.

A serious incident at a nuclear power plant could be expected to release large amounts of radioisotopes into the atmosphere. These materials would contaminate air, water, soil, and food crops, sometimes out to a distance of many hundreds of miles from the site of the explosion. In the case of Chernobyl, radioisotopes were carried for long distances and contaminated large areas of the Ukraine, Poland, and Western Europe. In certain areas, all dairy products had to be destroyed, because cattle were contaminated through eating grasses that had been contaminated.

Radiation hazards also arise in the production of nuclear fuel. The uranium that is used to supply nuclear reactors must be mined. Uranium miners suffer an increased rate of death from lung cancer. This is caused by their exposure to radon, uranium, radium, and other radioactive materials in the mines where the uranium is extracted.

NUCLEAR WASTE

Nuclear waste constitutes the greatest long-term risk of nuclear power generation. This problem is frequently dismissed by spokespersons for the nuclear industry as trivial. It is far from trivial.

The operation of a nuclear reactor results in the formation of tons of radioactive waste for every month of operation. Everything from the uranium fuel rods to concrete shielding, to cooling water, to the clothing worn by reactor operators becomes contaminated in the course of the plant's operation. This waste must therefore be guarded carefully and disposed of properly. Of particular concern is "high-level" radioactive waste. This consists of the most heavily contaminated waste, such as the fuel rods and any materials containing plutonium.

Despite four decades of searching, a satisfactory disposal site for high-level radioactive waste has not yet been found in the United States. Thus, reactors are busily producing new waste every day that they operate. Because no satisfactory long-term solution has been found, this waste is accumulating on reactor sites and in "temporary" holding areas.

To continue to operate nuclear reactors and to produce nuclear waste when there is no resolution to the waste disposal problem is ostrichlike behavior. It poses inadequately evaluated risks to ourselves, our children, or future generations. We strongly urge that all construction of new nuclear power plants cease and that steps be taken to decommission existing nuclear power plants and to dispose of their remains in a safe fashion.

To be sure, there will be hazards associated with going from nuclear power to other sources of power generation. A greater reliance on coal could result in higher levels of sulfate, particulate, and acid air pollution than now exist in many areas of the United States, unless state-of-the-art technologies are utilized to scrub the emissions from coal-fired power plants. Coal mining, like uranium mining, is hazardous and carries risks of occupational disease. These issues must be considered carefully, and the risks and benefits weighed. But we cannot continue on our present course.

The best escape from the nuclear cycle in which we now find ourselves is to go from reliance on nuclear energy and on fossil fuels to a new economy in which we will place our principal reliance on environmentally friendly sources of energy such as solar, wind, and tidal energy. The additional prospect exists that in the years ahead we may place increasing reliance on hydrogen technology to generate power. The principal waste product of hydrogen combustion is water.

The importance of energy conservation cannot be overstated. The more energy we conserve, the less we need and the less power production is necessary. If we can reduce the generation of power, our health, the health of our children, and the health of our planet will all be the better.

CANCER CLUSTERS AROUND NUCLEAR FACILITIES

■ ■ ■

Several clusters of cancer, principally childhood leukemias and lymphomas, have been reported around nuclear power plants. Early reports published in 1984 described an increased mortality rate from leukemia in persons living around a nuclear fuel reprocessing plant in the village of Sellafield in England. Other clusters have been reported in the United Kingdom and the United States.

The results of these studies have not been entirely consistent. Different types of leukemia and lymphoma have been seen in the various reported episodes. Also, there has been no documentation of excess release of radioactive materials from the plants into the surrounding environment. Therefore, a search for the mechanism of exposure still continues.

The most unusual finding in these studies was an excess rate of childhood leukemia and lymphoma among young children whose fathers had been employed in the Sellafield plant before the child's conception. This study showed that if the father had received a substantial radiation dose during the six months before conception of the child, cancer risk in the child was increased fivefold. There is still no good explanation for these findings. The biological mechanism by which pre-conceptional radiation of sperm might affect childhood cancer rates is uncertain. One possibility is that the fathers may have carried small amounts of radioactive material home on their shoes and clothing, thus contaminating their home environment. This chain of events might have been particularly likely among those fathers with the heaviest pre-conceptional exposures to radiation. Perhaps the resulting contamination of the home resulted in exposure of the children. This possibility has not been confirmed, and the investigations still continue.

ELECTROMAGNETIC FIELDS (EMFs)

■ ■ ■

Electromagnetic fields are a very different type of radiation from ionizing radiation. EMFs are low-frequency radiation and lie at the opposite end of the electromagnetic spectrum from X rays, gamma rays, and other forms of ionizing radiation, all of which are high-frequency radiation. EMFs are generated when electric current flows through a high-tension wire.

Low-frequency electromagnetic radiation is defined as radiation with frequencies below 300 hertz (Hz). This form of radiation includes the 60 Hz electromagnetic fields found in household electricity.

Electromagnetic fields had not been considered hazardous to human health until the 1970s. They are too weak to disrupt DNA or to cause direct genetic damage. They are not capable of generating significant amounts of heat within cells like microwaves or radar. For all of these reasons, electromagnetic fields were long considered to be harmless.

EMFs AND CANCER

■ ■ ■

The possibility that EMFs might be associated with cancer was first raised in 1979. At that time, investigators in Denver reported that children dying from leukemia and brain tumors were more likely to have lived in homes with high levels of electric current than healthy children in the same neighborhoods.

Since that time, there have been numerous studies of children and adults exposed to electromagnetic fields. The most elegant and

ELECTRIC AND MAGNETIC FIELDS

Electric fields are directly related to the level of voltage in an electric line. The higher the voltage, the stronger the electric field. Magnetic fields are produced by the movement of current down the electric line. Both types of fields are produced by electric transmission lines. They are also produced by electronic appliances of all types. Electric fields are easily blocked by normal building materials such as bricks, mortar, and wood. The strength of an electric field decreases rapidly with distance from the source.

Magnetic fields consist of a series of force waves in concentric rings around an electric current. Magnetic fields are produced by all electric charges. Like electric fields, magnetic fields drop off rapidly with distance from the source. Unlike electric fields, however, they are capable of penetrating most objects, including concrete. They cannot be easily blocked by building materials.

Exposure of the American population to electromagnetic fields has increased greatly over the past several decades. More and more electric transmission lines have been built, and they carry higher and higher voltages. Today, the most powerful transmission lines carry 765 kilovolts (kV). These 765 kV lines are the major lines used for long-distance transmission of large quantities of electricity.

meticulously detailed study to date is an investigation recently reported from Sweden. This study examined cancer rates in children who lived near high-voltage electric power lines. It found that leukemia rates in children living near these power lines were significantly increased, and a dose-response relationship was found. In separate studies of adults, an association between electrical exposure and brain cancer has been reported.

The mechanism by which EMFs could cause cancer is not yet clear. It has been hypothesized by medical scientists that EMFs may alter the membranes of cells within the human body and thus disrupt communication between cells. This could trigger unregulated cell multiplication and set cells on the path to cancer.

WHAT CAN YOU DO TO PROTECT YOUR CHILDREN AGAINST EMFS?

A reasonable approach to protect your children against EMFs is "prudent avoidance." This term was introduced by Dr. M. Granger

Morgan of Carnegie-Mellon University in Pittsburgh. The principle is that in the present state of knowledge, in which there is still much that we do not know about EMFs, it is wise to take reasonable precautionary measures until data suggest a need for more specific actions.

Approaches to prudent avoidance include the following:

- In dealing with magnetic fields, remember that distance is your friend. Magnetic fields from household appliances drop off very quickly within a few feet of their source. To minimize your exposures and those of your children, do not sleep or sit for long periods of time near electrical devices, particularly those with motors.
- With regard to the magnetic fields produced by video display terminals and color TV monitors, you should sit a minimum of 18 to 24 inches from the monitor and should turn it off when it is not being used. It is also wise not to sit close to the back or sides of a monitor even if it is located on the other side of a wall, in another room; remember that magnetic fields can easily penetrate most objects, including walls. The health hazards of cellular telephones are not yet known, but prudent avoidance seems a reasonable approach. Therefore we recommend that their use be minimized, especially by children.
- Water-bed heaters and electric blankets can be unplugged before you go to bed. If you feel that you must use an electric blanket, be sure to get one in which the current has been balanced so that the magnetic fields are canceled out. The close contact that a child has with an electric blanket over many hours of sleep each night can result in considerable exposure to EMFs.
- Finally, in the spirit of prudent avoidance, think twice before you purchase a home that is directly beneath or within 100 feet of a high-tension power line. Also, determine whether your child's school is under or close by a power line.

GAUSSMETERS

A useful way to cut through the uncertainty is to obtain direct information on levels of EMFs through the use of a gaussmeter. A hand-held instrument that reliably measures the strength of a magnetic field, a gaussmeter may be rented or purchased. Also, you can request that an official from your state or local health department come to your home or to your child's school to make direct measurements of magnetic fields using a gaussmeter. Field strengths can be measured in areas throughout your home and under nearby power lines. This information will serve as a guide to intelligent preventive action.

THE DIFFERENT TYPES OF IONIZING RADIATION

NATURALLY OCCURRING

Cosmic rays
Gamma radiation from the earth (terrestrial radiation)
Radon

MAN-MADE

Medical, diagnostic X rays
Medical, radiotherapy
Medical, radioisotopes
Fallout from atmospheric bomb tests
Occupational exposure
Nuclear power plant explosions
Radioactive waste

RADON AND HOME SALES

More and more, home buyers and renters are asking about radon levels before they purchase or lease a home. Because real estate sales happen quickly, there is often little time to deal with issues related to radon at the time of closing a sale. The best thing to do is to test for radon now and save the results in case the buyer is interested in them. Fix a problem if it exists so that it will not complicate the sale of your home.

If you are planning to move or to buy a house, call the radon office in the state where you will be living for the EPA pamphlet *Home Buyer's and Seller's Guide to Radon*, which addresses some common questions that arise during home sales:

- Buyers often ask if a home has been tested for radon and whether elevated levels were reduced.
- Buyers frequently want tests made by someone who is not involved in the home sale. Your state radon office or the regional office of the EPA can provide a list of qualified testers.
- Buyers might want to know the radon levels in specific areas of the home (such as a basement that they plan to finish).

Today many new homes are built to prevent radon from entering. Your state or local area may require these radon-resistant construction features, which usually keep radon levels in new homes below 2 pCi/L. If you are buying or renting a new home, ask the owner or builder if it has radon-resistant features.

9

TOBACCO

Each year 350,000 Americans die from smoking cigarettes. That's almost as many citizens as those who died in World War II. Tobacco, which kills more people each year than alcohol or drugs combined, is the single most important cause of disease and early death in the United States.

Lung cancer, long the most common cancer in men, now surpasses breast cancer as the leading malignancy in women. In addition to cancer of the lung, tobacco accounts for many cases of laryngeal, esophageal, pancreatic, and bladder cancer. Cigarettes, along with snuff and chewing tobacco, are major causes of cancer of the mouth. More than 500,000 Americans die each year of coronary heart disease. Between 20 and 40 percent of these deaths can be directly related to cigarette smoking. Each year more than 75,000 Americans die of chronic lung disease. Between 80 and 90 percent of these deaths are caused by smoking. Tobacco dramatically increases the risk of stroke, heart disease, and chronic lung disease. Whether measured in dollars or lives, the effects of tobacco on the American public are staggering. Each year we spend $25 billion on medical care for tobacco-related diseases.

Parents need to know that about 90 percent of all cigarette smoking begins in childhood and adolescence. If a person is not already a smoker by his or her twenty-first birthday, it is highly unlikely that he or she will ever become a smoker. It is essential that you do everything you can to keep your children and teenagers

PERCENTAGES OF CHILDREN IN
THE UNITED STATES WHO SMOKE*

	HAVE EXPERIMENTED WITH SMOKING	SMOKE REGULARLY
6th grade	23%	
8th grade	30%	9%
10th grade	37%	10%
12th grade	41%	17%

* Data from the Centers for Disease Control.

from beginning to smoke. But to do this successfully you need to know and understand the forces that are arrayed against you.

CHILDREN AND TOBACCO—
HOW AND WHY DO KIDS BEGIN TO USE IT?

■ ■ ■

The habit starts early. In 1991, 70 percent of all high school students in the United States had tried cigarettes. More than 30 percent of all students in grades nine through twelve had used tobacco, most commonly cigarettes, in the thirty days immediately before the survey. One-tenth of high school students across the United States reported use of smokeless tobacco.

Boys are more likely than girls to use tobacco, especially smokeless tobacco. White students were much more likely than black or Hispanic students to use tobacco. Tobacco use increased from 30 percent in eighth-graders to 41 percent in twelfth-graders (see table).

Seventeen percent of American high school students reported that they were regular smokers. Over the past decade, the number of boys who had started smoking has declined. But, tragically, there has been a steady increase in the number of young women who have begun to smoke. As a result of these trends, rates of tobacco use differ minimally between boys and girls in high school. Young women have achieved an equal risk of death.

Pressure from friends appears to be the most important factor that starts kids on their way to smoking. Study after study has shown that smoking typically begins as experimentation among children and young teenagers, usually initiated by a single influential teen. A kid's first cigarette is never pleasant. It tastes terrible, causes nausea and coughing. A youngster who refuses an offer of a cigarette may be called a "chicken" and risk being excluded from a group. This is incredibly strong pressure for a 12-year-old. Too often, the child who accepts an offer of a cigarette is seeking acceptance and hopes to appear more mature and adventurous.

Many studies have shown that children under the age of 10 are strongly committed against smoking. Educational programs aimed at young children have been successful in informing them about the hazards of smoking. Despite knowing these dangers, children begin to smoke as they grow older. The same kids who were strongly antismoking at age 9 are often regular smokers by age 11. Clearly, parents and the schools need to do more.

One singularly successful smoking prevention program has used peers to teach each other. In peer education programs, children play different roles. One child pretends to be the initiator and tries to persuade his or her friends to begin smoking. Another child plays the part of the person who is being offered a cigarette. This child is instructed in assertiveness and is taught to reply, "If I smoke to prove to you that I am not a chicken, all I'll really be showing is that I am afraid not to do what you want me to do. I don't want to smoke." In schools across the country these programs have proven extremely effective.

Cigarette advertising is clearly another factor that contributes to smoking behavior in children. Although the tobacco industry proclaims that they do not want kids to smoke, they spend billions of dollars each year on advertising campaigns that feature cowboys and cartoon characters. Not surprisingly, Marlboro and Camel are the brands most commonly smoked by kids. In California, for example, 59 percent of teenage smokers smoke Marlboros and 23 percent smoke Camels. Each year in the United States, approximately one billion packs worth $1.25 billion are sold to minors. Sales to children and teenagers amount to 3 percent of the tobacco profits ($221 million).

Tobacco companies advertise extensively in magazines read by children and teenagers—such as *Sports Illustrated, Rolling Stone, Playboy, The National Lampoon*, and *Mademoiselle*. All of this advertising is aimed at suggesting that smoking is associated with good looks, sexual attractiveness, and athletic ability. These appeals to freedom, wealth, and glamor cannot be without some effect. Why else would the tobacco industry spend billions on them?

Sponsorship of sports events is another route through which the industry reaches children and teenagers. Even though tobacco advertising is banned on television, the images and trademarks of the tobacco manufacturers permeate TV through brand-name sponsorship of televised sporting events or through pictures of cigarette billboards at the forty-yard line, in deep center field, and at stock-car races.

Sales of cigarettes to minors are illegal in most states across the nation, but these laws are rarely enforced. Programs that impose strict and well-publicized penalties on retailers who sell cigarettes to kids and that remove cigarette vending machines from areas frequented by children have reduced childhood smoking rates substantially.

A parent or older sibling who smokes exerts a powerful influence on a child. If a child sees that his or her parent smokes, there is a much higher likelihood that the child will begin to smoke. And if a parent and an older sibling both smoke, the child is four times more likely than other kids to smoke. Seventy-five percent of young people who smoke come from homes where one or both parents smoke.

PASSIVE SMOKING—A HAZARD TO CHILDREN

■ ■ ■

Children who live in households with smokers involuntarily inhale secondhand smoke. Secondhand smoke comes from the burning end of the cigarette. It contains the same toxins as mainstream cigarette smoke, including carbon monoxide, nicotine, tars, formaldehyde, and hydrogen cyanide. Air sampling surveys conducted in the homes of smoking parents have documented that children and other nonsmokers in these homes are exposed to all of these products of cigarette combustion. Levels of carbon monoxide, tars, and other combustion products are substantially higher in the homes of smokers.

Children who are exposed to passive smoke have more bronchitis, pneumonia, and viral respiratory infections. The amount of infection depends directly on the amount of smoke in the home. Children who live with two smoking parents have significantly more respiratory infections than children who have only one smoking parent. Because young children tend to be around their mothers more, maternal smoking has a stronger effect on children's respiratory infections than smoking by the father. The lowest rates of lung infections and asthma are found in children of parents who do not smoke at all.

LONG-TERM HEALTH EFFECTS OF INVOLUNTARY SMOKING

Children of smokers have small but significant decreases in their pulmonary function when compared with children whose parents do not smoke. They are especially likely to have obstructive changes in their lung function; these increase the risk for asthma and bronchitis. The lungs of children whose parents smoke grow more slowly. As a result, they fail to attain their full, genetically determined level of pulmonary function. This may predispose them to lung diseases and to premature pulmonary failure.

PASSIVE SMOKING AND CANCER

Studies in Greece and in Japan have found that nonsmoking women who live with smoking husbands have an elevated risk of lung cancer. Studies in the United States have found an association between lifetime exposure to passive smoking and the overall risk of cancer. These risks are greatest for persons whose exposure to passive smoke began in childhood and continued through adult life.

PASSIVE SMOKING AND HEART DISEASE

Nonsmoking wives of men who smoked had a substantially increased rate of death from heart disease. Although children who live with smoking parents are not known to develop heart disease in childhood, it is possible that early damage done to the hearts of children by cigarette smoke leads to increased risk of heart disease later in life.

In summary, children passively exposed to cigarette smoke share all of the problems of smokers; they are, in fact, smokers. They have increased respiratory tract symptoms and infections, decreased pulmonary function, and decreased lung growth. Passive cigarette smoking may result in a predisposition to development of chronic lung disease, lung cancer, and heart disease.

SMOKELESS TOBACCO—A CANCER HAZARD FOR CHILDREN

■ ■ ■

Smokeless tobacco refers to snuff, chewing tobacco, and other forms of tobacco that are placed in the mouth or nose and not ignited. About 10 to 20 million Americans regularly use smokeless tobacco.

WHO USES SMOKELESS TOBACCO?

Smokeless tobacco is used mainly by teenagers. In many parts of the country, especially in rural areas, the use of smokeless tobacco is a badge of manhood. A worn white patch in the back pocket of a pair of blue jeans indicates that the owner is the proud carrier of a can of snuff. A status symbol in too many schools, it is a pure product of the advertising industry. Sales of snuff have risen dramatically over the past ten years. The National Health Survey found in 1991 that 10 percent of all high school students in the United States had used smokeless tobacco. Almost 20 percent of high school boys had used smokeless tobacco as compared with only 1 percent of high school girls. The use of smokeless tobacco is especially common in rural states. For example, 31 percent of high school boys in Wyoming had tried smokeless tobacco.

The tobacco industry has conducted widespread, carefully targeted, insidious advertising campaigns that promote the mistaken notion that smokeless tobacco is safe. Although twenty-one states restrict the sale of smokeless tobacco to minors, no federal restrictions govern its sale. Snuff is frequently advertised during sporting events, including the Olympic Games, football games, and automobile races. Prominent athletes, musicians, and other celebrities are seen enjoying it, and it has been given away to teenagers at sports events and rock concerts. There are no warnings about health hazards on smokeless tobacco packages or in their ads.

THE HAZARDS TO HEALTH OF SMOKELESS TOBACCO

Smokeless tobacco is a proven cause of cancer. As early as 1761, John Hill, a physician in England, described cases of cancer of the nose and mouth in men who used snuff. In recent years, snuff has been a major cause of cancer of the mouth in the United States. Among persons who have used snuff for 50 years or more, the risk of cancer of the mouth is increased 47 times.

Laboratory testing of snuff confirms that it contains very high concentrations of proven carcinogens. The most important is a family of chemicals called the nitrosamines. Levels of nitrosamine in snuff and other forms of smokeless tobacco are much higher than the levels found in cigarettes, apparently as the result of the curing and fermentation of smokeless tobacco.

Regular use of smokeless tobacco has been reported to cause dental diseases, including foul-smelling breath, periodontal disease and erosion of the gum, and loss of teeth.

The most famous case of disease in a user of smokeless tobacco was that of Sean Marsee, a high school athlete in Oklahoma who had used snuff for many years and developed fatal cancer of the mouth. Sean's parents tried to sue the tobacco industry to recover the cost of the medical care for Sean's terminal illness. The tobacco industry argued successfully in court that it was Sean's own fault that he had smoked. They claimed that the millions of dollars that they had spent to advertise snuff in the state of Oklahoma had no influence on Sean's behavior. The jury believed those arguments. The parents received nothing.

SMOKING IN PREGNANCY

■ ■ ■

Smoking during pregnancy poses a serious danger for the unborn child. When you smoke, your unborn baby smokes. Study after study has shown that among women who smoke the likelihood of giving birth to a premature, low-birthweight infant is substantially higher than among women who do not smoke. Women who smoke are also at greater risk than other women of having their pregnancy end in a miscarriage or a spontaneous abortion.

Women who are smokers also often have a much more difficult

time conceiving a child than nonsmoking women of the same age. And the risk of not becoming pregnant at all—the risk of sterility—is elevated. Finally, parents who smoke have a higher than normal risk that their child will die of sudden infant death syndrome (SIDS).

Women who wish to become pregnant should make every effort not to smoke. Cessation of smoking increases fertility, decreases the risk of spontaneous abortion, decreases the risk of giving birth to a premature child, and decreases the risk that your child will die of SIDS.

RECOMMENDATIONS FOR PARENTS

■ ■ ■

The most important recommendation that we can make to you, as a parent, is that you do not smoke. If you smoke, then your children are smoking. If you smoke and you are pregnant, your baby is smoking. Your baby absorbs nicotine, carbon dioxide, and other substances in the smoke and these toxic chemicals pass into your baby's body. The greatest damage of passive cigarette smoke occurs in infants who are under 2 years old. These young children are especially vulnerable to smoke because their lungs are immature and their immunity to respiratory infections is not well developed. But even the healthiest babies suffer from exposure to tobacco smoke, and those with asthma and allergies need special protection because smoking can trigger attacks of coughing, wheezing, and shortness of breath in a baby.

To keep your children from smoking, be sure that your school takes an aggressive stance against smoking. There should be no cigarette machines in or near your children's school. If there are any stores or convenience shops near the school that sell cigarettes to minors, you should, first, try to persuade the owners not to sell cigarettes illegally to minors. If gentle persuasion does not work, contact the legal authority in your state. It is illegal in most states for store owners to sell tobacco products to minors; store owners who persist in this illegal behavior can be subject to bad publicity, stiff fines, and even jail time. It is your responsibility as a parent to insist that your child live in a smoke-free environment.

Remember that most use of tobacco begins in elementary school, junior high school, and the early years of high school. If you can keep your child from starting smoking through high school, the odds are very high that your child will never begin to smoke in later life. It is important that the school have organized peer counseling groups that advise children on the hazards of smoking, alcohol, drug abuse, and other risk-taking behavior. Peer groups are an extraordinarily effective mechanism for preserving the health of your children, and their growth should be encouraged.

RECOMMENDATIONS FOR PEDIATRICIANS

■ ■ ■

Pediatricians, acting individually and through the American Academy of Pediatrics, are encouraged to take action in their cities and states to counsel their patients and their patients' parents about the hazards of tobacco. No intervention is more effective than one-on-one advice that is given by a caring physician. To prevent the hazards of passive inhalation of cigarette smoke, pediatricians should always ask parents of children in their practice, particularly children with respiratory disease, if they smoke. If the parent does smoke, he or she must be counseled to stop smoking or at least to smoke away from the child.

Pediatricians should set an example by not using tobacco products themselves. Pediatricians should urge that sales of all tobacco products be banned in pediatric hospitals and other hospitals caring for children. They should encourage Congress and the U.S. Trade Commission to ban all advertising in all media for all tobacco products, and should encourage these agencies to sponsor counter-advertisements, particularly on television. They should urge strengthening of the health warnings that appear on cigarette packages. Such messages should specifically warn of the hazards of involuntary smoking. They should specifically warn of the hazards that cigarette smoke imposes on children. Pediatricians should work to increase the federal excise tax on all tobacco products and to urge Congress to dismantle the tobacco price support program.

To prevent the further spread of smokeless tobacco, pediatricians and the American Academy of Pediatrics should take action to:

- Require placement of strong health warnings on all smokeless tobacco products.
- Ban all advertisements for smokeless tobacco.
- Ban all free giveaways for smokeless tobacco products.
- Ban all sponsorship of sporting events by tobacco manufacturers.

Finally, pediatricians and the American Academy of Pediatrics should urge the players associations of the major professional sports leagues to discourage their member athletes from appearing in smokeless tobacco commercials. Children will not use smokeless tobacco if it is seen as the foul habit that it is and if they have no heroes with a pouch in their mouth.

Finally, every school and every hospital in the United States should be declared a smoke-free zone. Children should not smoke. Teenagers should not smoke. Health personnel should not smoke. Teachers should not smoke. No adults who work around children or teenagers should smoke. If children do not begin to smoke, then in a generation in this country there will be no adult smokers.

10

SOLVENTS AND PCBs

We encounter solvents everywhere in the home. They include alcohols, aldehydes, benzene, toluene, glycol ethers, trichloroethylene (TCE), perchloroethylene (PCE), n-hexane, formaldehyde, styrene, methyl ethyl ketone (MEK), and carbon tetrachloride. The common factor that links these chemicals is their ability to dissolve grease and other fatty substances.

Drinking water is an important source of solvent exposure. *Trichloroethylene*, a widely used industrial solvent, is found in thousands of water systems across the United States. Other solvents such as benzene and carbon tetrachloride are also found in drinking water. Children can be exposed to these chemicals particularly if they live near hazardous waste disposal sites, petrochemical plants, or other industrial facilities that dump industrial toxins. *Perchloroethylene*, the most commonly used dry-cleaning solvent, is also a common contaminant of drinking water. Millions of gallons of perchloroethylene are released into local water supply systems by dry-cleaning plants, and large amounts evaporate into the air.

Inhalation is a common route of children's exposure to solvents. Some hobbies may expose children to the solvents in airplane glue and some kinds of quick-drying paint. Children who operate small gasoline engines in lawn mowers and outboard motors will come into contact with the solvents in gasoline. It is important that work with solvents be performed either out of doors or in a well-ventilated area. Solvents can pass rapidly through the skin and produce high levels in the bloodstream within minutes after skin exposure.

HEALTH HAZARDS OF SOLVENTS

■ ■ ■

CENTRAL NERVOUS SYSTEM TOXICITY

Nearly all solvents can cause acute and chronic injury to the central nervous system. Inhalation of high doses of almost any solvent (including gasoline) can, within a few moments, cause dizziness, nausea, and hallucinations. If exposure continues for more than a few minutes, unconsciousness may result. A number of solvents, including gasoline, were used as anesthetic agents in the early part of the century.

Long-term exposure has been shown to produce chronic injury to the nervous system. Workers regularly exposed to solvents often experience dizziness, loss of coordination, headaches, and chronic drowsiness. They may also suffer from learning problems, decreased concentration, and impaired memory. In severe cases, actual shrinkage of the brain has been seen on X rays. Children can have similar symptoms and, in addition, irritable and aggressive behavior. Some of the worst cases of chronic exposure occur in children who sniff glue or gasoline.

PERIPHERAL NERVOUS SYSTEM TOXICITY

Certain solvents, notably n-hexane, methyl-n-butyl ketone (MBK), and carbon disulfide, have a particular affinity for peripheral nerves. Persons who have been exposed to these solvents (usually on their jobs) typically experience a tingling of the fingertips and toes followed by persistent numbing or altered sensation. This is followed by weakness of the muscles of the hands, forearms, and feet.

Damage to the peripheral nerves is usually repairable, except in the most severe cases. Brain damage usually cannot be repaired.

CANCER

Benzene was first shown to be associated with leukemia among workers in the 1890s. Recent work conducted by the U.S. Public Health Service has conclusively established that benzene can cause leukemia. Benzene can also cause lymphoma and other cancers of the blood-forming organs. Unleaded gasoline consists of about 5 percent benzene. This is one possible source for children. Their exposure to gasoline should be severely limited or eliminated.

Several other solvents cause cancer in experimental animals and are suspected of being human carcinogens. Perchloroethylene causes liver cancer in mice and leukemia in rats. Limited studies of perchloroethylene exposure among laundry and dry-cleaning workers show some excesses of cancer.

KIDNEY DISEASE

Many solvents are associated with the development of kidney failure following exposures in the workplace, in hobbies, or after intentional inhalation. Solvents that have been associated with kidney failure include carbon tetrachloride, trichloroethylene, perchloroethylene, carbon disulfide, and the glycol ethers. Acute kidney failure caused by solvents most commonly occurs after acute high-dose exposure—in the workplace, with heavy exposure at home in a confined space, following glue sniffing, or after accidental ingestion.

Chronic exposure to some solvents, including gasoline, has been associated with the development of chronic kidney disease. How this occurs is not clear. It is thought that prolonged exposure could be due to an immune reaction in which the immune system turns and attacks the altered kidney tissue.

LIVER DISEASE

Many solvents can cause acute toxic damage to the liver. Carbon tetrachloride is the best-known of these chemicals. It can also cause cirrhosis of the liver.

Other solvents that can cause liver damage after high-dose or chronic exposure include trichloroethylene and 1,1,1-trichloroethane. The toxic effects of solvents upon the liver are magnified by exposure to alcohol.

WHAT CAN PARENTS AND PEDIATRICIANS DO?

■ ■ ■

All parents should inventory their home for solvents. They are frequently found in the cellar, under sinks, in the garage, and in a workshop. Parents should go through the solvents in their home and remove them from areas where they might come into contact with children. Dispose of unwanted solvents in an ecologically safe manner (see the Household Inventory, Appendix 1).

It is important to reduce the use of solvents in the home. Hobby glues should be scrutinized to see that they do not contain harmful solvents. Chemical solvents used in a home workshop should be kept away from children. Solvents should always be used in an open, well-ventilated space. Benzene and carbon tetrachloride should never be used in the home under any circumstances. For these reasons, it is important to minimize children's exposure to dry-cleaning solvents. Whenever you bring materials home from the dry cleaners, allow them to air out for several days on a porch or in a room where children will not encounter the fumes.

Drinking water is the most pervasive source of solvent exposure for children. Parents should determine from their local health department what solvents are present in drinking water. If solvents are present, procedures for their removal from the drinking water supply must be explored. Frequently solvents can be removed from drinking water through aeration. Most solvents are more volatile than water, and when water is exposed to air and agitated, much of the dissolved chemical is liberated into the air.

Solvent ingestion by small infants can result in serious chemical pneumonia within hours. For this reason solvents must always be kept out of the reach of infants, toddlers, and other small children.

PCBs

■ ■ ■

The polychlorinated biphenyls (PCBs) are a family of synthetic chemical compounds that contain atoms of the element chlorine. The PCBs are clear, oily, nonflammable liquids. They resist heat and do not conduct electricity. For these reasons, they were widely used in large quantities as liquid insulators in transformers and capacitors from the 1930s until the mid-1970s. Smaller volumes of PCBs were placed in many millions of ballasts, the units used to trigger fluorescent lighting tubes.

Over the years, large quantities of PCBs have been released into the environment from the factories that produced the PCBs, from the factories that used PCBs to make electronic components, and from the breakdown of transformers, capacitors, and ballasts. The PCBs that have been released to the environment have washed into our harbors, lakes, and rivers, and settled to the bottom, where they persist in the sediment.

PCBs do not break down. Because they resist the microbes that naturally destroy most chemical compounds, they last for decade after decade. These hydrocarbons are soluble in fatty tissues, where they accumulate and move up the food chain. From the sediments in the bottom of lakes and rivers they are taken up by worms, shellfish, catfish, and other bottom-feeding animals including eels. When those animals in turn are eaten by game fish, the PCBs accumulate to even higher levels in the fatty tissues of those predator species. Finally, when eagles, bears, or humans, the predators who are at the top of the food chain, eat fish, they can accumulate high levels of PCBs.

HUMAN EXPOSURE TO PCBs

■ ■ ■

In 1960, a Swedish scientist named Soren Jensen, suspecting that PCBs were widely distributed, examined his wife's breast milk, his child's hair, and a dead eagle from the North Sea. He found substantial levels of PCBs in all three. Subsequent studies showed that PCBs are also distributed widely in North America, in Japan, and in other industrialized nations around the world.

The manufacture and use of PCBs was banned in the United States in 1976, but millions of tons of PCBs are still at large in the environment. Some of these are still contained in transformers and other electrical equipment. Additional quantities have already escaped into the environment and reside in the bottom sediments of bodies of water such as the Hudson River, the Great Lakes, New Bedford Harbor, the Tennessee River, and smaller streams throughout the United States.

THE HEALTH EFFECTS OF PCBs

■ ■ ■

High-dose exposure to PCBs produces a serious skin rash known as chloracne. Chloracne resembles the acne rash of adolescence, but it occurs in persons of any age and is deeper and more persistent.

Chloracne was first recognized in the 1930s and 1940s among industrial workers exposed to PCBs. A major community outbreak was seen in 1968 among residents of Kyushu Province in Japan. There, over 1,000 persons were found to have chloracne, liver problems, and central nervous system disease. The disease was traced to the use of cooking oil that had been contaminated by PCBs and related chemicals.

Children born to mothers who were exposed to PCBs during pregnancy were small and darkly pigmented. The glands of their eyes were inflamed at birth. Follow-up of these children has shown that their intellectual and behavioral development was slowed. The most severely affected children were dull; some were profoundly retarded.

The PCBs that caused the Japanese episodes were in heat exchangers used to heat rice oil. These PCBs had been heated to a high temperature and then run through pipes in a supposedly closed system in tanks full of rice oil. But pinhole leaks developed in the pipes that contained the PCBs; the oily, liquid PCBs escaped undetected into the cooking oil.

PCBs IN NORTH AMERICA

■ ■ ■

Concentrations of PCBs have been documented in fish in the Great Lakes. In Michigan, studies conducted by the Michigan Department of Public Health have shown clearly that the human body burdens of PCBs are increased by high consumption of Great Lakes fish. The Michigan Department of Public Health has issued strong advisories warning persons to limit their consumption of Great Lakes fish. Women have been warned not to eat Great Lakes fish during pregnancy or during the year or two preceding pregnancy.

Two groups of U.S. children have been followed developmentally from birth and their exposures to PCBs measured; one in Michigan, the other in North Carolina. In North Carolina, prenatal but not breast milk PCB exposure was associated with poorer performance on the tests of infant development from 6 through 24 months of age. Cord serum PCB level and maternal consumption of contaminated fish were both associated with poorer visual recognition memory performance. There was no relation with breast milk exposure.

PCBs IN BREAST MILK

■ ■ ■

Because fatty tissue concentrates PCBs, and breast milk has a high content of fat, PCBs are commonly found in high concentrations in breast milk. The recommendation of the American Academy of Pediatrics is that unless women have a history of exposure to PCBs, they should be encouraged to breast-feed their infants as usual. When a well-documented history of exposure to PCBs is obtained and the mother wants to breast-feed her infant, the mother's PCB level can be measured in about three weeks' time. The advice of state health department officials should be sought in the rare instances when a high PCB level is found.

PCBs AND CANCER

■ ■ ■

Adult workers in Taiwan, Japan, and the United States who have been heavily exposed to PCBs have chloracne as well as an increased incidence of cancer of the liver. PCBs are thought to cause liver cancer by serving as a promoter and by altering the metabolism of other carcinogens.

11

AIR POLLUTION

Levels of pollutants in our atmosphere are increasing at a troubling rate. Epidemiological studies in urban, suburban, and rural communities and laboratory investigations have clearly established that air pollution affects human health. Particularly strong connections between air pollution and asthma have been identified. Around the world, recent increases in the rates of asthma that parallel the increases in pollution have been reported. In addition, air pollution appears to be linked to other upper and lower respiratory diseases, including ear infections, chronic bronchitis, pneumonia, and lung cancer.

Air pollution dates back about three centuries, to the beginning of the industrial revolution. Factories were driven by burning fossil fuel, and the combustion products were heedlessly dumped into the atmosphere. Most people did not realize then that the atmosphere is not infinite. They were unaware that it is a thin shell of gases maintained in precise and delicate balance around the earth. As a result, the levels of smoke, soot, smog, acid rain, and greenhouse gases have gradually increased until they threaten both human health and the function of natural systems. Particularly since the end of World War II, the amount of these substances released into the atmosphere has soared.

To trace the history of pollutant deposition, earth scientists have taken core samples from the Arctic ice caps. By examining these samples, they have precisely fixed in time the flow of pollutants

FIGURE I: LEAD IN GREENLAND SNOW CORE

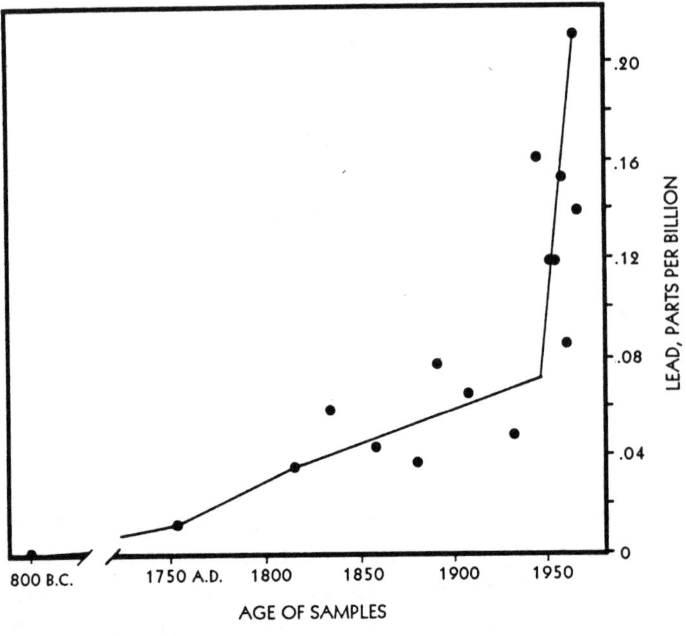

Source: Environmental Protection Agency

into the atmosphere across human history. Figure I shows the time course of lead pollution in the atmosphere as reflected in Greenland snow. Two thousand years ago virtually no lead was emitted into the atmosphere or deposited in the Arctic snow. Then, beginning about 1700 A.D., increased deposition becomes evident, and progresses steadily over the next three centuries. In the fifty years since World War II, there has been an enormous outpouring of lead and other air pollutants.

THE HEALTH EFFECTS OF AIR POLLUTION

■ ■ ■

A 5-year-old child inhales about 25 liters of air an hour and over 600 liters a day. As a result, substantial quantities of inhaled pollutants are deposited on the delicate membranes that line the respiratory tracts. Some of these are absorbed into the body. Air pollutants inflame the respiratory tract and lungs of children, producing coughing, wheezing, sore throat, shortness of breath, and asthma. Long-term exposure can diminish lung function and exercise capacity, lead to accelerated aging of the lungs, increase rates of chronic lung disease such as emphysema and bronchitis, and increase the risk of lung cancer.

THE NORMAL FUNCTION OF CHILDREN'S LUNGS

The central function of the respiratory system is to bring oxygen into the body and to eliminate carbon dioxide and other waste gases. With each breath, fresh air is brought into the body through the nose and mouth. After passing through the throat and pharynx, the air continues down through the trachea, the bronchi, and the bronchioles to minute sacs, the terminal alveoli, deep in the lungs. The nose, mouth, and upper airways serve as filters, removing the largest particles from the airstream, warming and humidifying the air. The trachea, bronchi, and bronchioles transport inspired air to the depths of the lung, further filtering it as it passes. These structures are lined with cilia—delicate, microscopic, hairlike structures that serve as active filters. The cilia trap small particles and pollutants and transport them back to the mouth. In this way they protect the delicate structures of the deep lung from harmful particles.

Ozone, nitrogen dioxide, and acidic particulates can damage the cells that line the airways. The passages swell and grow narrow. The movement of air into and out of the deep structures of the lung becomes labored. Some pollutants, nitrogen dioxide in particular, impair the normal activity of the cilia, allowing small particles to pass unhindered into the depths of the lung. This increases the risk of pneumonia and other respiratory infections.

THE SPECIAL VULNERABILITY OF CHILDREN

Children are particularly vulnerable to air pollutants for several reasons:

- Children's airways have small diameters. A pollutant that produces only slight irritation in an adult will significantly narrow the airways of a child and produce wheezing, bronchiolitis, and asthma.
- Because their metabolism is more active, children have a greater

need for oxygen relative to their size and weight than do adults. They breathe more rapidly and inhale more pollutants per pound of body weight.

- Children are outdoors more than adults and breathe more pollutants. When outdoors, they are more active and breathe faster. Their breathing zone is closer to the ground, where small particulates concentrate.
- Children focus less on their symptoms. They frequently ignore air pollution episodes that cause wheezing and discomfort in adults.
- The lungs of children are still growing. The lungs continue to grow through childhood and reach full maturity at about age 20. Repeated exposure to air pollution and repeated bouts of bronchitis, pneumonia, and asthma in childhood can limit the growth of the lungs and predispose a child to chronic lung disease.
- Finally, because they have more years of life ahead of them than adults, children have more time for the diseases initiated by early exposure to unfold and become manifest.

Some of the health effects of air pollution on children are acute and reversible; some damage may be permanent. We are particularly concerned with the recent dramatic worldwide increase in childhood asthma. The prevalence of asthma has increased by 33 percent in the United States over the past fifteen years. In 1991, over 2,000 children in the United States died of asthma. Increasing levels of air pollution appear to be one of the factors responsible for this epidemic. Yet pediatricians and allergists often fail to consider the role of pollutants in this increase.

SOURCES OF AIR POLLUTION

■ ■ ■

The nature of air pollution has changed over the past four decades. Thirty years ago, coal was the predominant source. Black smoke emitted by coal-burning industries darkened our industrial cities, particularly in the Appalachian states and the upper Midwest. Coal smoke, consisting of fine particles, sulfates, and acid mist, caused major air pollution disasters such as the killer fogs in Donora, Pennsylvania, in 1948 and in London in 1952. Five thousand

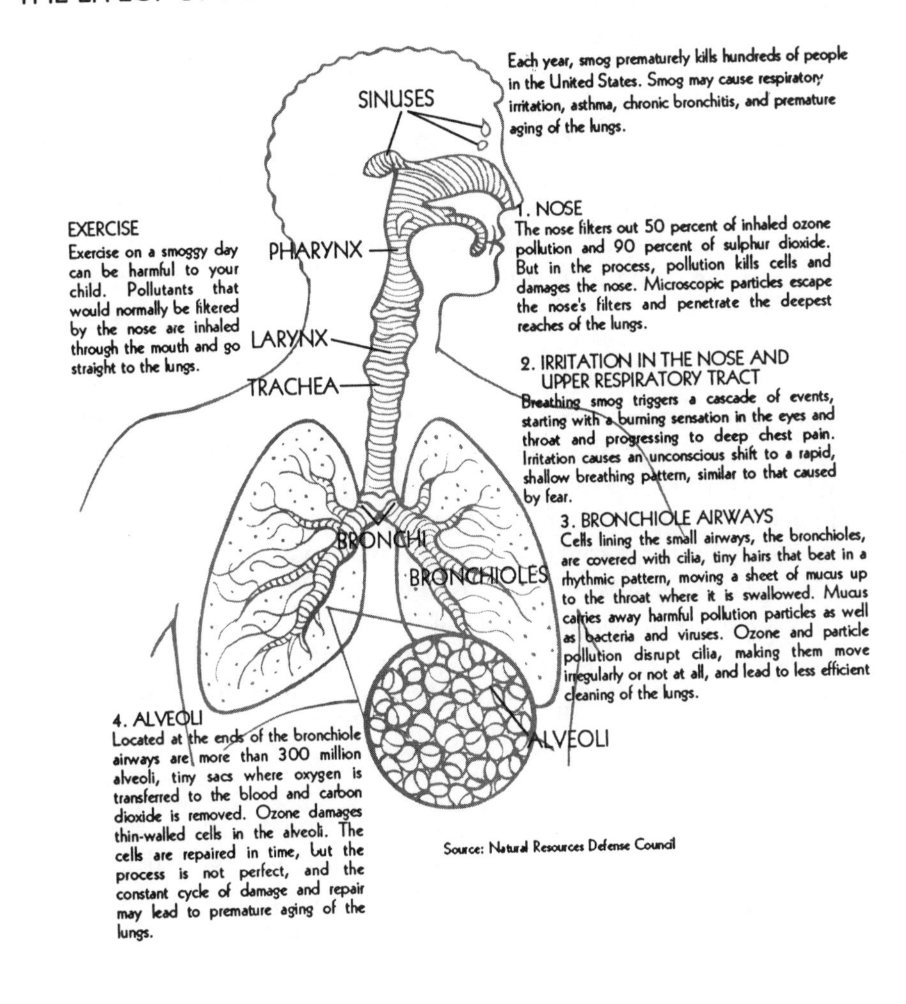

people were made sick in Donora, and 20 died. In four days the London fog killed more than 4,000 people.

Although coal is still an important pollutant in certain areas, the Clean Air Act of 1970 has substantially reduced coal smoke emissions. Nonetheless, the relief felt by scientists and the general public after the initial successes of the Clean Air Act was premature. Coal smoke has been controlled, but new sources of pollution have emerged. Air quality has continued to decline.

Exhaust fumes from cars, trucks, and buses are now the most important source of worldwide air pollution. In 1950, there were about 53 million cars on the world's roads. Four decades later, the global automobile fleet numbers over 430 million, a more than eightfold increase. In the United States, there are approximately 150 million private cars and almost 50 million trucks and buses on the roads.

Automotive exhaust is a complex mixture of thousands of chemical compounds. The significant components are nitrogen oxides (NO_x), ozone, sulfur dioxide, sulfuric acid, particulate matter, and carbon monoxide. Also of importance are toxic organic compounds, including formaldehyde, acetaldehyde, and benzene.

OXIDES OF NITROGEN

Nitrogen dioxide (NO_2), the brownish-red gas responsible for the classic smog haze of polluted cities, is a potent respiratory irritant. NO_2 is formed by the burning of fuel at a high temperature followed by rapid cooling. Automotive exhaust accounts for approximately three-fourths of the NO_2 released to the atmosphere each year. Gas stoves and kerosene heaters are other sources.

NO_2 is an important air pollutant in itself. It is also a major generator of atmospheric ozone. In the atmosphere, under sunlight, it reacts with hydrocarbon vapors, and ozone is formed.

OZONE

Ozone is a highly reactive, unstable form of oxygen. It is the single most important airborne hazard for children. Cars and factories do not emit ozone. It is formed in the atmosphere by a combination of nitrogen, hydrocarbons, and sunlight. Because ozone requires sunlight for its formation, ozone levels are highest in the hot summer months, and the highest concentrations are recorded during these months at midday and in the early afternoon. This is precisely the time of day when children are most likely to be playing outdoors. Ozone levels decline rapidly when the sun goes down.

In remote areas the concentrations of ozone are very low: 30 to 50 parts per billion (ppb). In heavily polluted areas, ozone levels frequently exceed 120 to 150 parts per billion. Levels of ozone are extremely high in the Los Angeles basin. The combination of vast amounts of automotive exhaust, intense solar radiation, and entrapping mountain ranges favors the formation of high levels of ozone. Similarly, high levels of ozone and other smog components are formed each summer over cities in the midwestern and eastern United States. This summer package of air pollutants forms in the Midwest and then moves across the country from southwest to northeast, picking up additional pollutants as it travels. The pollutant package has been traced up into New England and Canada.

Ozone damages the cells that line the respiratory tract, causing irritation, burning sensations, and difficulty in breathing during exercise. Children, the elderly, and persons with respiratory diseases as well as people who exercise outdoors are particularly vulnerable.

The federal standard for ozone exposure is 120 parts per billion. Ozone levels above 120 ppb violate federal law. But children and adults can experience wheezing and other respiratory symptoms at levels even below this standard. The federal ozone standard is definitely too high; it needs to be made stricter.

SUSPENDED PARTICULATE MATTER, SULFURIC ACID AEROSOL, AND AIRBORNE SULFATES

Airborne suspended particulates consist of solid and liquid particles less than 10 microns in diameter. (One micron is one millionth of a meter.) The tiny particles include ordinary dust, soot particles from diesel exhaust, automotive exhaust, and cigarette smoke. These compounds are produced by the combustion of any fuel containing sulfur.

Increases in airborne particulate levels are associated with impaired lung function in both healthy children and asthmatics. Increased levels of particulate pollution are also associated with more respiratory symptoms, asthma, pleurisy, and pneumonia. These effects have been noted in children at particulate levels well below the current federal standard of 150 micrograms per cubic meter. This standard also needs to be made stricter.

CARBON MONOXIDE (CO)

Carbon monoxide is a colorless, odorless poisonous gas produced by the incomplete combustion of fuel—coal, wood, charcoal, or petroleum. Automobiles are the major source of carbon monoxide. In 1990, automobiles in the United States released over 40 million tons of carbon monoxide; this is about two-thirds of the total CO produced.

THE FORMATION OF OZONE

Ozone is formed in the atmosphere through a complex series of chemical reactions that require the presence of sunlight. Because the reaction requires solar energy, the products are referred to as "photochemical smog." Although photochemical smog is found most commonly in hot cities with many automobiles and abundant sunshine, such as Los Angeles and Mexico City, it is encountered with increasing frequency in the Midwest, the Middle Atlantic States, New England, and Canada, especially during the summer months. During several recent summers, record levels of both temperature and ozone have been encountered in many cities, both large and small, in the eastern United States.

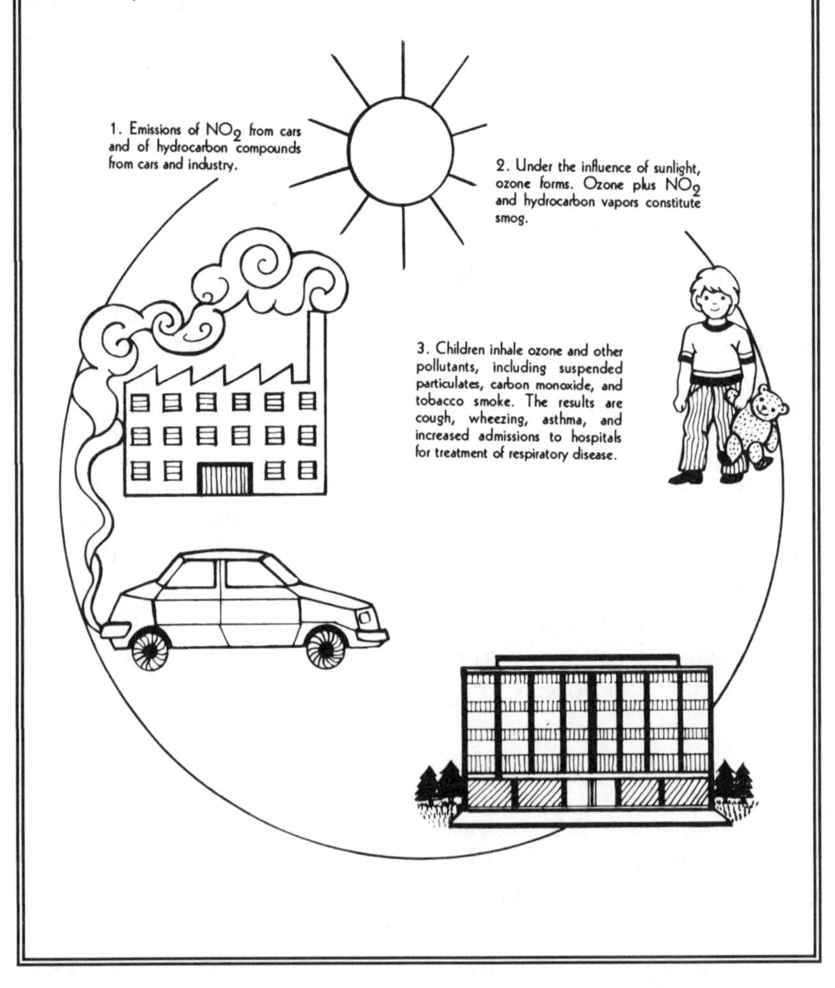

Once inhaled, carbon monoxide passes immediately through the lungs into the circulating red blood cells. There it binds tightly to hemoglobin and blocks the ability of hemoglobin to carry oxygen to the body's cells. Acute high-dose exposure to CO can be immediately fatal. This has happened when people used charcoal briquettes indoors during power failures. Chronic low-grade exposure to carbon monoxide, such as occurs in polluted cities, increases the risk of heart disease and stroke in the elderly and may increase the risk of heart disease for children. The developing fetus may be impaired by relatively low levels of CO that cross the placenta. Smoking can raise the CO levels of infants in utero. When a pregnant woman smokes, her baby smokes.

TOXIC ORGANIC MATERIALS

Automotive emissions contain a number of toxic organic materials. *Formaldehyde* and *acetaldehyde* are strong respiratory irritants. They redden eyes, cause noses to run and chests to burn. Chronic exposure to formaldehyde can cause cancer of the nasal sinuses and lungs. *Benzene* is toxic to the bone marrow and the blood cells. Acute high-dose exposure can rapidly destroy the marrow, where most blood cells are made. Chronic lower-level exposure causes leukemia and lymphoma. Unleaded gasoline contains approximately 5 percent benzene by weight. Some of this benzene is released into the air during the pumping of gasoline, and more is released during incomplete combustion.

DIESEL EMISSIONS

Heavy vehicles that burn diesel fuel, such as trucks and buses, emit a mixture of pollutants that differs from that of automobile exhaust. The two major toxic products in diesel exhaust are oxides of nitrogen and heavy black soot. NO_2 levels from diesel vehicles are substantially higher than those from automobiles and require special emission controls.

A number of cities in the United States and around the world have begun to impose strict standards on diesel emissions and now require engine modifications, treatment of exhaust, and strict controls of fuel composition for trucks and buses. When these approaches are followed conscientiously, the familiar black foul-smelling diesel exhaust has been substantially controlled.

WASTE INCINERATION

The burning of household and municipal wastes can release substantial amounts of pollutants into the air. Municipal incinerators can be a particular problem because of the large amounts of waste they consume and the huge amounts of carbon monoxide, NO_x, and metals that some of them can release. Incinerators can emit lead, nickel, cadmium, copper, and mercury, all hazardous metals. They can be contained in the "fly ash" that is released from the stacks and also in the solid residue left behind after burning. Some municipal incinerators can release the highly toxic organic compound dioxin and a related compound, furan.

Urban areas also are burdened with apartment incinerators. These small units incompletely burn the trash, throwing off large amounts of pollutants in the process. Most of these incinerators employ only minimal, if any, filtration.

The only effective response to the problem of waste disposal is reduction of the amount we generate, reusing the products instead of disposing of them, recycling when this is not feasible. Each of us has a serious stake in this problem, and a responsibility to reduce our contribution to the waste stream.

INDUSTRIAL EMISSIONS

Factories, refineries, incinerators, and power plants release enormous quantities of toxic pollutants into the atmosphere. These include hydrogen sulfide, benzene, mercaptans, and other organics released by oil refineries; sulfates from paper mills; sulfates and acid aerosols from coal-burning power plants; and metals and dioxin dispersed by municipal incinerators. These industries are responsible for a substantial fraction of all the sulfur dioxide and hydrocarbons emitted into the atmosphere each year.

Since 1986, industries in the United States have been required by law to publicly report data on their environmental emissions of toxic chemicals. This information is collected by the EPA and is published each year in the EPA Toxic Release Inventory (TRI). The TRI was created in response to the chemical disaster in Bhopal, India, in 1984. Over 2,000 people were killed in a single night when a chemical plant accidentally vented methyl isocyanate, a compound used in the manufacture of pesticides. The goal of the inventory and of the federal right-to-know legislation that supports it is to provide citizens and communities with information on the chemicals used, stored, and released in their neighborhoods. The chemical industry fought bitterly against establishing the TRI, and the legislation was passed by Congress on December 10, 1985, by only one vote. Chemical manufacturers and users must by law report to the EPA their environmental releases of some 330 toxic chemicals and waste substances. The EPA is required to make this information publicly available through the TRI. The information in the TRI is accessible to the public in print form and also through on-line computerized data bases.

COMMUNITY SOURCES OF AIR POLLUTION

Small businesses and local industries are important contributors to air pollution. Dry-cleaning shops release solvent vapors into the atmosphere. Auto body shops: paint fumes. Plastic molding plants: formaldehyde and other organic chemical compounds. Scrap-metal recycling plants: lead, cadmium, and mercury. Plating operations: chromium and nickel. Few of these releases are reported to the TRI. Major opportunities for pollution control exist in small businesses.

HOME SOURCES OF AIR POLLUTION

The use of products such as room fresheners, deodorants, and hair sprays can release substantial quantities of toxic gases into the atmosphere. Although each individual's use of these materials is small, when millions of persons use them, the total amount of air pollution released from home sources is significant.

INDOOR AIR POLLUTION

■ ■ ■

Most children spend more than half of their lives indoors. The importance of indoor air pollution has become increasingly evident in recent years as a result of efforts to "tighten" homes to make them more energy-efficient. With increased tightening, ventilation by outside air is reduced. Pollutants released into the home environment are trapped for longer periods of time and pose greater risks to children. Secondhand cigarette smoke, gas stoves, and wood-burning stoves and fireplaces are the major sources of indoor air pollution. Home products such as aerosols, air fresheners, cleaning agents, and certain consumer goods also contribute to the problem.

SECONDHAND CIGARETTE SMOKE

This is the single most important source of indoor air pollution. Most studies of children exposed to cigarette smoke suffer from substantial increases in respiratory illnesses and respiratory symptoms as compared with unexposed children.

A lighted cigarette releases more than 4,000 chemical compounds into the air. These materials include carbon monoxide, ammonia, nicotine, and hydrogen cyanide and carcinogens. (See Chapter 10.)

GAS STOVES

Gas stoves release nitrogen dioxide (NO_2) and other oxides of nitrogen (NO_x) into the home. Stoves with pilot lights are especially severe offenders. They release NO_2 and NO_x throughout the day and night.

Studies conducted in the United States and Europe have shown that children exposed to gas stoves, particularly stoves with pilot lights, have decreased pulmonary function and more respiratory symptoms and bronchitis. Similar effects can be seen in children exposed to gasoline or kerosene home heaters; these heaters also release NO_2 and NO_x as well as hydrocarbons, soot, and carbon monoxide.

WOOD-BURNING STOVES AND FIREPLACES

Wood-burning stoves and fireplaces emit particulates, carbon monoxide, benzene, formaldehyde, and other noxious materials. Children who are exposed to wood smoke have an increased frequency of chronic coughing and wheezing, and they have more asthmatic attacks than other children. These children may be at increased risk of lung cancer, because many of the tars and particulates emitted in wood smoke are similar to those found in tobacco smoke.

Only wood-burning stoves and fireplaces with excellent ventilation are safe. Fireplaces must be built with an adequate draft. Stoves must have high-quality functioning catalytic converters. Pollution control devices on wood-burning stoves should be checked and cleaned at least once a year.

In certain mountain valleys, wood-burning home stoves have been banned. In these settings, high concentrations of wood smoke are trapped between the hills during the winter months and cause severe local air pollution hazards. Families who live in such areas or are contemplating moving should inquire about local restrictions on wood-burning stoves.

CONSUMER PRODUCTS

Insulation, plywood, pressed-wood furniture, and new carpets have all been shown to release formaldehyde gas into the home environment. Formaldehyde is used extensively in the manufacture of these products. It is a potent respiratory irritant and a cause of lung and nasal cancer. In recognition of the hazards posed by formaldehyde to children and other home occupants many states have banned the use of formaldehyde-containing home insulation. But other sources of formaldehyde continue to be produced.

DUST

House dust contributes to indoor air pollution and can be a source of respiratory irritation in children. House dust can arise from many sources, including dirt particles brought in from out of doors and pets' hair and feathers. Exposure to dust, especially when combined with exposure to passive cigarette smoke and toxic fumes, can provoke asthma and other respiratory symptoms in children.

To control dust in the home, pediatricians frequently recommend that wall-to-wall carpets be removed and, when possible, replaced with small area rugs that can be thoroughly cleaned. Heavy curtains may also need to be removed and replaced with curtains that can be easily laundered.

These preventive measures, combined with cessation of smoking and reduction of home combustion sources, can substantially reduce children's exposure to indoor air pollutants. Reduction of passive cigarette smoking is probably the single most important preventive measure. Although the work of dust control can be quite onerous, the benefits can be rewarding, and are measured in less asthma and pneumonia and fewer trips to the doctor's office and the hospital emergency room.

CLEAN AIR LEGISLATION

■ ■ ■

The first federal clean air standards regulating certain air pollutants were established in the United States in the 1950s. The first major legislative breakthrough occurred in 1970, when Congress passed the Clean Air Act. This law serves as the basic legislation controlling air pollution in the United States. Under this act, which is administered by the EPA, federal standards have been set to limit exposures to major air pollutants—ozone, sulfur dioxide, particulate matter, nitrogen dioxide, carbon monoxide, and lead. For each of these materials, the administrator of the EPA is required by the act to establish a National Ambient Air Quality Standard (NAAQS). Each of these standards sets a legally permissible upper limit on the concentration of a pollutant in the air.

An extraordinarily farsighted and important provision of the Clean Air Act is that the standards developed under it are designed to protect the health of the most vulnerable groups within our population and provide an adequate margin of safety for these groups. In most cases, the most vulnerable group is children.

Individual states are allowed to establish air pollution standards that are stricter than the federal standards. In many cases, California has led the way in developing standards that are stronger than federal regulations.

The table below shows the current U.S. standards for the six major pollutants.

A major problem with the Clean Air Act of 1970 is that it does not regulate the amount of material that is emitted from automotive exhaust or industrial smokestacks. It regulates only the levels of pollutants that are actually found in the air. Therefore, the act does not get at the source of air pollution and does not provide incentives for cleaning up pollutants at their source.

To deal with this shortcoming, Congress passed the Clean Air Act Amendments of 1990. A major provision of this new legislation

FEDERAL STANDARDS FOR SIX MAJOR AIR POLLUTANTS

POLLUTANT	STANDARD
Ozone	120 parts per billion (ppb) calculated as a one-hour average)
Carbon monoxide	35 parts per million (ppm) calculated as a one-hour average
Airborne particulates	150 micrograms per cubic meter of air, calculated as a 24-hour average
Nitrogen dioxide	53 ppm, calculated as a one-year average
Sulfur dioxide	330 ppm, as a maximum permissible annual average; 140 ppm, as a maximum permissible 24-hour average
Lead	1.5 micrograms per cubic meter, calculated as a three-month average

is that it includes standards for source reduction. As a result, standards will be set that strictly control the amount of pollutants that can be released in automotive exhaust and industrial emissions. This legislation also contains incentives for recycling.

RECOMMENDATIONS TO GOVERNMENT AGENCIES

■ ■ ■

AMBIENT STANDARDS

The current federal ambient air standard for ozone of 120 parts per billion is inadequate. It provides no margin of safety. It does not fulfill the congressional mandate to protect the most vulnerable members of our population. This standard must be lowered promptly. As a first step, the American Academy of Pediatrics recommends that the current standard should be reduced to a level no higher than 80 ppb (averaged over a period of one hour). Moreover, because recent epidemiologic studies suggest that children's lungs may be affected by exposures to ozone even at concentrations below 80 ppb, the EPA urgently needs to sponsor additional studies to determine whether it will be necessary to reduce the ozone standard still further.

Federal standards for sulfates and particulates also fail to protect the health of our children. They too need to be made stricter.

SOURCE CONTROL AND ENFORCEMENT

Prevention of air pollution requires reducing the emission of pollutants into the atmosphere. Once nitrogen dioxide and the other constituents of ozone have been released into the air, its formation cannot be prevented. It is necessary, therefore, that the federal and state governments strictly enforce standards limiting automotive and industrial emissions of air pollutants.

There are two strategies for reducing automotive air pollution. Vehicles can be required to run more cleanly or the number of vehicle miles driven can be reduced. Both strategies should be pursued at once. Cars must be required to pass frequent inspections, and those that fail must be repaired or removed from the road.

Vehicle miles can be reduced only if private transportation is replaced by safe, clean, and accessible systems of mass transportation. Trains, streetcars, and buses emit far less pollution per passenger mile than private cars.

Strategies to discourage driving include increased gasoline taxes, bridge and highway tolls, traffic restriction days, and limitations on parking. If we are to keep the cities of the twenty-first century from being polluted parking lots, it is urgent that planning in all of these directions begin actively now. Land-use planning offers an additional approach to reduction of driving. In land-use planning, zoning laws are reexamined. Places of work are situated closer to the places where people live so that long commutes can be avoided.

POLLUTION ALERTS

State and local governments have a responsibility to issue pollution alerts in a clear and timely manner. These alerts need to warn specifically of the hazards that air pollution presents to children, and they must recommend appropriate short-term action. Parents and children must be warned of the dangers of strenuous exercise when levels of air pollutants are elevated.

ONE COMMUNITY'S BATTLE FOR BREATHABLE AIR

■ ■ ■

Boerum Hill, a neighborhood in Brooklyn, New York, had a severe toxic air problem for over ten years. Residents complained to city officials about an odor in the neighborhood resembling that of nail polish, and about frequent headaches and nausea. The source was an art supplies manufacturer, Ulano, that was releasing toluene into the air. Toluene is a highly volatile solvent with a strong odor. The Boerum Hill–South Brooklyn Clean Air Committee, a neighborhood organization, began to demonstrate while wearing gas masks, tracked the frequency of toluene emissions, and informed the state representatives. At first, little happened. Then, in 1986, the Emergency Planning and Community Right to Know Act was passed. This gave citizens the tool they needed. Consumers Union was alerted, and, using data from the EPA Toxic Release Inventory, they issued a report identifying Ulano as the top industrial air polluter in the city, responsible for 17 percent of the air pollution.

The Boerum Hill committee released the report at a joint press conference with Consumers Union. The New York Department of Environmental Conservation responded and announced that Ulano would be compelled to either build a new, cleaner incinerator or face stiff fines.

RECOMMENDATIONS TO PARENTS

■ ■ ■

INDOOR AIR POLLUTION

Parents should take specific steps to reduce their children's exposure to indoor air pollution. First and foremost, parents who smoke must make every effort not to smoke around their children. If you are addicted to tobacco and cannot stop smoking, then it is essential to go out of doors when you smoke. You cannot protect your children from air pollution if you smoke in the house where they live.

It is important to check stoves, fireplaces, and heaters for possible emissions of air pollutants. If you have a gas stove with a pilot light, have it disconnected.

If you have children with asthma or other respiratory diseases, dust control in the home is important. Sources of dust should be minimized or eliminated.

Outdoor Air Pollution

To prevent outdoor pollution in your state and community, you must begin by examining your own behavior patterns. Do you drive excessively when you could use public transportation? Does your car run clean? Does your furnace or fireplace pour pollutants into the neighborhood atmosphere? Are you attempting to reduce the amount of solid waste produced by reusing and recycling?

You may wish to join an environmental organization at either the local or national level. Because pollution is emitted by large and powerful industries, an individual parent can usually do little to reduce pollution at the source. But groups of thousands of committed citizens have had a major impact in reducing pollution in the United States and around the world. There are numerous regional and local groups organized to deal with specific issues (see Appendix 2).

Use the Toxic Release Inventory to learn what polluting industries may be present in your community or state. TRI information, available through the regional EPA office, although it has certain shortcomings, is extremely useful and quite accessible. It makes very interesting reading and can be of importance in the protection of your family.

RECOMMENDATIONS TO PEDIATRICIANS

■ ■ ■

- Pediatricians have a unique opportunity to lead in the struggle against air pollution. They should express their concern about the health hazards of air pollution to their elected representatives in state and federal governments. On a number of occasions, the American Academy of Pediatrics has spoken out about air pollution in public testimony and in strong position papers.
- Pediatricians who serve as physicians for schools and for team

sports should be aware of the health implications of pollution alerts and should provide appropriate counsel on these hazards to the children under their care. Outdoor games and track meets should not be held on high-pollution days.

▪ Pediatricians caring for children at special risk, such as children with asthma and cystic fibrosis, should be aware that current levels of air pollution may cause deterioration in these children's pulmonary function and may aggravate their symptoms.

▪ Pediatricians must at every opportunity urge children not to smoke and not to experiment with smoking.

THE TOXIC RELEASE INVENTORY AND RIGHT-TO-KNOW LEGISLATION

BACKGROUND

The goal of the federal right-to-know law is to enable citizens, community groups, and local governments to learn which toxic chemicals in what quantities are stored, used, and released in their neighborhoods.

Since its passage into law in 1986, the TRI has sparked extensive interest from the public, legislators, the press, regulators, and industry. The TRI data base is now widely recognized as a valuable source of environmental data. Armed for the first time with equal access to information, citizens are leading a nationwide movement to prevent toxic pollution and enforce environmental laws.

THE TOXIC RELEASE INVENTORY

TRI legislation requires large manufacturers to report publicly their environmental releases and off-site transfers of some 330 toxic chemicals and wastes. The releases are reported for each environmental "medium" (air, land, water, etc.). The EPA must make this information public in the first publicly accessible, on-line computer data base ever mandated by federal law.

LIMITATIONS

- Many common toxic chemicals are not included on the right-to-know list.
- Nonmanufacturers, small firms, and federal facilities are exempt.
- Annual reporting does not reveal peak release rates.

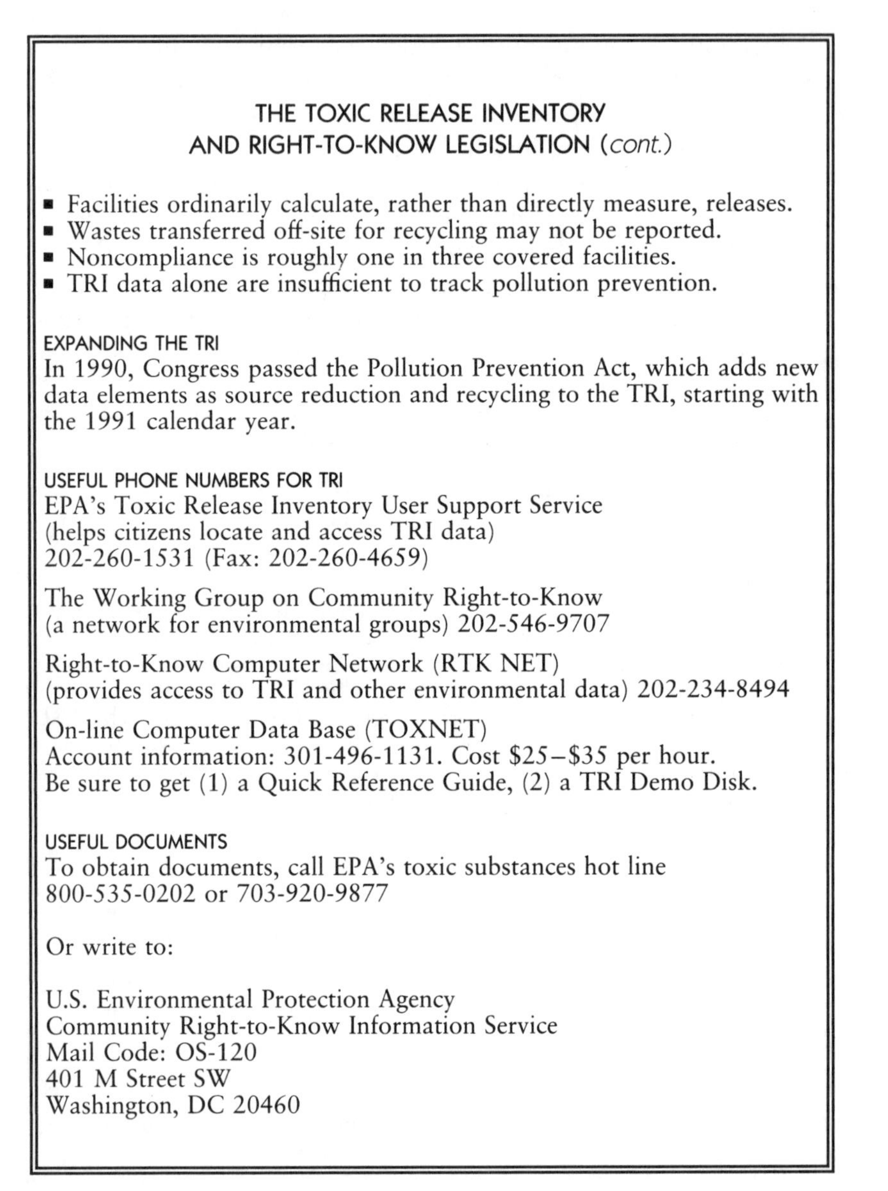

THE TOXIC RELEASE INVENTORY
AND RIGHT-TO-KNOW LEGISLATION (*cont.*)

- Facilities ordinarily calculate, rather than directly measure, releases.
- Wastes transferred off-site for recycling may not be reported.
- Noncompliance is roughly one in three covered facilities.
- TRI data alone are insufficient to track pollution prevention.

EXPANDING THE TRI

In 1990, Congress passed the Pollution Prevention Act, which adds new data elements as source reduction and recycling to the TRI, starting with the 1991 calendar year.

USEFUL PHONE NUMBERS FOR TRI

EPA's Toxic Release Inventory User Support Service
(helps citizens locate and access TRI data)
202-260-1531 (Fax: 202-260-4659)

The Working Group on Community Right-to-Know
(a network for environmental groups) 202-546-9707

Right-to-Know Computer Network (RTK NET)
(provides access to TRI and other environmental data) 202-234-8494

On-line Computer Data Base (TOXNET)
Account information: 301-496-1131. Cost $25–$35 per hour.
Be sure to get (1) a Quick Reference Guide, (2) a TRI Demo Disk.

USEFUL DOCUMENTS

To obtain documents, call EPA's toxic substances hot line
800-535-0202 or 703-920-9877

Or write to:

U.S. Environmental Protection Agency
Community Right-to-Know Information Service
Mail Code: OS-120
401 M Street SW
Washington, DC 20460

EPILOGUE: A HEALTHY PLANET FOR HEALTHY CHILDREN

We pediatricians choose to spend our days observing developing lives. As we watch them unfold, our gaze lifts past the immediate present. We are pressed to confront the continuity of life, to think of the generations that will succeed us and of the world that we will leave to them.

This book focuses on the steps you can take to reduce environmental risks encountered by your children at home and in their schools. This is important work, but it is not enough. We live in a wider realm, in which environmental changes are taking place at an increasingly rapid rate. It is these changes, daily coming into sharper focus, that will determine the nature of the lives our children and their children will lead.

Protecting our personal environment is essential, but this alone will not shield us. The disturbances in the global environment seep into our air-conditioned, lead-free homes and follow us to the seashore and mountains. The question of how best to protect the environment will dominate the political and economic agenda of this country for the next decade and century.

For the past fifty years we have focused almost exclusively on the conflict between the East and the West. As we raise our vision, we can now see the spreading spoilage of the planet as the principal threat to our lives. This peril crosses borders and spares no one. In this chapter we examine some of these major environmental threats: global warming, solid waste, desertification of forests, acid rain, and destruction of the ozone layer. We look at some of the economic forces that push us to spoil our land, and then sketch some appropriate actions. These problems have not come about accidentally. Strong forces have fueled them and explain their persistence. To deal effectively with these forces, individuals must join with others to change governmental, national, and international behavior. We point you in that direction.

Why has it taken so long to understand that the environment is in real peril? Why have we been caught unawares? One reason is that the natural world has always appeared, if not invulnerable, then extraordinarily resilient. Nature's strength and recuperative powers are visible everywhere. If a summer cottage is left without attention for a year, it will quickly be covered with weedy overgrowth, and surrounding forests rapidly envelop unused farmland. Nothing can match the strength of a hurricane or a flood. It is hard to realize that nature can be damaged.

But many of these forces exist in delicate balances that can be unsettled, and over time changes are brought about that do not heal. Overpopulation, uncontrolled technology, and the dispersal of chemicals have grievously wounded natural systems, in some cases past the possibility of repair. Here are some facts that sketch the outlines of recent damage to the planet.

- Since 1970, 200 million hectares of trees have been destroyed worldwide. This is equal to the area of the United States east of the Mississippi.
- In the same time span, the amount of desert has increased by 120 million hectares. This is equal to the area of cropland planted in China.
- In the same time span, the world's population has increased by 1.5 billion people.
- Each year industrial and agricultural activities generate 5 billion tons of solid waste, or 20 tons for each American citizen.
- We produce 700,000 tons of *toxic* waste each day in the United States, or 250 million tons per year.
- 150 million Americans live in places where the air quality is below standard.
- Half of the German forests are affected by acid rain and resultant tree death.
- The six hottest years in recorded history were 1981, 1983, 1986, 1987, and 1988.

Some of these changes have already made themselves felt in the way we live, in the quality of our daily lives, and in our health and vigor. Other changes have yet to make their effects obvious. In order to restore the place we live, we must understand the state of affairs on the planet, our home.

SOLID WASTE

■ ■ ■

Open a compact-disk package, or a parcel you have ordered from a mail-order catalogue, and notice what you throw away. Look at the volume of commercial mail that you dispose of unread each day, or the quantity of paper and plastic you discard when you come home from the supermarket. Look at the ground around a fast-food restaurant or an automated teller machine, or at the amount of trash you and your neighbors put at the curb for collection.

Most environmental damage occurs during the extraction of natural resources and during the disposal of its waste. The mining of materials and the cutting of timber are extremely destructive. Mining and logging take place primarily in remote areas, unseen by most citizens. One look at a strip mine, or the tailings of a smelter, and you will understand the terrible damage done when resources are extracted.

The damage done to our environment by the quantities of solid waste we generate is less obvious, but just as problematic. In the United States we generate 5 billion tons of solid waste a year from mining, farming, and manufacturing.

SOLID WASTE DISPOSAL

■ ■ ■

There are five ways to deal with solid waste: source reduction, reuse, recycling, incineration, and landfills. The traditional and—until recently—the cheapest way to dispose of waste was to dump it in the nearest landfill or river. A considerable portion of our wastes is toxic: pesticides, solvents, metals such as mercury and lead, motor oils, acids, and strong detergents. Putting these in an ordinary landfill raises the threat of their seeping into our water supply. We are running out of landfills, and we cannot live for long with continued pollution of our waterways.

INCINERATION

In the United States, we have recently turned to building incinerators. Incineration is not a form of recycling. It neither recaptures material for later reuse nor eliminates the need for landfills. Incineration really amounts to an aerial equivalent of a landfill.

Twenty percent of the initial mass of waste remains after incineration. This then requires landfilling, because the residues of incinerators are not suitable for reuse. Claims that burning waste is a source of energy must be treated with skepticism; most of the energy is required to incinerate the garbage, and little is available as heat.

Toxic products of incineration are the most serious cost of this method. Every five tons of waste produces a ton of ash. This ash has high concentrations of lead, mercury, cadmium, sulfates, and carcinogens.

Incineration is inefficient and expensive, and these costs are passed on to the consumer. According to the Worldwatch Institute report *State of the World 1991*, $8 billion invested in incinerators in the United States now would accommodate 25 percent of the solid waste output generated ten years from now. If we invested the same amount of capital in recycling and composting, we could take care of 75 percent of the solid waste.

REUSE

Reuse simply means cleaning the finished product and returning it to use. Reusing containers is the least energy-consuming method of recapture. Glass bottles are the best example. Making one aluminum can uses 10 times the energy of reusing a glass bottle. One bottle can be used as many as 50 times. This conserves the energy of 500 aluminum cans, or the equivalent of 250 gallons of gasoline.

Why haven't we moved to this technology? The makers of disposable bottles and cans and the beverage vendors have a great deal of influence on the economy. They have little interest in speeding the nationwide adoption of bottle-return laws and programs.

RECYCLING

Recycling means breaking down a waste product and then reconstituting it into useful stock. Recycling is most efficient when it returns the waste to its original state; recycled paper is a good example. Manufacturing new substances out of waste is far inferior from an energy point of view. Chairs or picnic tables made out of recycled plastic bottles serve a public relations rather than an environmental function.

Recycling requires capital investment in collection and processing, but it can reduce the amount of materials entering the waste stream. The logistics of recycling, from disposal to pickup, to reentry into the recovery stream, are in their infancy. In many places, the chain of processes is incomplete. We frequently read of enormous piles of newsprint filling warehouses. If the industrial capacity to handle the paper were built up, recycling newsprint could become cost-effective. Creating this capacity requires capital investment, and many communities have begun the collection process without investing in the industrial conversion capability. The recently announced federal policy to use paper containing at least 20 percent recycled fibers will provide an important stimulus to the recycling industry.

WASTE REDUCTION

The most effective approach to solid waste management is waste reduction. Accomplishing this absolutely essential goal will not be easy. It will ask us to make significant changes in the way we live. We have all been trained to be good (meaning voracious) consumers. A well-indoctrinated consumer equates the good life with constantly acquiring new products and discarding them at the first sign of wear or slipping out of style. The fashion and automobile industries have thrived on a population that traded in its cars every two or three years and spent a king's ransom whenever the definition of a stylish hemline changed a few inches.

The authentic benefits of true labor-saving devices like backhoes and washing machines have been extended to include caricatures that have wormed their way into our culture. We have, as a result, developed a market for battery-driven drink stirrers, back scratchers, and nose-hair trimmers. Our conditioned worship of "labor-saving" devices has drawn us to a sedentary life. How do we handle that? People drive to the corner store, and then join a health club for aerobics classes.

Because we cannot be burdened with bringing a shopping bag to the store, packaging of foods (notice the amount of plastic wrap in your supermarket order), hardware, and other goods has become a major sector of the economy. We not only dispose of our razor blade when it becomes dull; we throw away the whole razor. Nor do we want to make the effort to return bottles to the store for reuse, so we buy our soft drinks in cans or throwaway glass at a tremendous energy penalty. The manufacturing of a single aluminum can requires the energy in a half gallon of gasoline.

But there is growing evidence that many Americans are increasingly fatigued with ravenous consumption. We suggest that you as a parent examine your own possessions and ask yourself how much of what you own really contributes to a sense of meaningfulness, satisfaction, and well-being.

Then take a look at your children and evaluate how much they are driven by the need to buy and own consumer goods. Do they appear satisfied, confident, and fun-filled? Ask yourself how much of their durable happiness is associated with their possessions. Does your child need technical toys to keep from being bored? If the television set or the Nintendo is broken, can he or she find an interesting way to spend an idle evening? It is not too late to reeducate ourselves and our children in the wisdom and need to consume less. It is essential that we do so before we have no choice.

GLOBAL WARMING

■ ■ ■

In the preceding decade we experienced the six hottest years in recorded history. While there is some debate whether this is due to ordinary random variation in weather patterns, the great majority of earth scientists believe that this is a real and durable trend, and that unless it is altered, we are in for eventual catastrophe. Some scientists predict that the consequences of continued global warming include the melting of polar ice caps, the flooding of our coastlines, the reduction of food supplies, and the increased incidence of ultraviolet-related diseases like skin cancer.

Much of the predictions of what will happen to our global

temperature rely on mathematical models of the earth's atmosphere, using high-speed computers and actual data from meteorological stations. Mathematical models are simplifications of nature; they always produce a range of predictions, and they depend on many assumptions. These are the sources of the debate. A prudent person will ask what is the cost of acting as if global warming is occurring and what is the cost of acting as if it is not.

Almost all of our energy derives from solar radiation. This reaches our planet in the form of ultraviolet rays, and some of these bounce back off the earth's surface into space. The reflected radiation is in the form of infrared rays, a different part of the electromagnetic wave spectrum. There is a layer of gases in the earth's stratosphere, primarily carbon dioxide (CO_2), methane, water vapor, and nitrous oxide. This layer behaves like a pane of glass and reflects a considerable portion of the infrared radiation back to earth. If this did not happen, heat would radiate out into space, and the earth would be too cold to sustain life as we know it.

Due to increased combustion from human activity, the amount of these greenhouse gases in the reflecting layer is increasing. About 50 percent of the greenhouse gases consists of CO_2, which derives from the burning of fossil fuel. Technologically advanced societies consume much more energy and generate more CO_2 than less developed societies. Although the United States possesses about 5 percent of the world's population, we provide about 25 percent of the CO_2 to the stratosphere. Deforestation is the other major contributor to global warming. Trees use CO_2 to make carbohydrates. The removal of trees from the earth's surface deprives us of one of the great regulators of CO_2. Each time a tree is harvested and burned for fuel, we feel a double impact: the increase in CO_2 produced and the decrease in photosynthesis and CO_2 uptake.

WHAT CAN BE DONE ABOUT IT?

Since the industrialized countries are by far the largest contributors to global warming, it is here that the burden for action falls. While we express great concern over the impact of development in the Third World on global pollution, we cannot expect them to slow their development and remain embedded in poverty. Any serious international attempt to deal with global warming requires a sharing of resources with the underdeveloped peoples. Conservation is the most effective tool. By reducing the amount of energy wasted through leaky buildings, leaky pipes, and extravagant urban transport, we can decrease our reliance on carbon-liberating fuels, and the amount of air and water we pollute. And we do not have to substantially change our lifestyle to do so.

ENERGY

■ ■ ■

At the World Energy Conference in 1989, it was estimated that if we continued in our present patterns of energy use, by the year 2020 the world would consume 75 percent more energy than at present, and that most of this would come from oil, coal, and nuclear power. This is a forbidding scenario. We would be even more dependent on unstable Middle East governments for oil, and we would be forced to build many more nuclear plants. The amount of greenhouse gases and smog-causing chemicals would increase correspondingly.

Even though a continuation of the business of energy consumption as usual is a guarantee of a grim future, the outlook really is not bleak. We can reduce our dependence on dangerous sources of energy without reverting to a more primitive form of existence, or even making major sacrifices. We simply need to understand our consumption patterns and then select alternatives. Almost all of our energy derives from the sun. Each year our planet is bombarded with 15,000 times the earth's total energy requirements from that source. Thirty percent of this is reflected back into space, 50 percent of it is absorbed, and 20 percent fuels the evaporation of water from the lakes and seas and the precipitation of rain. Of all energy consumed worldwide, 18 percent comes from renewable sources such as firewood, charcoal, and peat, and 4 percent comes from nuclear plants. The rest, 78 percent, comes from fossil fuels. The average consumption of fossil fuel in this country is 40 barrels of oil for every man, woman, and child. In Japan it is 20 barrels. In the poorest countries the mean consumption is 2 barrels per year. We are using fossil fuel at 100,000 times the rate that it is being formed, and we are faced with a time not too far off when these supplies will be exhausted.

Generally there are two responses to this crisis. The first is to deprecate or ignore it and rely on the faith that technology will someday supply a solution. The second response is to call for reduced fuel consumption. This alternative is not an impossible or even a difficult task. Indeed, many industries have learned that fuel consumption can be reduced without penalty, and profits can be increased.

It is not generally appreciated that energy efficiency in this country has increased substantially in the past twenty years. Only a few years ago, experts were estimating that conservation could save 5 to 10 percent of energy consumption. In fact, we have decreased our consumption 24 to 44 percent, and we have just begun. Easy forms of energy conservation include the use of more efficient lighting schemes and of better motors and appliances. A number of hotel chains have learned that through installing low-energy lights and using rather than wasting heat generated by other processes, they can save hundreds of thousands of dollars per year.

A considerable amount of electricity can be conserved immediately through the use of compact fluorescent lamps. Electricity expenditures for lighting can be reduced 80 to 90 percent. The average household expends about $1,500 dollars per year for energy; about 23 percent, or $350, is used for lighting. Although these low-energy lamps are quite expensive initially, they pay for themselves in reduced electric bills in two to three years, and last ten times as long as the average incandescent bulb. The return to the consumer is perhaps $50 per unit over the lifetime of the lamp. In a single warehouse, Johnson & Johnson reduced their lighting costs by $14,000 per year by installing low-energy fixtures.

Industrial motors consume 60 to 70 percent of industrial electricity. New efficient motors can reduce consumption as much as 50 percent. Modern refrigerators consume 80 percent less electricity than their older counterparts.

Home energy conservation is an important area that has quick payoffs for the individual and for the planet as well. Buildings in the United States consume 36 percent of our energy budget and cost $200 billion per year. They generate 500 million tons of CO_2 per year. Energy efficiency could reduce CO_2 emissions by 50 percent and save $100 billion per year within twenty years.

Perhaps the quickest fix is insulation. This can pay for itself in about three years and represents a 30 percent return on the investment per year. Replacement of inefficient home heaters can save $35 for every $100 dollars in heating costs. There are many other simple steps that can be taken to reduce energy consumption without reducing our lifestyle at all. Hot-water heaters can be insulated for a pittance. Setback thermostats lower the temperature at night or when the house is empty and bring it up before you get up. Simply wearing a sweater instead of cranking up the thermostat is a healthy way to reduce consumption.

OZONE

■ ■ ■

Ozone is a gas consisting of three oxygen molecules. It has vastly different impacts on our health depending on where it is located. Ozone in the breathing zone, as discussed in Chapter 11, is toxic to human tissue. Ozone in the stratosphere serves to screen out ultraviolet radiation from the sun and protect us from the cancer-producing effects of these rays.

The high ozone layer is being damaged by synthetic products produced on earth. Chlorofluorocarbons (CFCs), chemicals that are used as aerosol propellants and in refrigerators, as insulating foam, and as degreasers in the electronic industry, rise to this level in the atmosphere. There, under ultraviolet radiation, the CFCs release chlorine. This in turn attacks and breaks down ozone, allowing ultraviolet radiation to penetrate through the ozone layer. CFC levels have risen rapidly in the past decades, and the ozone layer has as a result been severely damaged.

Recognizing the global threats from CFC releases into the ozone layer, a number of countries have agreed to reduce CFC use in aerosols. The goal is to decrease CFC production by 50 percent by the year 2000. This is a positive step, if a tentative one.

The single biggest contributor to CFC emissions is leaky automobile air conditioners. You can play a preventive part in improving this problem by using only repair shops that recycle CFCs and by not attempting to refill your air conditioner yourself. Newer automobile air conditioners are less damaging to the ozone. You can also write to your congressman asking for the most rigorous enforcement of the Clean Air Act and a higher tax on ozone-emitting chemicals.

DEFORESTATION

■ ■ ■

One-third of the earth's surface is covered by forest. Trees are vital to our existence as we know it. They provide cooling shade, slow erosion, take up CO_2 and pollutants, furnish food, fuel, building materials, and some medicines. At present, we are destroying trees to make room for cattle grazing, farming, mining, and development. In addition, the impact of acid rain and other pollutants is accelerating the process. The poorest of the world's population need firewood for heating and cooking. They are destroying rain forests at a rate much faster than the forests can regenerate.

In this country, federal lands are licensed to lumber companies who clear-cut entire forests, instead of selecting trees for harvesting. This harmful activity is subsidized by federal tax dollars. The government also builds the roads into these areas to allow the easy removal of the timber, another form of environmental damage. Taxpayers underwrite the management of these resources and then lose both the resources and the tax dollars.

Lumber companies want clear-cutting of timber because it is faster, allows the use of heavy machinery, and maximizes profit. The American taxpayer and then the entire world pay the price through the loss of trees' ecologic function. The timber industry also prizes huge straight-grained old trees. These historic hardwoods, which will take centuries to replace, are being turned into timber and plywood. When a clear-cut forest is reseeded, the old hardwood trees are replaced by fast-growing softwood species, arranged in neat rows for easy cultivation. This is the way that the face of our country is being reshaped to suit the convenience of timber interests.

There is a strong and growing reforestation movement. The annual cost of replanting would be about $2.4 billion. The United Nations, the World Bank, and others are participating in an international effort to restore the world's forests. There is convincing evidence that local reforestation is more effective than large-scale proprietary efforts.

WATER

■ ■ ■

When most of us turn on our kitchen tap, we expect clean, fresh water; we do not even think about it. This is not the case for most nations: more than half of the world does not have access to potable water. We have no reason to be complacent about our situation. It is changing, and not for the better. Our confidence in the purity of our water was shaken when the city of Milwaukee had an epidemic of bacterial contamination in 1993.

Half of our drinking water is supplied by surface waters (lakes, streams, ponds, and reservoirs) and half from groundwater (wells, springs, and aquifers). Increasing amounts of pesticides, solvents, and chloroform derivatives are showing up in our water. There are an estimated 2 million underground oil and gasoline tanks in the United States, 10,000 of which are leaking petroleum products. Additional sources of pollution are agricultural runoff, with pesticides, fertilizers, bacterial and organic wastes, and road salt and PCBs from industrial sources. We can no longer afford to use our rivers and lakes as dumps.

Groundwater as well as surface water is affected. The great Ogallala Aquifer, which extends from South Dakota to Texas, has been drawn down substantially by extensive irrigation of arid areas. A visit to a naturally dry area that has been turned into a resort by diverting enormous quantities of water from rivers and changing the ecosystem is a sobering experience. As you watch people swim in pools, play golf on irrigated grass, and hear the constant hum of air conditioners, you are eventually forced to think of the huge energy costs and environmental penalties, while just a few miles away the desert is waiting to reclaim the entire area. This is not only a problem for the West. The cultivation of lawns all over the country, a relatively new phenomenon, has used enormous amounts of water, energy, and pesticides, while depriving many species of their natural habitat.

There has, however, been some notable progress in improving the state of our waters. The Great Lakes, which contain one-fifth of the earth's surface fresh water, have had a severe pollution problem from industrial toxins and phosphate detergents. Over the past decade, bans on phosphate detergents, and improved sewage treatment have reduced the input of phosphate into the lakes, so that Lake Erie is now once again able to support the growth of fish and other living things.

WHY HAVE WE ALLOWED THIS DAMAGE TO OUR PLANET TO PROCEED THIS FAR?

■ ■ ■

Haven't enough environmental scientists warned us, and isn't there an abundance of evidence that we are heading for increasingly serious and possibly irreversible health and economic problems? Why, then, is our environment still being assaulted? We need to look without flinching at the reasons that have worked to hide the truth from us, or hide us from the truth. If we do, there is hope that we will take the hard steps toward building a sane relationship with our planet.

Civilized people see themselves as separate from nature. We have been taught that the natural world exists to be conquered, and that we are set apart from nature's strictures. This instruction is clear in Genesis: "Be fruitful and multiply, and replenish the earth and subdue it, and have dominion . . . over every living thing that moveth upon the earth." For too long, we willingly believed that the world's value lies mainly in its utility, that nature is a storehouse of raw materials waiting to be refined and developed.

Tied to this is another perilous belief: that our technology can conquer any problem, and it is almost always beneficent. We are taught that when we convert a natural substance into a product, we have created wealth. This is why we are here, and it is good. At the same time, we see nature either as a danger "red in tooth and claw" which must be tamed or as a problem. We believe that our scientists and engineers can solve any problem, given the time and money, and so why bother with the restrictions that developing a sustainable society might impose?

We require training in order to make decent estimates of risks to us from our environment. If a risk is not personally perceived, it is felt as remote and less threatening. Global warming only triggers a response when we have personal experience with it, such as the summer of 1988. Similarly, the risk to health from toxins that do not make us immediately and dramatically sick is perceived as low. The watery eyes and irritation in our lungs from sulfur dioxide can be pushed aside as we think about more pressing concerns. It becomes easy for our bodies and minds to adjust to the gradual increase in the intensity of threats to our health.

ECONOMICS OF ENVIRONMENTAL DEGRADATION

■ ■ ■

We must rely on reason to inform us of the level of risk posed by pollution. The best way to do this would be to attach a value to our resources and pin a realistic cost to their degradation. If this were done, then just as we make choices when we shop by balancing the need for a particular good against its cost, we could put these costs into our calculations and keep a running record of our national expenditures and wealth.

This obviously is the job of economists, who keep track of our national wealth and provide us with numerous indices of how we are doing. But few economists are concerned with the environment. This is largely due to the lack of any method of including our natural resources in calculations of our wealth or gross national product. With no metric for this important component of our bounty, economists tend to dismiss or forget it.

There is a reason that natural resources have not been counted in calculations of national product. When eighteenth-century neoclassical economists began to develop their theories of wealth, they saw the supply of raw materials as limitless. Neoclassical economists virtually ignored natural resources and focused their theories on the roles of labor and capital. And when we compute our gross national product, we ignore the state of our natural resources.

Robert Repetto, an economist with the World Resources Institute, gives an example of how this omission can mislead us: If a farmer cuts timber from his woodlot to build a barn, he will count the barn as a new asset in his private accounts and will also subtract the loss of raw timber. His accounts will show both an increase in wealth for the barn and a corresponding reduction for the loss of natural resources. Our government accounting handles this transaction differently. The barn will be counted as an increase in goods. But no loss of timber will be shown on the books. In this way our national wealth is distorted. Obviously a country with ample forests and pure water is economically better off than the same place after the forests have been cleared and the lakes poisoned, even if the books and annual statistical reports don't show it. What is missing is a way to attach a meaningful value for these resources to an estimation of wealth or evaluation of any plan to exploit them.

There is a cost for cutting timber, even if no one writes a check at that moment. If there were a national policy to clear-cut timber and this led to erosion and flooding, somewhere, sometime, someone would pay for it. If the residents were forced to move, their resettlement costs would be attributable to the clear-cutting and should be attached to it. If flooding resulted, the costs of repairing the damage would be a cost of cutting the timber.

Economists call costs of this type "externalities," and the process of attaching them to another agent "externalizing the cost." This is a somewhat astringent way of saying that someone else is paying for the damage. When we calculate the cost of a barrel of oil, we do not add in the cost of the Persian Gulf War. The cost may have been as high as $80 billion, or $23 per barrel of oil. But that cost shows up in the military budget and our deficit, not at the pump. It is "externalized" onto the defense budget, and instead of paying for it at the gas station, we pay for it when we pay our income tax. And we forget that it was part of the cost of "cheap" gasoline.

Another example: Let us say that the cost of manufacturing a battery without attention to the spread of lead in the factory air or in the community is $15. And let us say that the cost of making a battery in absolutely safe conditions is $25. The cost for safety is obviously $10. If the workers and neighbors pay the cost in terms of impaired health, part of the cost for manufacturing the battery is said to be externalized onto the workers and neighbors. They are the ones who will pay for it in increased neurologic and other illnesses, in medical and funeral costs.

One can readily see that externalizing costs dangerously misleads an individual or a society. And attaching the costs to the proper source could be a powerful drive toward sane environmental policies.

The progress of a civilization can to some degree be measured by how well it has internalized the costs of production. There were societies that externalized the costs of labor—they held slaves. Internalizing the costs of an educated workforce resulted in public education. Internalizing the costs of workplace safety led to regulation, compensation, and insurance; externalizing it led to sweatshops and child labor.

Internalizing costs is not a simple task. It depends heavily on the values of the group. What is the value of a human life? Of healthy air, of a beautiful horizon? Some economists have strained to rationalize this process, and much work remains to be done. But recognizing when a cost has been externalized is the first and most important step toward a sustainable society.

If our gross national product had a measure for the use and restoration of our natural resources, we would have a more accurate accounting of the state of our wealth. We could all then make more informed and healthy decisions about the use of resources. There are people working to develop such a system of accounting.

WHAT MUST WE DO?

■ ■ ■

Some things are clear. We must begin by understanding that there are real costs that we pay for pollution, even if they are not printed on each object's price tag. They are often attached to something or someone else. We need to "internalize" these costs and then consider them when making decisions. Our gross national product must be redesigned to include these costs and assets. This single step would have profound consequences for our national policies. We would know where we stand.

We badly need both national and international environmental policies. We need a deliberative national debate among our leaders, industry, scientists, and an informed public that will set these policies. In this way we can examine and destroy the noxious myth that we must choose between environmental protection and a sound economy. The jobs-or-owls debate is phony.

Then we can define the steps needed to accomplish national and international goals. If we develop national policies, we could use the federal government to stimulate the development of means to achieve our designated goals. If, for example, policy directed that electric cars were a positive step in reducing air pollution, the government, through its fleet purchases of vehicles, could stimulate the electric car industry, accelerate research in this area, and thus lower the costs of batteries and electric cars. Similarly, an environmental policy would act as a rational brake on harmful government subsidies for clear-cutting of timber, grazing on federal lands, and overuse of pesticides in agriculture.

An international environmental policy would steer the World Bank away from its current tendency to give loans to underdeveloped countries that stimulate the importing of manufactured goods from developed countries. Instead more loans would be granted to stimulate indigenous conservation of resources and the development of self-sufficiency in those countries.

An international environmental policy would place population control near the top of its agenda. There simply is no possibility of a decent life or healthy environment if the world's population continues to grow at its current rate. Poverty is a spur to population growth, and large families continue and extend the cycle of poverty. Education and a chance at a decent standard of living are the best incentives to control the number of offspring in a family.

It is clear that these rather dramatic departures from business as usual require a change in vision as much as new science or laws. There are signs that this is happening, and that increasing force is growing behind the need to build a sustainable as opposed to a consumer society. We believe this is a healthy trend, not just for the health of the environment but for individual health and happiness as well. It begins with individual changes in awareness.

Earlier in this chapter, we suggested that you examine your life and your children's. In Appendix 1 we present a household checklist for evaluating the health status of your residence. A similar inventory of one's personal status could be useful. Because that is a unique and private task, we will not furnish an exhaustive list of questions. But here are a few to challenge you: How much are your own wants or goals set by the advertising industry? What would happen to your life if you reduced your consumption by 15 percent? Suppose you reduced the number of cars in the family, kept them longer, watched less television, owned fewer television sets, and freed yourself from the tyranny of the annual fashion shuffle. What would your life be like? Would it be less interesting; would you laugh less?

APPENDICES

APPENDIX 1
THE HOUSEHOLD INVENTORY*

HOUSEHOLD QUESTIONNAIRE

■ ■ ■

THE HOUSE/THE APARTMENT

1. How old is your house?

1. Almost all homes built before 1945 contain leaded paint. If paint is intact and is not flaking, peeling, or chalking, it does not present a current risk.

2. Are there surfaces with peeling paint?

2. If surfaces are peeling or flaking, the paint should be tested and then removed by an experienced contractor. The improper removal of paint can increase the amount of lead in the dust of the home and sicken workers and residents. When lead paint is being re-

This appendix is based on material developed by Sophie Balk, M.D., Assistant Professor of Pediatrics, Albert Einstein College of Medicine. The original material appeared in the manual "Kids and the Environment—Toxic Hazards," edited by the Children's Environmental Health Network, California Public Health Foundation. The sponsors for this project were the Agency for Toxic Substances and Disease Registry and the California Department of Health Services.

moved, residents should be relocated, the rooms being treated should be isolated, and no one should move back in until the area has been cleaned thoroughly and tested for safety.

3. Are the windowsills peeling?
4. Do the window wells contain solid material?

3.–4. Windowsills and window wells are often sites of high lead content.

5. Is the plumbing more than 40 years old?
6. Is the plumbing less than 5 years old?
7. Do you have lead pipes?
8. Has your water been tested for lead?

5.–8. Older homes are more likely to have lead pipes and newer homes may have lead in the water supply due to leaded solder joints that have not had a chance to be coated by dissolved minerals.

9. Do you have a basement?
10. Are the basement pipes insulated?

9.–10. If the pipes are insulated, the insulation may contain asbestos.

11. Are any of the ceilings covered with sprayed-on or troweled-on material?

11. These substances have in the past contained asbestos.

12. Are there sleeping or playing areas in the basement?

12. Basements are the site of radon entry into the home. Basement bedrooms or playrooms increase exposure time to radon if it is present.

13. Are there cracks in the basement floor?
Walls?
Gaps between basement ceiling and walls?

13. Cracks or gaps provide entry to radon gas. They can be readily and inexpensively repaired.

14. Do you have one or more working fireplaces?
Does smoke enter the room when you use it?

14. Fireplaces that are inadequately ventilated are sources of indoor air pollution.

15. Do you have a wood-burning stove? Is it properly vented?

15. Wood-burning stoves must be adequately vented or they can introduce carbon monoxide and other combustion products into the room.

16. Do you have storm windows?

16. Tightly sealed homes may have higher levels of indoor pollutants.

17. Has your house been treated for termites in the past 3 years?

18. Do you know the agent used?

17.–18. You should know the agent used and its toxic properties.

APPLIANCES

19. Do you have a gas stove?

20. Does it have a pilot burner?

21. Do you use it for heat?

19.–21. Natural gas stoves are a source of nitrogen dioxide (NO_2), a respiratory irritant. Stoves with a gas pilot are the worst offenders. If your home has such a pilot, we recommend turning it off and replacing it with a spark pilot or using a butane grill lighter or a match. Gas stoves are dangerous when used to heat the living space.

22. Do you use kerosene space heaters?

22. Kerosene space heaters add combustion products and particulates to the indoor air. Their use should be avoided. Quality electric or oil-filled radiators are nonpolluting.

23. Do you use a gas clothes dryer?

23. Gas clothes dryers should be adequately vented.

24. Do you have hot-air heat?

24. Hot-air heaters should be cleaned and inspected and their filters changed as recommended by the manufacturer.

25. Do you have an electronic air precipitator?

25. Some electronic precipitators can increase the amount of ozone in the residence.

26. Do you have a furnace humidifier?

26. Furnace humidifiers can be sources of airborne bacteria.

GROUNDS

27. Do you use pesticides on your lawn?

28. Do you use a proprietary lawn pesticide service?

27.–28. Some pesticides are neurotoxic; some are carcinogens. Attractive lawns can be had without wholesale use of these toxins. We do not recommend the use of proprietary lawn services.

CHEMICALS

29. Do you store pesticides in the house?

30. When you are through with them, do you dispose of them through a hazardous waste facility?

29.–30. Do not store pesticides in the house. Buy only as much as you need, and dispose of the rest in an environmentally safe manner.

31. Do you keep old prescription drugs in the medicine cabinet?

31. Dispose of old prescription drugs.

32. Do you keep motor oil or gasoline in the house or garage?

33. Do you keep solvents such as alcohol, toluene, dry-cleaning, or degreasing materials in the house?

32.–33. These products should not be stored in the house, or in the garage if it is attached to the house. They are sources of indoor air pollutants.

34. Is your home insulated? Do you know what type of insulation?

34. Formaldehyde is a component of urea-formaldehyde blown-in foam insulation. It can cause eye and respiratory irritation. If you have such insulation, or these symptoms, you may want to test your air

for formaldehyde. EMSYS/Air Quality Research, P.O. Box 14063, Research Triangle Park, NC 27709, sells a home monitor.

SMOKING

35. Does anyone in the house smoke?

36. How many people?

37. What is the total number of packs consumed per day?

38. When driving with children, does anyone smoke in the car?

35.–38. The most important cause of indoor air pollution is smoking. Smoke-free homes breed healthier, smarter children.

HOBBIES

39. Are the following hobbies practiced in the home?
Making fishing weights?
Making self-loading bullets?
Making stained-glass windows?
Making pottery?
Making jewelry?

39. These hobbies can release heavy metals or solvents into the air that are toxic to the hobbyist and others in the home. They should be carried out only in well-ventilated areas, away from children, and the hobbyist should change his or her clothes before entering the home.

40. Do you use any of the following products: toilet-bowl cleaners, room deodorizers, polishes, varnishes, or paint thinners?

40. The use of these products should be minimized. They should be stored outside the home.

APPENDIX 2 MAJOR ENVIRONMENTAL ORGANIZATIONS IN THE UNITED STATES

The following list presents information on just a few of the better-known national and regional public-interest organizations. In most cases the descriptions of their activities were provided by the organizations themselves. Many have offices or chapters in cities across the United States, and will be listed in local telephone directories. They can be an important source of information on environmental hazards in your area and can provide seasoned support for organizing efforts to control toxic environmental hazards.

Poison-control centers are a particularly important resource for parents. Frequently they are staffed by pediatricians or pediatric nurses. They are knowledgeable about acute toxic exposures and ingestions. Often they also have information on chronic exposures and environmental hazards to children, and they provide referrals for specialized advice. They are usually listed at the front of your local telephone directory.

Children's hospitals, medical schools, and schools of public health are increasingly likely to have persons available on their staffs who are knowledgeable about environmental hazards to children. In seeking advice from these organizations, parents should ask for the department of either environmental health or preventive medicine.

ALLIANCE TO END CHILDHOOD LEAD POISONING

227 Massachusetts Avenue NE, Suite 200
Washington, DC 20002
202-543-1147
Fax: 202-543-4466

The Alliance is a national nonprofit public-interest organization created to launch a comprehensive attack on the epidemic of childhood lead poisoning. The Alliance was formed in 1990 by national leaders in pediatrics, public health, environmental protection, low-income housing, education, minority rights, and children's welfare.

The Alliance's mission is to bring all resources to bear—other organizations, scientific and technical knowledge, public policy, economic forces and community action—to raise awareness and change perceptions about childhood lead poisoning and to develop and implement effective national prevention programs.

HAZARDS/ISSUES ADDRESSED:
- Education
- Policy support
- Technical assistance and advocacy to reduce lead in the environment of children

AMERICAN ACADEMY OF PEDIATRICS

141 Northwest Point Boulevard
Elk Grove Village, IL 60009-0927
1-800-433-9016
708-228-5005
Fax: 708-228-5097

The American Academy of Pediatrics is the principal professional organization of pediatricians in the United States, Canada, and Latin America. It was founded in 1930 and has 40,000 members in 66 state and local chapters that span the Americas.

Since its inception the Academy has been a major advocate for the health of children and a guiding force and source of strength for pediatric physicians. It has established standards of practice for many issues in child health, including immunization, nutrition, control of infectious diseases, injury prevention, and poison control.

The Academy's Committee on Environmental Health is a major resource to pediatricians and other medical care providers concerning environmental hazards to children.

PUBLICATIONS:
Pediatrics—monthly professional journal
AAP News
Newsletters, guides, and handbooks on specific issues and problems in child health

THE AMERICAN CANCER SOCIETY

1599 Clifton Road NE
Atlanta, GA 30329
404-329-7686

The American Cancer Society is dedicated to the prevention of cancer from all causes, including environmental causes. Volunteers in communities nationwide participate in collecting health data from their friends and neighbors. Regional offices coordinate assistance for patients with cancer (mainly transportation for treatment) and promote education in the awareness of early signs of disease. The ACS conducts educational programs for doctors and members of the public on the prevention, early detection, and treatment of cancer.

TYPES OF ACTIVITY:
Health effects/risk assessment
Education of consumers or employees
Education of professionals and/or business managers

PUBLICATIONS:
Cancer Facts and Figures—annual report

AMERICAN LUNG ASSOCIATION

Environmental Health
1726 M Street NW, Suite 902
Washington, DC 20036-4502
202-785-3355

The American Lung Association (ALA), the nation's oldest voluntary health organization, is committed to fighting lung disease and to the promotion of lung health.

Since the early 1980s, the ALA has embarked on a program utilizing its network of local lung associations to inform the public about the sources, health effects, and control strategies for a variety of indoor pollutants, including pollutants contained in household and office products, and building materials. It is preparing a booklet for physicians to help them determine whether indoor air quality problems may be causing specific cases of illness. The ALA has developed a variety of print and audiovisual materials related to indoor air quality in homes and buildings. The ALA is also working to ensure the passage of federal legislation that requires adequate federal support for research on indoor air pollutants and their health effects, support for enhanced public information programs, and, where necessary, regulatory controls.

HAZARDS/ISSUES ADDRESSED:

- Outdoor air pollution and smog
- Indoor air pollution from consumer products and building materials

PUBLICATIONS:

Air Pollution in Your Home (1990, 12 pp.)
Indoor Air Pollution Fact Sheet: Household Products (1986, 4 pp.)
Indoor Air Pollution in the Office (1987, 12 pp.)
Toxic Chemicals in the Air: Indoors and Outdoors (1986, 6 pp.)

AMERICAN PUBLIC HEALTH ASSOCIATION

1015 15th Street NW
Washington, DC 20005
202-789-5650

The American Public Health Association is the world's largest organization of public health professionals with 55,000 members. It is concerned with a broad set of issues affecting personal and environmental health. It represents these concerns and provides expert testimony to the U.S. Congress and government agencies. Through its Environmental Section, it promotes cooperation among health disciplines to protect the environment and helps to shape national environmental health policies. Its Occupational Health and Safety Section promotes a healthy and safe working environment.

HAZARDS/ISSUES ADDRESSED:

- Indoor air pollution from consumer products and building materials
- Home pesticides
- Household poisonings
- Smog formation due to volatile organics
- Environmental illness
- Household hazardous waste

PUBLICATIONS:

Methods for Biological Monitoring: A Manual for Assessing Human Exposure to Hazardous Substances

American Journal of Public Health (publishes peer-reviewed original works covering all aspects of public health science and practice)

The Nation's Health—monthly report on policy issues and government activities

Policy papers on indoor air pollution, home pesticides, smog, and environmental illness

Numerous other books, monographs, and reports (publications catalogue is available upon request)

CENTER FOR SAFETY IN THE ARTS, INC.

Art Safety Information
5 Beekman Street, Room 1030
New York, NY 10038
212-227-6220

The Center for Safety in the Arts is a national clearinghouse for research and education on hazards in the visual arts, performing arts, educational facilities, and museums. The CSA has a variety of programs offering assistance in finding out about hazards in the arts and what to do about them. These programs include: The Art Hazards Information Center, *The Art Hazards News* (a four-page newsletter), educational programs, and consultation programs.

Well-known industrial diseases caused by hazardous chemicals, unfortunately, are also found among artists, craftspeople, theater technicians, museum conservators, teachers, and sometimes even children who are using art and craft materials without adequate precautions. In many instances, the users of these art and craft materials do not even know that they are using hazardous chemicals.

Performing artists—actors, dancers, musicians, singers—also experience a wide variety of occupational illnesses and injuries. Most of these art-related injuries and illnesses can be prevented through education about the causes of the problems and following suitable precautions. The Center for Safety in the Arts can help provide this education through its various programs.

HAZARDS/ISSUES ADDRESSED:

- Indoor air pollution
- Home pesticides
- Household poisonings
- Smog formation due to volatile organics
- Environmental illness

PUBLICATIONS:
The Art Hazards News—newsletter

A comprehensive listing of books, pamphlets, articles, and data sheets on health hazards in art-related fields is available upon request.

CHILDREN'S ENVIRONMENTAL HEALTH NETWORK

5900 Hollis Street, Suite E
Emeryville, CA 94608
510-540-3657
FAX: 510-540-2673

The Children's Environmental Health Network is a national multidisciplinary and multicultural project focusing on the prevention of childhood exposures to environmental hazards.

GOALS:

- to make pediatric environmental health a routine component of primary care for children and to emphasize prevention and early diagnosis of environment-related illness in children
- to stimulate research on the health effects of environmental exposures on children

BACKGROUND:
The Children's Environmental Health Network was founded in 1989 to educate California health practitioners about pediatric environmental health. Early involvement of the pediatrician and other primary care providers is crucial for prevention of environment-related diseases in children. However, health practitioners do not routinely receive training in environmental health in medical education.

To fill this gap in medical training, the Network has been vigorously involved in organizing seminars, symposia, and courses for health practitioners and in developing teaching materials for pediatricians, nurses, and parents.

PUBLICATIONS:
Kids and the Environment: Toxic Hazards Manual. This manual was first developed as part of the physicians training course on pediatric environmental health.

CITIZENS CLEARINGHOUSE FOR HAZARDOUS WASTE

P.O. Box 6806
Falls Church, VA 22040
703-237-2249

The Citizens Clearinghouse for Hazardous Waste (CCHW) is the only national environmental organization started and led by grass-roots leaders. The CCHW was founded in 1981 by Love Canal leader Lois Gibbs. Love Canal taught that the best policy comes from the bottom up, from grass-roots efforts when the people who are most directly affected speak for themselves. While other groups lobby for changes in national and state policy, the CCHW directs all of its energies and resources toward helping people work effectively at the local level.

HAZARDS/ISSUES ADDRESSED:

- Indoor air pollution from consumer products and building materials
- Home pesticides
- Household poisonings
- Smog formation due to volatile organics
- Environmental illness
- Household hazardous waste

PUBLICATIONS:

Fact Packs on household hazardous waste and on lawn care and pesticides
Drinking Water Filters: What You Need to Know

CONCERN, INC.

1794 Columbia Road NW
Washington, DC 20009
202-328-8160

CONCERN is a nonprofit, tax-exempt organization founded in 1970. It provides environmental information to community groups, public officials, educational institutions, private individuals, and many others involved in public education and policy development. Its primary goal is to help communities find solutions to environmental problems that threaten public health and the quality of their lives. To this end, CONCERN's primary activity is the development, publication, and distribution of "community action guides," which define major issues, explain relevant legislation, describe successful regional, state, and local initiatives, give resource information, and recommend specific action guidelines.

HAZARDS/ISSUES ADDRESSED:

- Home pesticides
- Household poisonings
- Household hazardous waste

PUBLICATIONS:

Household Waste: Issues and Opportunities (1989, 30 pp.)
Waste: Choices for Communities (1988, 30 pp.)

CONSUMERS UNION OF THE UNITED STATES
101 Truman Avenue
Yonkers, NY 10703
914-378-2000

Consumers Union is actively involved in health effects/risk assessment, identification and development of nontoxic alternatives or substitutes, legislation-lobbying, public policy research, education of consumers or employees, and litigation.

Consumers Union is a nonprofit organization established in 1936 to provide consumers with information and advice on goods, services, health, and personal finance; and to initiate and cooperate with individual and group efforts to maintain and enhance the quality of life for consumers.

HAZARDS/ISSUES ADDRESSED:

- Indoor air pollution from consumer products and building materials
- Home pesticides
- Household poisonings
- Smog formation due to volatile organics
- Environmental illness
- Household hazardous waste
- Recycling

PUBLICATIONS:

Action Kit: Lead Hazards and Children (1983)
Citizens Guide to Biotechnology (1990)
Consumer Reports—monthly magazine rating products and services
Is Your Water Safe to Drink? (1988, 390 pp.)
Radon: A Homeowner's Guide to Detection and Control (1987, 370 pp.)

ENVIRONMENTAL DEFENSE FUND
1616 P Street NW
Washington, DC 20036
202-387-3500

The Environmental Defense Fund is one of the major national environmental organizations in the United States. Founded in 1967 to achieve the banning of DDT spraying on Long Island, the EDF's 200,000 members are active and independent in their support of activities that include health effect/risk assessment; legislation-lobbying; public policy research; education of consumers and employees; litigation.

HAZARDS/ISSUES ADDRESSED:
Indoor air pollution from consumer products and building materials
Home pesticides
Household poisonings
Smog formation due to volatile organics
Environmental illness
Household hazardous waste

PUBLICATIONS:
Membership newsletter
Numerous books (list available upon request) on toxins including acid rain, biotechnology, energy policy, environmental toxins, global warming, ozone depletion, solid waste, recycling, and water policy

ENVIRONMENTAL HEALTH NETWORK, INC.
Great Bridge Station
P.O. Box 16267
Chesapeake, VA 23328-6267
804-424-1517

A grass-roots organization that links up with other environmental groups. It focuses on toxicants, air pollution, and occupational health.

ENVIRONMENTAL LAW INSTITUTE
1616 P Street NW, Suite 200
Washington, DC 20036
202-939-3800

The Environmental Law Institute's goals include advancing environmental protection by improving law management and policy. It educates professionals and citizens, and arranges meetings of all stakeholders to work out solutions.

PUBLICATIONS:
Environmental Law Reporter
Environmental Forum
National Wetlands Newsletter

FRIENDS OF THE EARTH
218 D Street SE
Washington, DC 20003
202-544-2600

Friends of the Earth espouses nonviolent action to protect natural resources.

PUBLICATION:
Friends of the Earth—magazine

GREENPEACE
1436 U Street NW
Washington, DC 20009
202-462-1177

Members of Greenpeace are conservationists who believe that verbal protests against threats to environmental quality are not adequate. Initiates active, though nonviolent, measures to aid endangered species. Monitors conditions of environmental concern, including the greenhouse effect, radioactive and toxic waste dumping, and a comprehensive test ban for nuclear weapons. Conducts research and lobbying efforts and media campaigns. Maintains a speakers' bureau.

HAZARDS/ISSUES ADDRESSED:
Industrial threats to marine life
Degradation of the environment
Health effects of environmental pollution

PUBLICATION:
Greenpeace—quarterly

INFORM, INC.
381 Park Avenue South
New York, NY 10016
212-689-4040

Founded in 1974, INFORM is a national, nonprofit environmental research and education organization that identifies and reports on practical ways to improve the environment and public health. Recent activities in the field of toxics in products include a directory of organizations concerned about problems of toxic chemicals in products and current case study research on corporate efforts to develop and market less toxic products.

Decisions made by business, government, environmental, and community leaders across the United States inevitably affect the health of our country's environment. These decisions need to be based on accurate, thoughtful information on key land, water, and air quality problems facing our industrialized society. Most essentially, decision makers need facts on those realistic practices that could solve environmental problems.

HAZARDS/ISSUES ADDRESSED:
- Indoor air pollution from consumer products and building materials
- Home pesticides
- Household poisonings
- Smog formation due to volatile organics
- Environmental illness
- Household hazardous waste

PUBLICATIONS:
Tackling Toxics in Everyday Products: A Directory of Organizations (1992)
Burning Garbage in the U.S.
Reducing Office Paper Waste
Business Recycling Manual
Cutting Chemical Wastes
A Citizen's Guide to Promoting Toxic Waste Reduction
INFORM Reports—quarterly newsletter

LEAGUE OF CONSERVATION VOTERS
1707 L Street NW
Washington, DC 20036
202-785-8683

The League monitors the voting behavior of Congress.

PUBLICATIONS:
Greengram—newsletter
LCV National Environmental Scorecard

LEAGUE OF WOMEN VOTERS EDUCATION FUND

1730 M Street NW
Washington, DC 20036
202-429-1965

The League of Women Voters is a nonpartisan, political organization that encourages the informed and active participation of citizens in government and influences public policy through education and advocacy.

The League's tax-deductible Education Fund provides nonpartisan services to voters, as well as balanced and objective information on topics of concern.

HAZARDS/ISSUES ADDRESSED: House pesticides
Household poisonings
Household hazardous waste

PUBLICATIONS:
Household Hazardous Waste: A Guide to Detoxifying Your Home (1989, 89 pp.)
America's Growing Dilemma: Pesticides in Food and Water (1989, 20 pp.)
Crosscurrents: The Water We Drink (1989, 18 pp.)
Groundwater: A Citizens Guide (1986, 24 pp.)

MOTHERS & OTHERS FOR A LIVABLE PLANET

40 West 20th Street
New York, NY 10011
212-727-4474
Fax: 212-675-6481

Mothers & Others for a Livable Planet is a national organization devoted to helping parents act on their concerns about environmental issues affecting the health of their children, particularly the overuse of pesticides in food production.

Mothers & Others has been working on the issue of pesticides and food safety since early 1989. That year, the Natural Resources Defense

Council published an influential report, "Intolerable Risk: Pesticides in Our Children's Food," which documented how children were being legally exposed to pesticides in their diets at levels above what the government itself considered safe. Concerned about the information in that report, actress Meryl Streep and some of her neighbors in a small Connecticut town organized the first local Mothers & Others group to start educating themselves about pesticides in food. Inspired by that effort, the NRDC created the national Mothers & Others Project, which made the information in the "Intolerable Risk" report accessible to the general public.

Mothers & Others is currently working to build public support to change the food production system in this country by reducing reliance on pesticides and to ensure a safer food supply and to better protect the environment, the health of farmers and farmworkers, and the long-term productivity of American farmland. Mother & Others has launched a major consumer education campaign to focus consumer demand on safer food.

PUBLICATION:
The Way We Grow: Common-Sense Solutions for Protecting Our Families from Pesticides in Foods.

THE MOUNT SINAI–IRVING J. SELIKOFF OCCUPATIONAL HEALTH CENTER

5 East 98th Street, 12th Floor
New York, NY 10029
212-241-9738

The Mount Sinai–Irving J. Selikoff Occupational Health Center provides medical evaluations for workers who want to know if their health problems may be related to conditions at their job. Services include: assistance in evaluating a workplace and suggesting ways of eliminating dangerous conditions; written information about specific hazards you face at work; advice on how to reduce or eliminate work conditions that are causing problems; educational programs for unions and workers on workplace health issues; help in getting workers' compensation and other available legal benefits; and social work services to help with the social, psychological, and financial problems caused by work-related health problems.

HAZARDS/ISSUES ADDRESSED: Occupational illness and injury
Health effects of work environment
—physical/chemical

NATIONAL AUDUBON SOCIETY
700 Broadway
New York, NY 10003
212-979-3000

One of the oldest and largest environmental organizations, the Audubon Society focuses on issues dealing with natural resources, rivers, wildlife, and forests.

PUBLICATIONS:
Audubon—magazine
Audubon Activist

NATIONAL WILDLIFE FEDERATION
1400 16th Street NW
Washington, DC 20036-2266
202-797-5440

One of the oldest and largest of the environmental organizations, the NWF initially focused on fish and game management and natural resources, but has expanded its agenda to include toxicants, urban environmental issues, sustainable development, and environmental health.

PUBLICATIONS:
National Wildlife
Ranger Rick

NEW YORK COMMITTEE FOR OCCUPATIONAL SAFETY AND HEALTH
275 Seventh Avenue, 8th Floor
New York, NY 10001
212-627-3900

The New York Committee for Occupational Safety and Health, Inc. (NYCOSH), a coalition of activists, professionals, and local labor unions, was founded in 1978 to fight for every worker's right to a safe and healthy job.

The staff helps workers learn how to protect themselves by teaching them about hazards in the workplace—from gasoline fumes and crumbling asbestos to less apparent threats, such as radiation and indoor air pollution.

And to reinforce the struggles of workers in the shops, NYCOSH vigilantly monitors the Occupational Safety and Health Administration, as well as state and local legislative activity, reminding lawmakers that every day an estimated 240 Americans die from on-the-job accidents or job-related illnesses.

By banding local unions together with health professionals and activists, NYCOSH has helped foster a sense of shared goals and accomplishments in the rapidly expanding safety and health movement.

HAZARDS/ISSUES ADDRESSED: Indoor air pollution from consumer products and building materials
Environmental illness
Occupational health and safety

PUBLICATIONS:
Death on the Job (Monthly Review Press, 1984, 276 pp.)
Double Exposure: Women's Health Hazards on the Job and at Home, ed. Wendy Chaukin (Monthly Review Press, 1984, 276 pp.)
Getting Job Hazards Out of the Bedroom: The Handbook on Workplace Hazards to Reproduction (PHILAPOSH, 1988, 66 pp.)
Office Work Can Be Dangerous to Your Health, J. Stellman (Fawcett, 1988)
Ventilation: A Practical Guide (for Artists and Others), N. Clark, T. Cutter, and J. McGrane (Center for Occupational Hazards, 1984, 117 pp.)
Numerous fact sheets are also available upon request.

NATIONAL INSTITUTE OF ENVIRONMENTAL HEALTH SCIENCES

P.O. Box 12233
Research Triangle Park, NC 27709
919-541-3345

NIEHS is a component of the U.S. National Institutes of Health. It is the principal federal agency for biomedical research on the health of environmental agents. Sophisticated new research tools enable NIEHS-funded researchers to look at a broad range of environmentally related diseases. While cancer-related research remains vital to the NIEHS mission, expanded opportunities include studies to examine the effect of environment on reproductive health, neurological and endocrine disorders, immune disorders, respiratory problems, and aging, among others.

HAZARDS/ISSUES ADDRESSED:

- Human health effects of environmental exposures
- Biomarkers
- Reproductive health
- Neuroendocrine/neurodegenerative disorders
- Airways hypersensitivity disorders
- Environmental equity
- Lead poisoning
- Agricultural chemicals
- Air pollution

PUBLICATIONS:

Environmental Health Perspectives—a scientific journal
Monographs
Conference proceedings

NATURAL RESOURCES DEFENSE COUNCIL

40 West 20th Street
New York, NY 10011
212-727-2700

The Natural Resources Defense Council is a public-interest organization involved in health effects/risk assessment; identification or development of nontoxic alternatives or substitutes; legislation-lobbying; public policy research; education of consumers or employees; education of professionals and/or business managers.

HAZARDS/ISSUES ADDRESSED:

- Indoor air pollution from consumer products
- Exposure to home pesticides
- Household poisonings
- Smog formation due to volatile organics
- Environmental illness
- Household hazardous waste
- Effects of chemicals in products on waste treatment technology

PUBLICATION:
The Amicus Journal—quarterly

PHYSICIANS FOR SOCIAL RESPONSIBILITY
1000 16th Street NW
Washington, DC 20036
202-785-3777

Physicians for Social Responsibility began in the 1960s in response to the medical consequences of nuclear warfare. It has been an effective educational and advocacy organization and more recently has broadened its program to include environmental threats to health. It has become influential in informing the medical and legislative communities.

PUBLICATIONS:
PSR Quarterly

SCIENTISTS INSTITUTE FOR PUBLIC INFORMATION
355 Lexington Avenue
New York, NY 10017
212-661-9110

This organization attempts to provide improved communication between scientists and citizens, to foster more informed public opinion and decision making.

PUBLICATION:
SIPIscope—magazine

SIERRA CLUB
730 Polk Street
San Francisco, CA 94109
415-776-2211

The Sierra Club is a national public-interest organization involved in legislation-lobbying; education of consumers or employees; regulation; identification or development of nontoxic alternatives or substitutes.

HAZARDS/ISSUES ADDRESSED:

- Prevention of ecological degradation
- Home pesticides
- Household poisonings
- Household hazardous waste

PUBLICATIONS:

Hazardous Materials/Water Resources Newsletter (quarterly, Sierra Club, 12 pp.)
Sierra—a monthly magazine

UNITED STATES PUBLIC INTEREST RESEARCH GROUP
215 Pennsylvania Avenue SE
Washington, DC 20003
202-546-9707

U.S. PIRG is the national lobbying arm of the state PIRGs, representing more than one million citizens. Nonprofit and nonpartisan, U.S. PIRG investigates problems, educates the public about solutions, and lobbies for reforms that preserve the environment, protect consumers, and renew American democracy.

U.S. PIRG is funded by the individual membership contributions of thousands of citizens across the nation. These funds are used to hire a staff of lawyers, scientists, and other public-interest professionals.

Activities include legislation-lobbying; public policy research; education of professionals and/or business managers; identification or development of nontoxic alternatives or substances.

HAZARDS/ISSUES ADDRESSED:

- Indoor air pollution
- Exposure to home pesticides
- Environmental illness
- Clean water
- Product safety
- Recycling standards

PUBLICATIONS:

The Picture's Getting Brighter All the Time: Recent Improvements in DC Public School Art Room Safety (August 1988)
Not a Pretty Picture: Toxics in Art Supplies in Washington, DC, Area Public Schools (April 1986)

THE WILDERNESS SOCIETY
900 17th Street NW
Washington, DC 20006-2596
202-833-2300

Purposes of the Wilderness Society include the establishment of the land ethic as a basic element of American culture and philosophy, and the education of a broader and more committed wilderness preservation and land protection constituency. Focuses on federal, legislative, and administrative actions affecting public lands, including national forests, parks, and wildlife refuges, and Bureau of Land Management lands. Programs include grassroots organizing, economic analysis, lobbying, research, and public education.

HAZARDS/ISSUES ADDRESSED: Destruction of wildlife habitat
Water pollution

PUBLICATION:
Wilderness—quarterly

WORLD RESOURCES INSTITUTE
1709 New York Avenue NW
Washington, DC 20006
202-638-6300

This organization conducts research on reconciling economic growth with sustaining the environment.

PUBLICATIONS:
Environmental Almanac
World Resources

WORLDWATCH INSTITUTE
1776 Massachusetts Avenue NW
Washington, DC 20036
202-452-1999

This influential organization is involved in the study of global environmental issues.

PUBLICATIONS:
State of the World—annual
Worldwatch—magazine

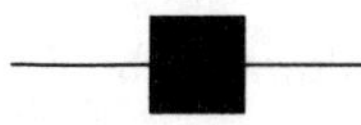

APPENDIX 3
GOVERNMENTAL ORGANIZATIONS

Executive Office, Council on Environmental Quality
202-395-5794

Department of Energy
Office of Assistant Secretary for Environmental Health
202-586-2407

Department of the Interior
Office of Public Affairs
202-208-6416

Department of Labor
Occupational Safety and Health Administration
Office of Public Information and Consumer Affairs
202-523-7075

U.S. Environmental Protection Agency
Communications and Public Affairs
202-260-7963

Consumer Products Safety Commission
202-492-6600

Food and Drug Administration
301-443-5006

Agency for Toxic Substances and Disease Registry
404-639-0700

Centers for Disease Control
Center for Environmental Health and Injury Control
404-488-7300

Senate Subcommittee on Health and the Environment
202-224-6176

House Subcommittee on Health and the Environment
202-225-4952

EPA Regional Offices
Address inquiries to the EPA Regional Offices at the following addresses:

(CT, ME, MA, NH, RI, VT)
EPA Region 1
John F. Kennedy Federal Building
Boston, MA 02203
617-565-3232 (indoor air)
617-565-4502 (radon)
617-565-3744 (asbestos)
617-565-3265 (NESHAP)

(NY, NJ, PR, VI)
EPA Region 2
26 Federal Plaza
New York, NY 10278
212-264-4410 (indoor air)
212-264-4410 (radon)
212-264-6671 (asbestos)
212-264-6770 (NESHAP)

(DE, DC, MD, PA, VA, WV)
EPA Region 2
841 Chestnut Building
Philadelphia, PA 19107
215-597-8322 (indoor air)
215-597-4084 (radon)
215-597-3160 (asbestos)
215-597-1970 (NESHAP)

(AL, FL, GA, KY, MS, NC, SC, TN)
EPA Region 4
345 Courtland Street NE
Atlanta, GA 30365
404-347-2864 (indoor air)
404-347-3907 (radon)

404-347-5014 (asbestos)
404-347-5014 (NESHAP)

(IL, IN, MI, MN, OH, WI)
EPA Region 5
230 South Dearborn Street
Chicago, IL 60604
Region 5 Environmental Hotline:
1-800-572-2515 (IL)
1-800-621-8431 (IN, MI, MN, OH, WI)
312-886-7930 (outside Region 5)

(AR, LA, NM, OK, TX)
EPA Region 6
1445 Ross Avenue
Dallas, TX 75202-2733
214-655-7223 (indoor air)
214-655-7223 (radon)
214-655-7223 (asbestos)
214-655-7223 (NESHAP)

(LA, KS, MO, NE)
EPA Region 7
726 Minnesota Avenue
Kansas City, KS 66101
913-551-7020 (indoor air)
913-551-7020 (radon)
913-551-7020 (asbestos)
913-551-7020 (NESHAP)

(CO, MT, ND, SD, UT, WY)
EPA Region 8
999 18th Street, Suite 500
Denver, CO 80202-2405
303-293-1440 (indoor air)
303-293-0988 (radon)
303-293-1442 (asbestos)
303-294-7611 (NESHAP)

(AZ, CA, HI, NV, AS, GU)
EPA Region 9
75 Hawthorne Street, A-1-1
San Francisco, CA 94105
415-744-1133 (indoor air)
415-744-1045 (radon)

415-744-1136 (asbestos)
415-744-1135 (NESHAP)

(AK, ID, OR, WA)
EPA Region 10
1200 Sixth Avenue
Seattle, WA 98101
206-553-2589 (indoor air)
206-553-7299 (radon)
206-553-4762 (asbestos)
206-553-1757 (NESHAP)

APPENDIX 4
STATE RADON CONTACTS

Alabama 800-582-1866
Alaska 800-478-4845
Arizona 602-255-4845
Arkansas 501-661-2301
California 800-745-7236
Colorado 800-846-3986
Connecticut 203-566-3122
Delaware 800-554-4636
District of Columbia 202-727-5728
Florida 800-543-8279
Georgia 800-745-0037
Hawaii 808-586-4700
Idaho 800-445-8647
Illinois 800-325-1245
Indiana 800-272-9723
Iowa 800-383-5992
Kansas 913-296-1560
Kentucky 507-564-3700
Louisiana 800-256-2494
Maine 800-232-0842
Maryland 800-872-3666
Massachusetts 413-586-7525
Michigan 517-335-8190
Minnesota 800-798-9050
Mississippi 800-626-7739
Missouri 800-669-7236
Montana 406-444-3671
Nebraska 800-334-9491
Nevada 702-687-5394
New Hampshire 800-852-3345 ext. 4674
New Jersey 800-648-0394
New Mexico 505-827-4300
New York 800-458-1158
North Carolina 919-571-4141
North Dakota 701-221-5188
Ohio 800-523-4439
Oklahoma 405-271-5221
Oregon 503-731-4014
Pennsylvania 800-237-2366
Puerto Rico 809-767-3563
Rhode Island 401-277-2438
South Carolina 800-768-0362
South Dakota 605-773-3351
Tennessee 800-232-1139
Texas 512-834-6688
Utah 801-538-6734

Vermont 800-640-0601
Virginia 800-468-0138
Washington 800-323-9727
West Virginia 800-922-1255
Wisconsin 608-267-4795
Wyoming 800-458-5847

For more information on how to reduce your radon health risk, ask your radon office to send you these guides:
Home Buyer's and Seller's Guide to Radon
Radon in Schools
Radon: A Physician's Guide
Consumer's Guide to Radon Reduction
Technical Support Document

If you plan to make repairs yourself, be sure to contact your state radon office (see above) for a current copy of the EPA's technical guidance on radon mitigation, *Application of Radon Reduction Techniques for Detached Houses.*

APPENDIX 5
REFERENCE BOOKS

Samuel Hays. *Beauty, Health and Permanence.* Cambridge, Eng., and New York: Cambridge University Press, 1987. A masterful review of the history of environmental thought.

Lester Brown. *State of the World 1992*, Worldwatch Institute. New York: Norton. Yearly review of environmental topics.

Al Gore. *Earth in the Balance: Ecology and the Human Spirit.* Boston: Houghton Mifflin, 1992. Interesting viewpoint on global environmental issues.

Jeremy Rifkin. *Biosphere Politics.* San Francisco: HarperCollins, 1991.

World Resources Institute. *The 1992 Information Please Environmental Almanac.* Boston: Houghton Mifflin, 1992.

Jon Naar. *Design for a Livable Planet.* New York: Harper & Row, 1990.

Chivian, Eric, Michael McCally, Howard Hu, and Andrew Haines, eds. *Critical Condition: Human Health and the Environment.* Cambridge: MIT Press, 1993.

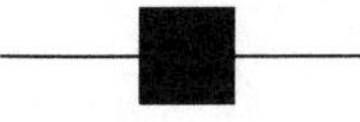

APPENDIX 6
PERIODICALS

The Amicus Journal
Natural Resources Defense Council
40 West 20th Street
New York, NY 10011
Quarterly

Audubon Activist
National Audubon Society
700 Broadway
New York, NY 10003

Environment
1319 18th Street NW
Washington, DC 20036
10 issues per year $48

EPA Journal
Superintendent of Documents
Government Printing Office
Washington, DC 20402
Bimonthly $8

Worldwatch
Worldwatch Institute
1776 Massachusetts Avenue NW
Washington, DC 20036
Bimonthly $15

Greenpeace
Greenpeace
1436 U Street NW
Washington, DC 20009
Bimonthly $15

Garbage
Old House Journal Corp.
435 Ninth Street
Brooklyn, NY 11215
Bimonthly $21

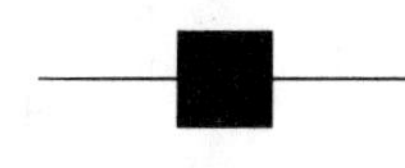

INDEX